College & University
CHAPLAINCY
21st Century *in the*

College & University

CHAPLAINCY

21st Century *in the*

A Multifaith Look
at the Practice of Ministry
on Campuses across America

Edited by Rev. Dr. Lucy A. Forster-Smith
Foreword by Rev. Janet M. Cooper Nelson

Walking Together, Finding the Way®

SKYLIGHT PATHS®
PUBLISHING
Nashville, Tennessee

College and University Chaplaincy in the 21st Century:
A Multifaith Look at the Practice of Ministry on Campuses across America

2013 Hardcover
© 2013 Lucy A. Forster-Smith
Foreword © 2013 by Janet M. Cooper Nelson

Library of Congress Cataloging-in-Publication Data

College and university chaplaincy in the 21st century : a multifaith look at the practice of ministry on campuses across America / edited by Rev. Dr. Lucy A. Forster-Smith ; foreword by Rev. Janet Cooper Nelson.
    pages cm
  Includes bibliographical references.
  ISBN 978-1-59473-516-5 (hc)
  ISBN 978-1-68336-011-7 (pbk)
  1. College chaplains. 2. Church work with students. 3. Universities and colleges—Religion. 4. Universities and colleges—United States. I. Forster-Smith, Lucy A., 1953–
  BV4376.C65 2013
  259'.24—dc23

                    2013028266

10 9 8 7 6 5 4 3 2

Manufactured in the United States of America

Cover Design: Kelley Barton
Interior Design: Kelley Barton
Cover Art: © iStockphoto.com/Qweek

SkyLight Paths Publishing is creating a place where people of different spiritual traditions come together for challenge and inspiration, a place where we can help each other understand the mystery that lies at the heart of our existence.

SkyLight Paths sees both believers and seekers as a community that increasingly transcends traditional boundaries of religion and denomination—people wanting to learn from each other, *walking together, finding the way.*

SkyLight Paths, "Walking Together, Finding the Way," and colophon are trademarks of LongHill Partners, Inc., registered in the U.S. Patent and Trademark Office.

Walking Together, Finding the Way®
Published by SkyLight Paths Publishing
A Division of LongHill Partners, Inc.
An Imprint of Turner Publishing Company
4507 Charlotte Avenue, Suite 100
Nashville, TN 37209
Tel: (615) 255-2665
www.skylightpaths.com

CONTENTS

FOREWORD

Rev. Janet M. Cooper Nelson
Brown University, Providence, Rhode Island

In the mid-1990s, religious life at Brown University clearly needed new structure. One idea proposed was renaming the chaplain, creating the post of Dean of Religious Life. At a meeting with the new provost I asked his opinion of the idea. After a long pause he said, "There are three officers in this university whose roles I actually understand: the president, the provost, and the chaplain; everyone else seems to be a dean of something." The room erupted in hearty laughter. The chaplain's historic title was retained and the work moved forward. However, the provost's clarity about chaplains is not widely shared, as these vignettes illustrate:

- A student researching the history of peace activism asks why the Christian Association and Rev. K. Brook Anderson would have been at the center of campus nonviolence work in the 1950s.

- Lindsay Harrison's 2011 poignant memoir, *Missing*, about her mother's suicide, describes the chaplain leading the campus bereavement group, saying, "She couldn't have been further from the buttoned-up, conservative, tight-lipped clergywoman I'd been expecting."

Rev. Janet M. Cooper Nelson is chaplain of the university at Brown University in Providence, Rhode Island, where she also teaches at Alpert School of Medicine. She is engaged in several national initiatives focused on higher education, religious literacy, interfaith understanding, and medical ethics, especially end-of-life care, and maintains ready access to poetry, scriptures, and a quiet beach.

- At a 2008 Yale Divinity School conference exploring a new phenomenon of "workplace chaplains," faculty were startled by the observation that university chaplains are also considered workplace chaplains.

Consternation about the work of America's academic chaplains derives in part from inexperience with religion in general and from the rapidly changing role of religion on campus. While chaplains serve the university's core mission most directly through their care of individuals, they also play a major role in creating and nourishing the overall campus climate. These tasks require increasing nuance as universities welcome an unprecedented diversity of identity, belief, and culture, creating a rare—and urgent—opportunity to engage differences with compassion and curiosity lest we produce educated cynics amid clashing sub-cultures.

The chaplain's work now occurs in myriad languages of belief and culture, often well beyond those of the chaplain's formation. Skill and trust are required; neither the faint-hearted nor the easily daunted is likely to be an effective guide

As the academic year begins each fall, we herald academic integrity, endeavor, and service to society. We renew our profession of the academy's "statement of faith," expressing our willingness as scholars to become a community that, however imperfectly, strives to create a welcoming, equitable, inclusive, and engaged academic climate. We urge everyone to take up this credo and to practice the academic disciplines and engage in community building, preparing diligently for the work that will measure us beyond the university's gates: the very transformation of society.

Brown University's eighteenth-century charter expressed the aspiration "that the rising generation may be able to discharge the offices of life with usefulness and reputation." Such lovely words rarely produce objection. But agreement about how to measure the "usefulness" and "reputation" of higher education is not easily achieved. Technocrats see education as training for the emerging professional class and tend to measure academic capacity by a graduate's employment and financial success. Philosophers understand education's privilege as a moral obligation: the learned will discern their moment in history, transform its ills, and anticipate the future with useful innovation and compassion. Universities struggle to embrace this wilderness of visions and hopes with equality and without prejudice. Within this forest, part of a chaplain's work may be to aver that these time-honored tasks are both sacred work and our historic purpose.

Stunningly for those who conceptualize higher education as an artifact of privilege, our colonial forbears, facing a vast literal wilderness, devoted scarce resources to establish our oldest American universities. While varied religious visions fueled this work—the Congregationalists founding Harvard; the Anglicans, William and Mary; the Baptists, Brown University—their impulse was common. In our nation's eighteenth- and nineteenth-century wilderness many others raised their voices as religious leaders, aspiring to clear space and to build educational institutions with enduring foundations.

These great schools stood thriving in the twentieth century even as a new cohort of campus clergy emerged. No longer presidents of these institutions but serving as their chaplains, these religious leaders were charged to insure that their institutions and those who studied within them took up work of worth and significance. Such remarkable voices as Rev. Dr. Howard Thurman at Boston University, Rev. Dr. George Buttrick and Rev. Peter Gomes at Harvard, and Rev. William Sloane Coffin at Yale exhorted, comforted, and fiercely interrogated their communities. They decried the unrighteousness of discrimination, racism, imperialism, privilege, and exclusivity that was found within the academy and the nation. Their voices resounded from the hallowed halls of ivy with the scriptural authority of biblical patriarchs and the animating revolutionary fervor of the nation's founders. Essential catalysts for integral change, these towering prophets spoke in pulpits from within the academy. Ironically, their voices articulated a rationale for clearcutting of much of the forest from which they emerged. As the twentieth century concluded, these prophets grew quiet through death or retirement. Much of the work they urged was moving forward—but would their like ever be seen again?

In the ensuing silence a new, quieter conversation became audible. New women and men were preaching ethics and worth in deconstructed political language that was feminist, postmodern, and more. Faculties, administrative structures, and student bodies changed dramatically as universities grew horizontally rather than vertically, with extended reach. As the late 1960s gave way to the '70s and '80s, previously excluded communities began to arrive on campus in significant numbers. Their joyful advent was accompanied by a pruning away of archaic patriarchy and hegemony to create space for the newly arrived, exposing societal isms for which the campus still lacked immunity. The vast new work of embracing the previously marginalized embodied much of the prophetic dream of the earlier generation, but religion's voice in the work grew quiet.

Admissions officers traveled broadly to increase numbers of under-represented minorities and inadvertently increased campus spiritual diversity as well. While personal piety continued to be protected on campus, faculty and students alike learned quickly to park religious identity and discourse off campus. Race, sexual orientation, ethnicity, culture, gender, and socioeconomic status formed the locus of campus discourse on identity. Religion was relegated to the periphery.

But in the opening decades of the twenty-first century the feared vanishing of campus religious life has abated, and dynamic work, shaped by comparison to the role and work of a previous generation, is underway with energy and vision. In *College and University Chaplaincy in the 21st Century* we hear for the first time the reflections of some of the American university chaplains who are the architects of this reconstruction. We marvel with them at the dynamics of spiritual transformation in the last fifty years of American higher education, as they reveal some of the radiant hope, humor, and struggle implicit in all of it.

The contributors to this book offer an unflinching view of this time of dramatic campus change. With rare candor they share their struggles to reshape pastoral formation to honor the trust of modern constituencies. We hear reverberations of lost authority; we hear honesty, integrity, vulnerability, vision, and faith. We hear the heart-felt campus dilemmas—personal and institutional—as well as the nation's social and cultural debates. We hear the whispered fears and dreams of students and faculty. We hear chaplains striving to dispel exclusionary shadows and to offer a radical welcome to those who never dared to expect it. As preaching presidents and radical chaplains did before them, these men and women continue to raise concerns of worth and worthiness.

The difficulty of these contributors' work is amplified in some cases by their identities and training. Some arrived at university among the ranks of those once ignored, barred, or repudiated. Their current appointments to the prestigious posts of former dons confirm the effectiveness of the prophetic reforms of the twentieth century, but earlier life at society's margins also informs their work.

Whether in building their own careers, advising students, or establishing programs, we see a concern to protect progress and prevent retrenchment on the positive gains of the past century. We also feel the weight of history's gaze. Those who are pioneering new work can find it exhausting and lonely. But these campus leaders are resilient, animated, and visionary in their work to motivate the academic community to ameliorate religious, racial, cultural bigotry; to foster medical research; to protect the environment; to promote economic stability and comprehensive health care; and all the while they continue their perennial work to relieve hunger, homelessness, and greed.

These chaplains write of their shared hope with the Prophet Isaiah "to sustain the one who is weary with a word" (Isaiah 50:4), but they take up this work in a land of rare beasts and unique adventures.[1] From precarious perches chaplains urge forward the work of both the newly arrived and the long established, both those who never imagined they would have the opportunity to earn a university degree and the established conservators of academic tradition and wealth. They urge humane perseverance in catastrophe, natural and political; they offer comfort in illness, trial, and tragedy; they provide historical and spiritual wisdom to encourage capacious, liberal vision.

In this strong collection we hear new voices doing new work. Over their shoulders we view the scope of the modern university's vision. Surely readers will rest secure in the knowledge that our nation's campus chaplains are at their posts, nourishing worthy scholarship and scholars as they strive together, as Langston Hughes says, to dream a world.[2] American higher education, while radically refashioned, remains animatedly faithful in preserving ancient wisdom and pursuing new justice.

INTRODUCTION

Rev. Dr. Lucy A. Forster-Smith

I sat in the Adams House at Princeton Theological Seminary with twelve colleagues, all chaplains in higher education, considering themes for a book we hoped to write about our work. As we brainstormed topics from student ministry to institutional dynamics to mentoring to multifaith engagement, one of the chaplains stopped the conversation with this comment: "We are hired by colleges and universities to oversee a dimension of human experience, the religious dimension, that many in our institutions doubt even exists." We all sat nodding. Then a second chaplain added, "That's true. And when the institution drops to its knees in crisis situations, it looks to us. We are used as confessor, pastor, confidante. We are then discarded." A third chaplain said, "The institutions that ordain us ask us to prove we are doing ministry. We, unlike those working in a congregation, have to justify our work. Our ordaining bodies have no idea of the crises of faith present in our work, the hunger at the heart of those we serve."

For over thirty years I have served as a chaplain in higher education settings. Though I am an ordained minister in the Presbyterian Church (U.S.A.), few of my seminary courses prepared me to take up this work. I have the privilege of working with young people making some of the most important decisions of their lives as college students, from determining their future career to embracing their sexual identity to discerning their deepest values and what Sharon Daloz Parks has called their "worthy dreams": "an imagination of self as adult in a world that honors the potential of the young adult soul."[1] More often than many would think, students are also developing their religious and spiritual values and practices at this critical juncture in their lives. Supporting young people at this moment of personal and spiritual development has always been an explicit role of college chaplains. Yet little has been written about the work of chaplains in this setting: how we do our work, how we think about the ways we enter the lives of those in our care, how it impacts us, how it challenges and captivates us. This book arose out of conversations among chaplains who serve on college and university campuses across the United States—from the reality that our story has not been sufficiently told.

It has been almost fifty years since the work of religious professionals on college and university campuses received sustained attention. In 1969 the Danforth Study of Campus Ministries published a work entitled *The Church, the University, and Social Policy*;[2] the same year, Princeton University chaplain Ernest Gordon published his memoir, *Meet Me at the Door*.[3] Since that time, much has changed on campus, in the religious landscape of America, and in the way chaplains inhabit their work.

This book arises at a moment when the American campus contains a remarkable religious and spiritual diversity. The contributing chaplains come from a variety of religious backgrounds, but we also are asked to serve religious communities that our seminary or rabbinical training never prepared us for. Most of our campuses are secular; some are vigilant in their secularity and struggle to respond to students who yearn for religious and spiritual support in a complex and violent world. The support and perspective chaplains provide to our academic communities have never been as important as they are right now. There is also a vital need for a new generation of chaplains who are guided by the experience and learning of remarkable practitioners.

This book offers a rare glimpse into the spiritual life that that finds its way into unexpected places on college and university campuses across America. Bringing multiple faith perspectives to the context of higher education, this book addresses questions about chaplains' work today:

> If traditional roles within the university no longer define our jobs, then what is the vocation and contribution of chaplains both now and into the future?
>
> Are chaplains here so we can care for the lost, emotionally fragile, or crisis-bound students? Are we here so we can shepherd a religiously diverse campus?
>
> How do chaplains sustain and deepen our own religious and spiritual commitments while caring for the diverse religious and spiritual needs of the academic community?
>
> As mentors, how do chaplains support and challenge the next generation of global citizens?

Each chapter addresses perspectives that arise at the intersection of religious practice, campus culture, the challenges of a secular context, and the individual ways chaplains inhabit their roles.

Our work as chaplains places us at the intersections of tradition and innovation, secularity and the sacred, and in some ways, hope and despair. The contributors to this book bring to it years of programmatic, pastoral, theological, and administrative experience. They are respected colleagues, brilliant thinkers and practitioners, radical and adventurous leaders. They were sought out for their thoughtful engagement with their work and also for an ability to make their professional experiences accessible. They—and I—all believe that this book will serve to encourage a new generation of chaplains on campus and will also enable our colleagues to know more about the enterprise of supporting a spiritually longing generation of students.

Part 1, "Chaplaincy in a Changing World," tells four stories of chaplains at work in the rapidly evolving, multicultural, multifaith context of the twenty-first-century campus—stories that ask, How does one best inherit a role made famous in a more radical past?

How does "chaplain" change meanings when adopted by a Roman Catholic woman or a Muslim man? How can the chaplain best support the community during a devastating crisis?

Part 2, "Multifaith Chaplains, Multifaith Campuses," offers the perspective of three chaplains for whom the intersections between their own faith cultures and those of the diverse campus communities they serve become powerful experiences, both for themselves and for their students.

Much of a chaplain's work focuses on supporting students, colleagues, and institutional life in ways that those we care for may not even be aware of. Part 3, "A Heart for the Community," describes three contexts for these important endeavors. From cultural-immersion pilgrimages where chaplains accompany students through deeply transformational experiences to the daily work of reminding individuals and institutions of their higher calling, to responding with grace in moments of crisis, these chaplains share perspectives and practices—some visible, some invisible—that enrich the lives of their communities.

In part 4, "Caring at the Crossroads," chaplains reflect on the many ways our work falls outside of clear categories and how this liminal state can serve as a source of strength—a perspective enhanced, in some cases, by our own multiple personal, religious, and cultural identities. The contributors of these chapters are harbingers of new patterns, new thinking, and a new appropriation of roles.

Part 5, "The Chaplain and the Secular," raises important questions about the role of religious leaders in the context of today's secular educational institutions: How do chaplains inhabit our religious identities while also honoring institutional assumptions about our role and work? How might chaplains help modern institutions reconcile their religious roots with the secular assumptions that shape higher education today? What is a chaplain's role when faith feels silenced in the academy?

Throughout, the chapters in this book ask, What surprises are in store for those who step into this field? To borrow from theologian Frederick Buechner, what "deep gladness" awakens in the heart of those who give their lives to becoming chaplains?

The chaplains who have contributed to this book come from a range of colleges and universities across the United States. They are Roman Catholic and Protestant, Jewish and Muslim. Some are ordained, others not. They are African American, white, Asian American, and those serving Hispanic/Latino communities. Some of the chaplains are straight and others gay. The institutions they serve range in size from several hundred students to tens of thousands of students and are remarkably diverse: historically African American, Ivy League, small liberal arts, denominationally affiliated, and research institutions. With contributions from all parts of the United States—East Coast and West, Midwest, South, rural, large cities, small college towns—the book provides a landscape view of chaplains' work. Yet even with this amazing diversity, the contributors share remarkably similar ideals and aspirations.

As editor of this book, I have had the privilege of guiding a remarkable project. The writers met in retreat settings to develop, draft, and edit (and calm writers' jitters). Over the past three years, the writers have gathered annually in order to determine the book's scope and direction. In what was probably one of the most compelling professional development opportunities for most of us, we were able to identify key themes that should be represented, imagine the audience for the book, recognize where we needed to seek additional writers, and encourage each other as we developed ideas. Having a multifaith constituency of chaplains provided particular religious or spiritual identities with a global and multifaith reach.

ACKNOWLEDGMENTS

Along the way, many people have offered guidance, awakened insight, and posed generous questions. One of those people is Sharon Daloz Parks, the project advisor, who helped in untold ways as the project began and who directed the chaplain-writers' gaze to the horizon of our work: the big questions and worthy dreams our work is about. Another guide was Kate Daloz, our writing consultant, who brought us from the wide horizon of our work experiences back to the page, helping us take care to write with energy, imagination, and precision. And it is the writers themselves, these chaplains of magnificent capabilities, their work, and their vocation that animate this book.

This project owes its life to Lilly Endowment Religion Division, particularly Chris Coble and Craig Dykstra, who recognized the need for this book, imagined its contribution, and supported it generously. It was propelled by the remarkable Program for the Theological Exploration of Vocation's interest in cultivating leaders for church and society. The request for this book came from those we serve: students. With their exploration of work and vocation, they wondered where the resources on college and university chaplaincy were. We trust this book will provide a source of insight, guidance, and education for those who are engaged in or exploring chaplaincy as their vocational path. We hope it will inspire some to take up this work as their own vocation. We hope it will prompt other campus religious leaders to tell their stories.

The contributors and I thank our institutions for releasing us from some of our responsibilities to allow us time to write, think, ponder, and share these reflections. We thank our spouses, partners, children, and colleagues for their support for this project. We thank our students and colleagues for the privilege of joining your journey. And we recognize that the Holy One, the Source of all life, the Generous Host of our days, winks through this book. With deep awe we bring it to birth, trusting the work of the academic communities across the globe to guide, infuse, and tend the vision of generations to come.

CHAPLAINCY
IN A
CHANGING
WORLD

MY DREAMSICLE JOB
Good Humor and
Becoming a Chaplain

Sharon M. K. Kugler
Yale University, New Haven, Connecticut

B rian came from a very small town in western Tennessee. As he sat in my office, he was visibly upset, a first-year student with some fairly typical adjustment issues. He was clearly now a small fish in a big pond at Yale, convinced that he did not belong, that he could not match the caliber of those around him. His baseball cap was pulled down as low as it could get to cover his eyes. His body language was stiff. He was tense and hurting. I said, "Brian, before we talk, would you like something? Some tea, water, maybe an ice cream?" He looked at me and said, "Ma'am, if I could have a Dreamsicle, that would be great."

So as he munched, we proceeded to talk. And once again I had to stifle an internal smile at the presence of an ice-cream bar in the midst of the day-to-day work of this vocation. Though at first glance it may seem silly, the ice-cream bar in this heartbroken boy's hand is a powerful entry to something holy. It had given us an opening and given me a way to connect with the ache in his soul.

Sharon M. K. Kugler is head chaplain at Yale University in New Haven, Connecticut, and a past president of the National Association of College and University Chaplains (NACUC) and of the Association of College and University Religious Affairs (ACURA). Her happiest moments in this work are when she is nurturing community in surprising ways, like cooking and serving enormous vats of chili at large gatherings of students: "It's magic!"

In 2007, upon my second interview for the university chaplain position at Yale, I was anxious to meet students, longing to know if I would be as fond of them as I was of those at Johns Hopkins. On a frigid January night, we were having an interview in the living room of one of Yale's famous Harry Potter–looking residential colleges. The room was decorated beautifully with classic Early American furnishings. It was cozy and warm, but it felt stranger than anything I had experienced in a college setting before. The diverse group of graduate and undergraduate students from many religious backgrounds clearly cared deeply about chaplaincy and religious life in general on campus. They were serious and earnest, and I was enjoying their thoughtful questions. I started to relax.

Then this happened: "You know, Ms. Kugler," one student said quietly, "I googled you." *Oh dear*, I thought. *What is coming next?* "Yes?" I said. "Well," he answered, "I read that you have a Good Humor ice-cream cart right outside of your office in Baltimore. Is that true?" *Oh well*, I thought, *it's all over now.* Yale had found out about my love for the goofy and whimsical. I glanced down at my teacup—it was real china and bore the unique seal of the residential college. I thought of my office at JHU. My collection of snow globes and religiously themed action figures would never fit here in the Ivy League. *Well, it was a nice run*, I thought. As I mentally prepared to head home, proud to have come as far as I did in the search process, I looked at the student and answered honestly, "Yes, I do have a Good Humor cart right outside of my office. Would you like to know why?" "Well yes," he replied, "but I especially want to know if you would bring it with you if you were to come to Yale." I exhaled. It was going to be okay after all. We were going to understand each other.

ICE CREAM AS ICEBREAKER

Though it had caused me a moment of panic, I was grateful that the student had offered me the opportunity to explain the presence of the cart and my taste for kitsch. When people walk into my office, they are often briefly distracted by an Elvis snow globe or the Last Supper clock or my Jesus action figure or the string of chili lights hanging from the ceiling or the Ten Plagues finger puppets. Sometimes they ask for the stories behind the items they see; at other times they don't focus on anything other than what they need from me in our precious moments together. Like the ice cream, though, it's not a gimmick. Besides being treasured gifts given to me by students and colleagues over the course of the last twenty-seven years in ministry, my collection is an expression of my personality, my taste for the unexpected and silly.

For me, the collection serves as something of an icebreaker. Sometimes people get worried that there's an ulterior motive to conversation with a religious person, that they'll be pushed toward the religious person's understanding of what faith is. That's not what I offer. I'll have conversations about faith, spirituality, or community, but my lead is offering a kind of presence, of meeting people where *they* are. I want my visitors to shed any apprehension or feeling of distance that might be connected to a visit with the university chaplain. No matter what brings them to my office, walking in with a laugh relaxes, welcomes, and opens them. It puts them in a mode of experiencing *me*, as opposed to "a chaplain," however they might have imagined that figure.

No matter what they were imagining, I almost certainly don't fit the model. To start with, I'm not ordained and I'm not a man. If they know I'm Roman Catholic and that I'm a mom and a grandma and therefore obviously not a nun, they're even more confused. People are puzzled about what chaplains do anyway, and my story is especially unique.

I've grown accustomed to standing on the outside of what was once considered normative for chaplaincy. In fact, my unusual route to chaplaincy and the fact that I have had to continually reaffirm, even to myself, what a Catholic laywoman is doing in a role traditionally held by those who are ordained has actually been one of my greatest resources. What I've learned over the years is this: my only option in doing this work is just to be myself and to be as present as possible for those I encounter.

"My career in ministry," just the phrase itself, still feels a bit awkward to use as a set of words that even remotely refers to me.

I am a Roman Catholic laywoman who has been on a remarkable journey of blessing, lifelong learning, and service. It just so happens that this journey has been one of priestly ministry, but without the formal title. Throughout my life, I have been fortunate to have doors opened to me by people who trusted more than I did that personality and instinct could be as valid a route to ministry as ordination.

CALLED TO SERVE

Upon graduation from college in 1981, armed with a bachelor of science degree in mathematics, I joined the Jesuit Volunteer Corps, a program devoted to service, with special emphasis on linking faith with social action. I was placed in Cleveland, Ohio, which might as well have been the moon for me. A true "California girl" from the sublime suburbs of San Francisco, I had never seen a housing project in my life, much less heard the term "wind-chill factor." I was assigned to work as a patient advocate at a free clinic on Cleveland's east side, serving battered women and children. I naively believed that all I had to do for these women was to affirm their self-worth, pray with them, share Maya Angelou's poetry, and they would be saved from their horrific predicaments. Everything I knew about domestic violence came through the limited lens of my undergraduate sociological studies and my feminist sensibilities. These women patiently taught me my first lesson of many in humility. It is a wonder they did not eat me alive.

After two years in Cleveland working at the free clinic and in a shelter for battered women, I received a call from my alma mater, Santa Clara University, a small Jesuit school in northern California, asking me to consider returning as an associate campus minister and to be part of a team of eight people, mostly clergy, in the university's campus ministry office. It was a wonderful and unexpected gift, but I was nonetheless filled with doubt.

The director of campus ministry must have read my mind. "Sharon," he said when we initially spoke on the phone about the position, "you are called to serve. If you do indeed answer that call, you are performing ministry." That moment was the first of several genuinely empowering moments I had at SCU that influenced the direction that the rest of my life would take. Until then, I had never considered that I could have a vocation. Here I was, already learning that the term is defined by our actions, not the other way around.

I surrendered to the unfamiliar notion of "calling," and Santa Clara was the ideal place to do so. "Servant ministry" was a term I had never heard but one I embraced as a model. I preached twice a month, studied sacred texts with fellow team members, led retreats for freshmen, and was the designated "sex-talk lady" in the residence halls, giving workshops on the issues of contraception and moral decision making. I felt most alive when I could bring about or witness moments of spiritual growth and awakenings in the students I served.

Because I was on the docket to preach regularly in the Santa Clara Mission Church, I often trembled at the thought of what this meant. A Roman Catholic laywoman preaching was something for which I had no compass. I did, however, have colleagues who believed I could and should preach. They gave me the opportunity to learn, and they were also willing to take whatever flak the hierarchy of the church tossed their way. I felt supported as I plunged eagerly into the nearly always painful yet also wonderful spiritual release that goes hand in hand with sermon construction and delivery. I could not believe my good fortune.

Each day was a time of huge learning and great fun. I participated in conferences and seminars with my clergy colleagues and felt like a true member of a ministry team. From the start, my colleagues treated me as an equal. It was a wonderful training ground for anyone, but especially for a young woman like me. The staff was inclusive in nature, justice oriented, and very willing to work collaboratively in every way. The hours were long; no job or task was ever deemed too trivial not to be done by everyone or anyone, and above all we believed in inclusion, compassion, creativity, and possibility. It was a model that informed many professional decisions I would come to make over the course of my career.

LEARNING TO BECOME

It was the fall of 1983. I was in heaven, loving every minute of the work. My life was opening before me in brand-new, unanticipated spiritually profound ways. I was also a newlywed. My husband and I had only been married a year when I took this position, and he had bravely moved across the country from his beloved hometown of Cleveland, Ohio, to start this adventure in our lives. Then, two months into my new job, another adventure began for us: we discovered that I was pregnant with our first child. I was overcome by anxiety. I did not know how I would be able to do it all. I had found work that was filling my heart and feeding my soul daily, but I was conflicted about how to be fully present both to that work and also to lovingly and responsibly raising a child. I felt completely overwhelmed, as if I was going to melt under all the pressure. I was barely able to accept *myself* in a new role that it had never occurred to me to hope for, let alone to feel the acceptance of others—and now I was also entering the unknown territory of parenthood.

I need not have worried so much because two remarkable things happened. The first was my husband's complete willingness, without giving it a second thought, to stay home with our firstborn as I continued to work in campus ministry. This was a solution that we were lucky to even have as an option in our lives. We lived in university housing, and because of that, we could make ends meet with one salary. This also allowed me to see my baby daughter as much as possible during the day.

The second remarkable thing happened when I poured my heart out to my Jesuit boss. He heard me out. Then he said, simply and firmly, "Sharon, we hired you to come here and *be you*. That means that whatever is unfolding in your life is what you will bring to this work. If you are to be a mother, then you will bring that reality, that unique understanding to this work." I had never received such a freeing gift in all my life.

I was being invited simply to become. This affirmation is something that informs how I approach my work even now, all these years later. I realized that perfection wasn't the goal and that nurturing a certain kind of openness for the next unknown playing out in my life, in this instance motherhood, was all part of the beautiful mystery of becoming. When I have a conversation with a young person today it is directly informed by that moment when I knew that who I *was* was, in fact, enough.

As I settled into my role at Santa Clara, the Jesuits encouraged me to pursue a master of divinity degree (my math degree was not terribly applicable to my newfound vocation), but shortly after beginning the process, I hesitated. Thirteen months after my daughter was born, my mother died. I was a bit of an emotional wreck. But there was another source of pain: I could not get beyond the fact, that in my case, an MDiv would never materialize into ordination. I felt that I would always be just short of fully belonging in ministry, just outside of the real or authorized ones who could answer God's call.

As housing prices began to soar in California and university housing lost its allure, we longed for a more settled existence. It was time to make a big move and start another adventure. In the mid-eighties my husband, our young daughter, and I moved to Baltimore, and my life continued to take some very unusual twists and turns.

My first ministry position in Baltimore was, true to form, an unconventional one. I was selected to be the founding director of a hospice for people struggling with AIDS. It was 1987; the world was still coming to grips with how to handle the crisis. This project was unique because it was sponsored by a number of church groups and synagogues in response to some horribly hurtful things that other "religious" voices had put forth about AIDS and those suffering with it. The board for this project consisted of former college chaplains and campus ministers, among others. In the course of the interview process, we talked about the impact of servant leadership in ministry. I think that is why they took a chance on me. Once again, I found that when I trusted myself to simply, honestly share what I had to offer, the way forward presented itself.

The hospice did not yet physically exist when I took the job. I had some seed money to begin initial planning, but for the most part I had to work from the ground up to build the program and to find a proper facility. I set policy and guidelines, learned local and federal housing and nursing care laws, and did a fair amount of fund-raising, along with recruiting and training volunteers. By the time the hospice opened, we had managed to create a welcoming, warm, and loving environment. When one is around a person in the last stages of AIDS, the unmistakable presence of God is reflected in the eyes of that person in the most lovingly simple ways. For me, and for the others who spent time in this most heart-wrenching of places on the margins of society, this ministry was one the purest forms of blessing we had ever encountered. The sense of community we felt as a result of this blessing was nearly indescribable. I felt that I had never done more important or tougher work.

In early March of 1993, nearly four years after leaving the hospice and after a series of part-time ministry consultant jobs, as well as the birth of our second child, I received a phone call that really did change my life. A former colleague from the hospice board who was also serving at Johns Hopkins University as the United Methodist campus minister called to ask me if I was interested in coming in as a consultant to the university. They had just made some changes in the chaplaincy and were on the verge of more in the wake of the resignation of the university chaplain and the subsequent restructuring of her position. I agreed to help, but only for a short time. I had my doubts about going back to salaried work and was really happy being a stay-at-home mom. My life was plenty full—or so I thought.

I cannot quite say for sure why I decided to take a risk and begin work at Johns Hopkins, I just know that I felt a strong pull back into ministry in higher education. The unknown next stage of becoming was again playing itself out, and I followed my gut.

I ended up serving as the Johns Hopkins university chaplain from 1993 to 2007 and then, accompanied by my Good Humor cart, I became the chaplain to Yale University in 2007. In the midst of my time at JHU, I had finally had the opportunity to finish my master's at Georgetown University. What I discovered in campus chaplaincy in 1993 was the exciting new frontier of doing this work in a multi-faith setting where religious and spiritual diversity were redefining the approach and understanding of college and university chaplaincy. Nurturing multiple communities across many faith traditions brought a new dimension of excitement and purpose to this call, and I discovered that I had a good instinct for it. As a matter of fact, I loved it.

THE HOLINESS OF A GOOD HUMOR CART

The Good Humor cart was with me from the beginning. At Johns Hopkins, I started by renting one each year as a way to ease the tension during freshman orientation, when families were preparing to say good-bye to their daughters and sons. Offering something that lightens the mood and nurtures our inner eight-year-old had been an immediate hit. I always took care to make sure that the cart was filled with whimsical offerings, like Choco-Tacos and Dreamsicles and that they would always be kosher so everyone could enjoy. It was only in September of 2001 that the cart began to take on another, deeper meaning and to become one of the holiest objects at the Interfaith Center.

Long after freshmen orientation had come and gone in 2001, the cart for some unexplained reason had yet to be picked up by the rental agency. On September 11, like so many others, we held each other and stared with disbelief at the images on television. Students, some who had loved ones in the Twin Towers, poured into the Interfaith Center. The rabbis and the imam were there too, along with some of the Buddhist and Christian campus religious advisors. We all looked at each other in horror, speechless and stunned. As the day wore on and we learned of the fate of so many, I noticed a kind of pacing taking place at the Interfaith Center. Students were walking back and forth in the multipurpose room, restless, seemingly aimless. This was a new state for them—these brilliant young souls who were so very accomplished already now confronted something that their considerable intellects could not quite process. They were stopped in their tracks and at a complete loss.

The one thing that stood noticeably apart from the solemn grip of the day was the presence of the Good Humor cart. Those standing near it in silence or speaking to one another in hushed tones helped themselves to its contents. Muslim students who looked as if they were going to melt from fear, especially women wearing the hijab, clustered together next to the cart. Students, regardless of religious affiliation, were receiving small, much needed comfort from this simple presence in the corner of the Interfaith Center. It was indeed a sacred object, not silly in the least.

Today, the Good Humor cart is commonplace in my office at Yale, as it was at Johns Hopkins. In normal, routine times, the Good Humor cart serves as the great equalizer. People from all parts of the university community are drawn to it. Everyone, from freshmen to the grounds crew, knows it's there and they stop by gratefully. Sometimes they join in conversation or just smile, wave, and take their popsicle. Either way, I don't care. I see the ice cream as a gift that has no strings attached. It's here just to lighten people's days, to express a different sort of hospitality. It is fun, it is kosher, it beckons, asks nothing, and gives so much. The grounds crew, custodians, security guards, and plumbers, the deans, rabbis, priests, and imams all enjoy its contents. Students from all points on the globe have discovered its pull, recalled its unconventional and comforting elixir, and have spread the word about it. It is the welcome wagon that says welcome over and over again.

BEING PRESENT WITHOUT GETTING IN THE WAY

There is a story of a priest in Italy who walked up to two men who were chiseling stone and asked them what they were doing. The first man said, "I am chipping at a rock," and the second said, "I am making a cathedral!" This story makes me smile as I recall one of the many articles that were written upon my appointment to be the chaplain to Yale. It lamented the end of the prophetic era of chaplains and interpreted my somewhat different approach to chaplaincy as one lacking in much depth to inspire young adults. It is true, I don't lead many protest marches or deliver thunderous sermons. But no less than my predecessors did, I still see my work as building a cathedral.

I find myself in an unusual spiritual and ministerial place. I never claim to be anyone that I am not. I am not and cannot be an ordained person through my Catholic religious community. I make that very clear to people who seek my assistance. Though I felt a kind of pain about my non-ordained status for many years, that distinction has come to mean less and less to me and, it seems, to others. A clergy colleague of mine once said to me, "Sharon you were ordained the first time a young person in trouble came to you and you did not look away." Perhaps this is so, and if it is, what a beautifully simple way to understand priestly ministry.

I have reached a certain peace regarding the fact that I am indeed an odd bird among chaplains. It challenges me nearly every day to be very clear about who I am as a person of faith in one particular tradition, as well as who I need to be as one who serves and guides *all* others in a boisterous multireligious university community. I have become the "pastor" of a most unusual flock, and I pastor this flock in a most unusual way and I feel blessed nearly every day to be doing so. I have for a while now secretly referred to myself as the "Nike Chaplain." As the slogan goes, I just do it.

An essential part of my job when offering pastoral care in moments of crisis is to be present, but to not get in the way—to be the person with tissues in my purse or a bottle of water at hand, but never to let the moment become about myself. No matter how horrible the situation, I'm the one who is not going to look away or abandon someone in a time of need. My presence in the room at that moment is about creating a space where it feels safe for someone to fall. Sometimes people want a prayer, sometimes they want anything but that. It's not up to me to know in advance what they'll need: you don't go in wearing a hat that says, "I'm here to do this"; you wear a hat that says, "I'm here to just *be*; take what you need."

Through all its twists and turns, I have built my career on a very simple belief: what matters most is to care for people in surprising ways, step outside of what is expected, and trust in the smallest of loving gestures offered with sincerity and without fanfare. My training as a chaplain came in different forms: some seminary, some academy, lots of cooking for crowds, lots of creative experimenting, and lots of listening. I remain heavily influenced by the notion of servant leadership and have never forgotten its importance in my daily work with people. The core values of the "ministry of presence" or "creative loitering" are at the very heart of my work. I've noticed that my best moments as a chaplain have been a result of making a connection with someone, not in a conventional way, but through laughter, presence, and smile, and that those can have as much weight as holding someone's hand and explicitly praying with them.

A few years ago I received an e-mail from a young Muslim student whom I came to know quite well starting in his freshman year at Yale. His name is Umar, and he aspires to work in the field of public health with the poorest of populations in a developing country. He wrote to tell me how the chaplaincy had impacted his perception of the world. He grew up in a sheltered environment and was taught by the imam in his mosque to fear those who didn't share the same beliefs, to trust no one outside his own religious community. His story is not unique; I have heard the same from time to time from Christians and Jews. People tend to fear what is unfamiliar. It is natural for us to feel ill at ease with what we do not know or understand. This student went on to say that those sermons of mistrust he had grown up believing now felt farfetched and skewed from his actual lived experience since starting college. For him, the idea of living in a religiously diverse setting no longer seemed a point of separation; rather it was a broader, truer idea of humanity, and he embraced it.

Umar then went on:

> In Islam, the idea of *nur* or divine radiance is often ascribed to those who exemplify sincerity and humanity. Many traditions speak of pious scholars and individuals who were recognized not so much by their physical characteristics, but by the *nur* that was manifest in their being. Students in search of knowledge would flock from different areas of the Islamic world to compete to be in the presence of these individuals, to have a portion of their light. The humble abode of the Yale

University chaplain's office, situated in the basement of
Bingham Hall alongside empty classrooms and a laun-
dry room, reveals nothing of the radiance that illumi-
nates from it. The chaplain's office has had a profound
effect on my own spiritual growth and in formulating
my views on humanity; it is that *nur* which has attracted
me there almost every day these past two years.

Umar's words reminded me of that Jesuit who simply encouraged
me just to become who I was meant to be in this work. My unusual
route to chaplaincy came about because others invited me into this
work with the promise that just being myself would be enough. All
these years later, it is a lesson I continue to relearn as my own life
continues on its twists and turns: I am a chaplain who is a mother,
a grandmother, a collector of kitschy snow globes, an experienced
chef who has produced hundreds of gallons of chili, a leader of a
community when it mourns and when it celebrates, a twelve-year
cancer survivor, and a lover of a good edgy joke. I bring all those
elements of myself to my work every day, whether I'm laughing
with someone, offering a tissue to wipe their tears, or just setting
up chairs for an event. There is a reflection by Benedictine sister
Joan Chittister concerning the Gospel story of the loaves and fishes:
"When we go out of ourselves to make a connection with the other,
we not only attend to the needs of the other, *we become more than we
were when we began.*"[1] I am awestruck by the knowledge that, Good
Humor cart and all, I have, in fact, *become.*

CHAPLAINCY IN DISPLACEMENT AND HOMECOMING
After Katrina

Rev. Gail E. Bowman
Dillard University, New Orleans, Louisiana

*O*ur *campus had been closed and empty for four months: four months of horror and hope and uncertainty and absurdity and deep appreciation; four months of being everywhere—people scattered as if a bomb had gone off and blown people all over the country to places we never thought to be. It had been four months of having no address, searching for one another, and asking whether the university would cease to exist, or relocate, or be reconstituted on an empty cruise ship docked in the Mississippi River. Then finally it was agreed: Dillard would reopen at the Hilton Riverside in January 2006. When we got there, we found each other changed and with enormous work ahead of us. But there was also a huge sign hanging high in the hotel atrium, in white on blue, our blue,* Dillard *blue: WELCOME HOME, DILLARD UNIVERSITY.*

BEFORE THE STORM

It would have saved me some time in 1998, when I came to Dillard University from Spelman College in Atlanta, if someone had just

---

Rev. Gail E. Bowman, JD, is the director of the Campus Christian Center at Berea College in Berea, Kentucky. She moved to Berea recently after serving as chaplain at Dillard University in New Orleans for fourteen years, and she grew up in Des Moines, Iowa. She has several published sermons and one book, *Praying the Sacred in Secular Settings*.

gone ahead and told me that people in the Deep South consider northerners uncivilized. I thought I had been living in the South already. They don't call Atlanta "Hot Lanta" for nothing. But so far as New Orleanians were concerned, living in Atlanta is no credential whatsoever for knowing and understanding "the South."

Southern schools—southern black schools in particular (we call them HBCUs: historically black colleges and universities)—are very stylized. They are deeply traditional, cautious in regard to change; they are proud; they are protected. To live in the South is to enter into another country with an almost constant recollection of slavery, its issues, and its aftermath of threat- and violence-enforced segregation. Today, the strength of southern cities and the HBCUs in them is partly a result of how whites perceived the black populations and how those black populations perceived themselves.

Coming out of the Civil War, Atlanta rose in economic markers while New Orleans declined. For that reason, as well as others, a certain amount of disdain bubbles between the two cities to this day. Atlanta perceives itself as the embodiment of the New South, with an upwardly mobile energy that skirts discussions of race in order to pursue aspirations of becoming an international powerhouse. Many Atlantans consider New Orleans a throwback city, raggedy and mired in old ways of being.

However, when New Orleanians speak of Atlanta, it is with a tone of mild puzzlement, the way you might speak of an estranged family member who "forgot their roots." When other cities (like Atlanta) modernized, New Orleans kept itself. It kept the French Quarter, Tremé, and the Marigny; it kept its habit of stuffing almost anything edible into the fryer; it continues to be a place where strangers may call you "baby" or "honey"; and it continues to study and try to protect its own cultural complexity and sophistication, which is immense. New Orleans is French, Cajun, Creole, African, Native American, Spanish, Caribbean, and more. It is religiously diverse, festive, family oriented, endless in appetite, and absolutely up to the task of warmly welcoming guests of all kinds at a moment's notice. Even with slavery's vestiges still ever present, it is oddly free. It is what many people are looking for when they want an experience of the South.

So I arrived on the campus of Dillard University with some "issues" I was aware of and others I couldn't have guessed. I was Dillard's first female chaplain, and single, in a city where most African American female clergy do ministry with their pastor husbands. I was a northerner with a strange accent, strange words, syntax, and thinking. Also, I was coming from Atlanta, which was as good as proof that I didn't know where I was.

Right away, I liked the students. Many were eager and ready to refurbish Sunday worship to be more reflective of their home experiences and to embrace contemporary black gospel, which had become a worldwide phenomenon. What I didn't realize was that since many people didn't understand what I was saying (or why I was saying what I was saying), either because of my accent or word choice, during my first year or so most of my communication was nonverbal. They couldn't follow my accent, I spoke too quickly, and my thinking was just unusual enough that much of what I said was surprising. But, apparently, people at Dillard decided I was worth keeping because of my smile, because I began to learn their names, and because I seemed to appreciate them as they were (I did!). So they decided to civilize me and teach me how to be their chaplain.

During the early years, I softened and slowed my speech and allowed it to contain more emotional content. Then I fused what I had come to understand with what I said and what I did. I learned not to start the prayer that begins the school year until I saw the dark blue shirts of the housekeepers and groundskeepers as they filed into the auditorium, because they so appreciated hearing us thank God for the work of their hands and the sweat of their brows. I carefully included those who planned and prepared, cooked and served, in the grace at special dinners, recognizing that community is *everybody*. The rank and file's interest in having the unrestricted exuberance of contemporary gospel music included in the baccalaureate worship persuaded me to include some, after a few years, despite the president's standing prohibition. It was wonderfully well done, and almost everybody appreciated it, but we do have a photograph of the president leaning over the baccalaureate preacher, mid–musical jump-up, to ask me, "Who approved this music?"

Every school is different. Every school is special. To be a chaplain is to pay attention. When I paid attention, I noticed that, at Dillard, the religious person is assumed to be inherently valuable. There's an unshakable appreciation that is based not on the individual but on the role. From time to time, groups of students would be asked to do the community-defining exercise of determining who should get a spot on a limited-seat spaceship leaving earth, with earth's total destruction imminent. No matter how we rewrote the scenario, the minister was always included. The minister could be female, infertile, haughty, inarticulate, drunk, or dying—it didn't matter. There was no concept of civilization going on without the minister.

An Opportunity for Change

In addition to being reshaped myself, it was not long before I had no choice but to try to reshape Dillard. Almost as soon as I arrived, I noticed that DU was not a safe environment for LGBTQ students, faculty, or staff. I had been warned about this before I came, and it was as bad as I had feared. My first year, people came to me literally under cover of darkness to let me know that they were gay or transgender or whatever it was. I realized they wanted someone to know this in case they ever needed to be helped and in case there was ever an opportunity for a change to be put in place.

The opportunity for a change came suddenly and unexpectedly in the second year. There was an incident among some males who were visibly involved in the ministry and, as it turned out, were experimenting with same-sex physical relations together. Suddenly, everybody knew, and students began coming to me, imploring me to condemn homosexuality as demon possession from the pulpit. However, that was not what I believed then, nor is it what I believe now.

For months, all I did was receive students in my office arguing with me as I tried to reframe the conversation about sexual orientation. People turned on me, including some who worked in the office. Sunday worship attendance melted down quickly as word got out that the on-campus ministry had done the Unacceptable—taken a stand that the "everybody" community also included LGBTQ students, faculty, and staff.

Through all this turmoil I was calm on the surface, but I was walking the floor at home. Jesus and I had some of our roughest, truest, and most earnest conversations during that time. The students and others pushed me and pushed me and pushed me until I felt as though my adored sixty-six books of the Bible had shrunk down to a lily-pad-sized theological singularity on which I stood, surrounded by peril. But what that last tiny piece of Word said was:

> *You shall love the Lord your God*
> *with all your heart*
> *and all your soul*
> *and all your mind*
> *and your neighbor as yourself.*

What I came to understand in my 3 a.m. squabbling with the Almighty was that there are good reasons to agree or disagree with my stance. I was not going to get a universal kiss of "Sure, you're right." To be a real chaplain I needed to take a stance, study that stance, pray on that stance, check in Upstairs on that stance, and then stand. I needed to stand still and let the winds rage and the intimidating absence of familiar markers not move me, and I did.

Together the university and I passed through four miserable years, at odds with each other. Then, when it looked as though we would simply continue to disagree, the Dillard University student body elected a gay *and out* young man, a marvelous young man, as Student Government Association president. When I heard the election results, I was floored. As I made inquiry, I realized that some of our students, along with some of the faculty and staff, had enough experience of LGBTQ individuals elsewhere, including in high school, that they were comfortable with a definition of community that included them. We were not prepared to answer all of the questions (e.g., what about same-sex marriage?) but we were ready to redefine ourselves, and I had a new and vitally important piece of what it means to be a chaplain within me. Dillard and I had changed each other, and Dillard was still Dillard.

GOD'S KATRINA

In the fall of 2005, new student orientation went wonderfully well. We had a new group of first years: big and strong and pleased with their choice of school. The seniors, the class of 2006, had that "I'm about to graduate!" strut going from the moment they returned to campus. The student population was at an all-time high, nearing twenty-one hundred. We had good people in place in a number of critical positions, and we had a new president. But by the end of the first week of classes we were pulling almost everybody off the campus as Hurricane Katrina took a turn in the Gulf of Mexico and headed in.

We were aware of the doomsday scenario. We knew that a category 3 or above hurricane had the potential to overwhelm the levees and send storm surges roaring up from the Gulf and into the city through water superhighways dug to ease the work of the oil and gas industry. We had evacuated before and had a location for our students arranged at a sister United Methodist School—Centenary College in Shreveport, Louisiana. However, we had never had to evacuate this quickly or this thoroughly (it was always assumed that the president and senior cabinet would remain in the city), we had no communication alternative in place if we lost the 504 area code, and we had only a partial plan for the eventuality of not being able to return for months. Somewhere (who knows where now?) there was a list of who was to travel with whom, but that list had not been shared with me or others in support positions. Also, there was no system for notifying the campus community of steps being taken beyond the decision to leave.

On the Saturday before Katrina, I was in my office, blissfully writing a sermon while the funeral of the past head of the New Orleans Urban League was being conducted in the sanctuary. I found out that the students were leaving when the bus my office had hired for a community service event was turned back at the gate. What I didn't know was that *seven* hired buses left Dillard University late Saturday afternoon, heading for Centenary College, filled with the 250-plus students who were not able to get themselves out. I continued my sermon work until word came that the worship for which I was preparing was canceled. I went home to bed. I woke up at 3 a.m. and turned on the local weather. When the broadcaster said, "This would be a good time to put your ax in your attic," a frisson went down my back. Fully awake now, I got up and made plans to leave. Family in Des Moines helped me find a 7:30 p.m. flight out of Jackson, Mississippi. When I turned the corner coming from my garage to drive past my little house, I was certain I would not see it as it was again, so I kissed it good-bye.

The traffic out of the area was epic, a Noah's ark ragtag cavalcade of people trying to get themselves, their families, their neighbors, their vehicles, their pets, and their horses out. All interstate lanes were heading north, east, or west in "contraflow," and all lanes were crawling. When I finally got to Jackson and to more gasoline, I had been on the road more than twelve hours and had missed the flight. I drove to the airport anyway. A kind man told me he might be able to get me out in the morning, but it was also possible that the airport would close before then. So I got back in the car and kept driving north—another 210 miles to Memphis. In Memphis I found a Motel 6 with an available bed, fell into it, and slept. In the morning, with Katrina roaring into most of the places I held dear, I headed on to my extended family members anxiously waiting for me in Des Moines.

On Tuesday night, the day after Katrina, I got a call from Dillard's brand-new president, Dr. Marvalene Hughes, who had somehow tracked me down. Among other things, Dr. Hughes wanted to know why I wasn't in my designated emergency position, which was with the provost, since I was in the Division of Academic Affairs. This was the first time I had ever heard I was supposed to evacuate with the provost. I wondered why my designated emergency position wasn't with the students, but I didn't say so. It was not a time for proposing rewrites to the emergency plan; we had bigger concerns.

What followed was about a week of being on daily conference calls with the leadership. There were tons of issues: getting the stranded emergency crew off the campus; getting permission to send someone in by boat to assess the campus; figuring out where the students were; figuring out where the faculty and staff were; deciding what to do about holding classes; and communicating our location, plans, and existence to the larger community. Eventually, there were two factions on the calls: the logistical side—those who were trying to deal with the insurance company (among other things, we had "interruption of business" insurance), the federal government (what should we do with our students' financial aid that had already been received?), and the accrediting body that makes the institution viable; and the people side—how can we communicate with our community?

A Network of Prayer

Those early days after Katrina remind me, now, of the story about the six visually challenged men encountering and describing their first elephant. For the man who touches the trunk, the elephant is a long flexible hose. For the man who encounters the ear, the elephant is a big hairy fan, and so forth. There was no way several people with different roles in the university were going to be able to move forward in unison. My thoughts were coalescing around the "elephant." What does an experience of this kind do to a community, and what might I do to help?

Within about ten days the provost, Dr. Bettye Parker Smith, decided to reassemble her team in Atlanta. We lived in a hotel within walking distance of an office of one of the university's insurance companies. Eight of us worked at a round table in the company's conference room, with the provost in an office nearby.

It felt odd to me to be so isolated from the rest of my colleagues. Dillard is small and intense. We ordinarily spent very long hours on campus, and our encounters with one another informed not just my professional existence but my personal one as well. I was used to being with other people and speaking often—public prayers, small group conversations, teaching, preaching, and at this point in a normal school year, welcoming. But now, all of the venues where I normally operated were missing. My presence was clearly appreciated, but the small group of deans and managers with whom I was working certainly didn't need a sermon.

We still had students, lots of students, in Shreveport at Centenary, but as we began to realize, we had students (and faculty and staff) *everywhere*. Word continued to trickle in: some alums in this city have located a pocket of Dillard students at the local university, or such-and-such a school in this or that city has been trying to find Dillard to let us know they have ten Dillard students safe and sound.

One of our student leaders took a carload with him when he evacuated to Memphis. They slept on the floor in his mother's living room for a few days, then took themselves to the University of Memphis, asked to be enrolled, and were. Another student heading north, also with a carload, realized he had a business card from a University of Northern Iowa grad school recruiter in the pocket of his jeans. He called the recruiter, asked if he could bring his little group there, and they were welcomed into the University of Northern Iowa.

Understand, we did not know all of this in the days immediately following the disaster. It would be months later when the stories would begin to come out. Unbelievable as it may seem, schools all over the country took in our students, along with Xavier students, Tulane students, Loyola students, and students from other Katrina-affected schools from all over the Gulf Deep South. These "host schools" readily provided these young people, most of whom arrived without transcripts or paperwork beyond an identification card, with what we could not provide. Most of those schools did not charge the guest students. Many of the schools had to put together material and counseling support for guest students who were without belongings, upset, and homesick. And the host schools set out to provide this help while respecting and maintaining their guests' original school identities. It was *stunning*.

In the magnitude of all this, with each day overwhelming us from a new direction, I found a means of being chaplain that was not so much "doing for" my community as it was representing my community through my choices. I did what I believed any of us would do if we were able. First, I read a whole lot of Bible every day. I have a One Year Bible that provides a reading from the Hebrew Scriptures, Christian Scriptures, Proverbs, and Psalms for each day of the year. The daily reading is about four pages, which, spiritually, is like trying to get a drink of water from a fire hose. But there's something powerful about being overwhelmed, knocked down, and rolled around daily by a whole lot of Word. Evacuating, I had decided I would do my daily four pages without fail until I was back home again, so that was the Bible I had packed. Second, I entered into (or was ushered into) a status of ceaseless prayer for Dillard and for the vast number of people who were displaced, mourning, struggling, despairing, and having to make immensely hard decisions based on very little actual information. I went into this place of prayer and remained there because there was more company there than anywhere else on earth. That web of prayer—all-people prayer—was tangible, audible, generous, and profound.

I have never had such an experience in my life. Ever since the day as a young woman when I dared God to talk to me and was startled silly to have God accept that dare, I have had no choice but to believe in the power of prayer. I believe that the world is encased in an international network of prayers of different languages and faiths, weaving together our spiritual existence like a tapestry that all are invited to share. But I had never had that tapestry become a force that welcomed me, called me by name, and carried me as it did in those months. It took care of me so I could try to take care of us.

I tried to make gratitude tangible. Every morning I would write a note to someone who had done something nice for us or for me the day before, and I would mail the note on the way to work. There was never a morning when I had to strain to find an act of kindness to celebrate.

I soon found a church. Just up the street from our hotel, St. Matthew United Methodist saw me every Sunday morning that I was in town even though I am not UMC. It felt odd to be nonfunctional in a worship setting, but I was. Fortunately, the pastor never asked me to do anything but "be." I could just enjoy the worship, and I did. A couple of times, completely unbraided by the music and the Word, and its relevance to our ongoing situation, I remained in the pew after the service and cried. That was the only place I cried. And both times, someone came, sat next to me, put an arm around me, and maintained a peaceful silence until I was done.

There was more than enough need for prayer to go around. Our students at Centenary were being gradually brought out—sent home or to other schools—by means of a local telethon and the great generosity locals had been offering since the storm. As one bus evacuating students had been on its way to Shreveport in August, its brakes overheated. The driver got everyone off, but without any belongings. Then they all watched as the bus burned down to the tires. Dr. Hughes, our president, learned about this and turned around in the midst of her own evacuation to go to the students. As a result, she ended up driving through the teeth of part of the actual storm. Shreveport citizens had learned of the fire and supplied our students with everything they needed and even the bags to put it in.

And so the autumn continued. Eventually, students began to find me, and once one had my cell number, almost everybody did. The others from my office found me after the storm through text messaging—which was new to me. While I was in Des Moines, I asked my niece to teach me how to text, and I added that to my communication options. Intent on their own challenges, students did not call or text me a lot, but when a need arose, they got in touch. One day a student contacted me to let me know another of our students, being host-schooled at Morehouse in Atlanta, was both ill and discouraged. Within not much more than an hour I found out where he was and knocked on his residence hall door. When the door opened and I saw his expression of surprise and gratitude, I felt more like a chaplain than I had in weeks.

When our website was finally up, the provost and I agreed that messages from the chaplain would be appropriate. So I began doing occasional short pieces for the web. There were not that many—maybe seven or eight in total—and I have no copies and little recollection of what I wrote. All I remember is that I always wrote with one of two thoughts in mind: that the power of what we were together had survived and would rise again, and that those speaking about what had happened to us with disdain and smugness were not in concert with the will of God. By this time more of the university administration was in Atlanta and we had moved to a temporary office space; we'd had a disaster recovery team on campus, had been visited by a special team of library experts (we ended up shipping almost all of the remaining books to Dallas while the library was renovated), and we were working to obtain special permission from the federal government and accrediting body to run two semesters of classes back-to-back with no break, with commencement in the first part of July.

Facing Loss

When a victim of a natural disaster says they lost everything, they're not quite telling you the truth—although they are telling *a* truth as they have experienced it. If they had really lost everything, they wouldn't be in a position to tell you about it. Nevertheless, in a society that prizes "things," losing a whole lot of things at one time can be startling. There is grief, absolutely, and there is pain. You hurt for yourself, and you hurt even more for others who had less to begin with and don't have the wherewithal to get themselves back on their feet. But there *is* such a thing as losing everything, and because of that truth, the worst of Dillard University's Katrina semester was not the emergency evacuation, or the flooded campus, or the people dispersed all over the place, or the chaotic conference calls with everybody talking and nobody listening, or the future that seemed to take a sharp turn into nothingness at least twice a day.

In November, one of our juniors took advantage of the one-day opportunity extended to students to come to campus and see if any of the few salvaged belongings were theirs. On his way back to his host institution, Tennessee State, his car was sideswiped by another car. Our student's vehicle rolled, and a physician following both vehicles was so indignant he chased the car that caused the accident rather than staying with the student. It might not have helped, but it's hard to give back the notion that it would have been good to have the doctor kneeling at our student's side after he was thrown from the vehicle rather than racing up the interstate barking on his cell phone.

Our student died at Grady Hospital five days later, with all of the displaced Dillard students in the Atlanta area keeping insistent vigil in the waiting room. By that time we all knew his daddy, his mom, and his auntie, all of whom had traveled up from Dallas. It cost $25.9 million to remove the debris from Hurricane Katrina and its aftermath—downed trees, drowned computers, destroyed furniture, defeated buildings—from the campus of Dillard University, but our first serious loss as a result of Katrina was that young man. That loss forced us to pause and truly mourn, because it was the first one we couldn't repaint or gut or tear down and throw away or "bring back better." I went back to Des Moines for Thanksgiving, but on the following Saturday I was in Dallas, speaking at his funeral.

Like some others, I was brokenhearted by that death. We had stood up through all of that immensity of destruction. I had despaired over the loss of life in the city and the region and over the horror. If CNN knew the convention center was filled with people without food, water, sanitation, and ventilation, how could the federal government claim this was news to FEMA? But I had consoled myself in the knowledge that, despite tremendous risks, we had not lost any students. Now we had.

Part of what happens with disaster is that people wonder what it means. This is why untouched others theorizing aloud about God's punishment as the reason for a disaster can be so cruel. The victims' defenses are down. Their very reason for existing can be in question. In a situation like ours, you feel immense guilt that people and things that seemed entrusted to your care—lives and heirlooms and ways of being—were lost. Your previous state of grace as you believed it to be is gone; everything that was once anchored is now bobbing loose. Since the awful has happened, *anything* can happen. And *anything* can be pretty bad.

In Atlanta for almost four months after Katrina, I talked with many members of the community—students, faculty, and staff. I even spoke with the president in her visit to us in Atlanta (she was based in Washington, D.C.). I was rarely *in* the role of chaplain, but I was never *out of* the role of chaplain. People needed to tell their stories, but they also needed a space in which to ask, directly or indirectly, what it all meant. They asked: *Should I leave this situation or should I stay? Should I pray differently? What does it mean if I can't bring myself to pray at all? Should I be embarrassed because my losses were less than those of others? Is it okay to say that this was just more than I can bear? Is it okay to say that I am experiencing this as a gift?* We were dumped into a sea of spiritual, philosophical, and logistical variability—individually, family by family, and collectively.

Coming Home

Nevertheless, by the end of November we were finally set. Dillard would continue to exist, in New Orleans and on our campus, following restoration. We would spend six months living together in a hotel, paid for by the university. The hotel would provide a cafeteria area just for us. Classes would be held in the exhibition center (divided into cubicles) across the street, and on local campuses where wet labs were available. The administrative headquarters would be just over a mile from the hotel in a building owned by Tulane University. There would be no classes on Fridays, to allow extra time for faculty and staff, almost all of whom had lost their homes, to sort through the endless red tape of insurance companies, FEMA claims, city permits, and contractors' requirements. Most of us would return to the campus in the fall of 2006, but the leadership would remain downtown for another year after that.

Worship would resume in one of the hotel meeting spaces, but we would need to set up the room and break it back down every Sunday. The university rented one room just for our *stuff*—which included our drum set, keyboard, and Communion pieces. The flag store on Magazine Street had reopened, so I bought a large, colorful, Native American–style jagged-edged flag with a blue cross as its center. That flag came to symbolize worship in places other than our sanctuary; it means "worship on the road." Finally, it was decided that the host schools that had taken in our students would be celebrated at commencement until the last hosted student graduated.

The return to campus began in late June 2006, as the two back-to-back semesters at the Hilton ("the Hillard" as some students called it) were wrapping up. The first location to be engaged was Lawless Chapel, where the roof had failed in places but no floodwaters had penetrated. It was the only building on campus that had not flooded and was the traditional location for seniors to gather and be briefed for rehearsal, baccalaureate, and commencement; the noisy and happy graduating seniors pouring into Lawless signaled a return to normalcy.

Baccalaureate and commencement at Dillard are outdoor events, with the processional up the grassed middle of campus between a double row of live oaks called the Avenue of the Oaks. Consequently, one of the major jobs was to get the campus "ready for its close-up." At the time of commencement weekend, although all of the buildings were freshly painted, with flood marks and search marks covered, no other building was open. Sanitary facilities other than those in Lawless were a long row of port-a-potties. Dead trees, storm debris, one downed building, and all of the landscaping and dead grass had been removed. Only one of the massive trees in the Avenue of the Oaks had gone down; there was a baby live oak in its place, and another baby live oak planted in front of the residence hall where the student who died in November had begun his time at DU. Sand and new dirt had been spread and covered with sod. The graduating seniors processed over bright green grass carrying flags bearing the name of each host school in the colors of that host school. There were 376 flags.

AFTER KATRINA

When we returned to campus in the fall of 2006, although the shock and hard decisions were behind us, life became more difficult. The physical restoration was under way, but some of the priorities were puzzling. Lack of communication related to these decisions contributed to low morale. Part of the morale issue had nothing to do with the university. A wrecked region is a lot to take in, and it's a lot to live in as well. Part of the problem *did* have to do with us, however, in that the leadership was devoted to technical challenges (of which we had a slew), and we could not, would not, authorize anyone to take on the challenge of figuring out who we were, now that Katrina had changed us forever.

In his book *Leadership on the Line*, Ronald Heifetz speaks of the difference between technical challenges and adaptive challenges. In a technical challenge, there are identifiable experts who can be brought in to address the issue at hand. Example: Cable's out? Call the cable guy. But in an adaptive challenge, people need to change their behavior, to adapt. There is no "them" to call to perform this job. Example: Nation mired in segregation and Jim Crow threats and violence? People must change, and they must do so together. The further complication with an adaptive challenge is that in such a challenge, people typically refuse to authorize anyone to do the work of eliciting change. This is the dilemma from which Rev. Dr. Martin Luther King Jr.'s "Letter from a Birmingham Jail" sprang. In the midst of trying to do the work of desegregation, he was also called on to explain who (if anyone) authorized him to do it.

At post-Katrina Dillard, our adaptive challenge is about "becoming." We cannot possibly be precisely who we were; too much has happened. But if we are changed, then *how* are we changed? And since so much of our identity at Dillard is defined by our relationship with God, we cannot go forward without trying to craft theological significance from our experience.

Searching for Meaning

From the time of Katrina, through that fall, after our return, and since, people have struggled to sum things up in a word. Some tried calling Katrina's floodwaters "baptism," but the salt water was just too filthy and there were far too many drownings for that word to work for many. Was it "exile," with the opportunity the nation of Israel found and claimed to sharpen its definition of itself while living as strangers in a strange land? "Exile" did not quite seem to be the right word because we had remained in our native land (although not our native city) and had been among many people who had dedicated themselves, selflessly, to helping us. If not "baptism" or "exile," perhaps it was "displacement" (swapping sacred language for secular). However, would calling ourselves "displaced" skewer us in the past, forever seeking pity rather than proclaiming strength? Or was it just "a thing," just an event or series of events, interesting and difficult but not ultimately significant? We did not find that likely. It is an intimidating experience for a people with a strong history of faith to need to ask aloud what God is doing in their midst. This was and is true even though we are the descendants of a stolen and enslaved people, who passed painful generations of waiting for understanding and for change. But that legacy of waiting for understanding does not necessarily render us enthusiastic about waiting again.

Yoruba (Nigerian/West African) philosophy or theology provides for a three-step process in the creation of each human. First, Obatala makes our physical bodies. Then we travel to Ajala to choose our *ori*, which is the seat of both our personality and our destiny. Finally, our life force or soul is given from Olodumare. The important and critical step here is that we *choose* our destiny. When we struggle on earth, it is partly because before we were born, we agreed to take on some of the tasks humanity must achieve in its process of becoming. With its frequent consideration of what kinds of life events may have been put in motion prior to our births I often find Dillard to be more than a little bit Yoruba.

The challenge, then, is that if we *chose* this destiny, this Katrina-ravaged destiny—if we agreed to be among those who would shoulder this burden—we do not want to have endured this difficult experience without completing the task we assumed. I am not surprised to find us, still, seeking some kind of divinely informed position in regard to the post-Katrina journey. We don't want this all to have been about nothing more than renovating our buildings and planting new trees. We know enough about God to suspect God has a greater purpose, a deeper task for us, in mind.

Part of the fulfillment of this task has already left the campus in the hands and minds and lives of our Katrina-era students who have graduated. But it would be responsibility avoidance of the highest order by those of us who remain behind to leave it at that. The experience was so profound, so reducing, so uplifting, so enlightening, we all expected to be changed. Change was absolutely there; we remember the feel of it on our fingertips. But soon, the jobs of many days, the necessary tasks, and the tyranny of the habitual stole in and muted that transformative encounter.

The Chaplain's Role "After"

When the community cannot afford to feel, the chaplain must feel. When the community finds itself without words, the chaplain must speak in word or deed. Over time, I have begun to follow through on the things that floored me about our experience, in an effort to keep an echo of the change we almost found alive.

The first thing that floored me was the empowerment. We have had a student body that encountered the highly unexpected and the possibly unfair and dealt with it in grand style. They expected and accepted God's help and handled themselves. In December of 2005, the university held a Christmas party at the Hilton for faculty and staff, and we got to see each other, all in one place, for the first time in four months. What struck me at that party was, again, the empowerment. People had followed the High Holy One through fire (or, literally, through water) and come out the other side. We were faith tested and tough, and we knew it.

The other thing that floored me was connection. All of us met people we would not ordinarily have met, went places we would not ordinarily have gone, and had our lives intertwined with each other and with strangers and former strangers in startling ways. We gained an understanding of what it might be like for others in similar (and worse) circumstances; that knowledge is a gift of great price. Like the prophets of old, we were burned in the process, but we made contact with the Most High. I have not forgotten that tangible experience in the tapestry of prayer, and it distracts me. Since finding it, nothing else quite satisfies. I am being wooed by that unity in diversity, the sheer risk of proximity to difference that was absolutely intended, and I cannot help but try to represent it in my community.

I keep trying to find a language all the factions in our community can speak so we can better understand each other. I am more interested in efforts to get us talking with each other than anything else. I am convinced that the lines of separation between administration and students and faculty and staff and alums are binding us up. I have no precise idea why it is so important for this little group of people in this little colored school in New Orleans to live up to the extraordinary opportunity we have been given to think and engage one another differently, but I am convinced of the importance of this. God invites us to be a community that became empowered on the inside and connected with the outside, and even the partial attaining of this destiny, *which we chose*, would be pleasing in the sight of the Most High.

Katrina pushed me into new territory, beyond what I or my community considered the norm for its chaplain. Apparently, I decided to stay there. Since our return, while trying to stay in the background, I did some things differently. I facilitated focus groups among the faculty, and those results are being employed by the president of the Faculty Senate. I issued a "Call to the Chapel" for a morning-long discussion about our identity and our future. The students picked up some of what was determined in that conversation and are carrying it forward. In the role of the Student Government Association's advisor, I encouraged the students as they sought "a place at the table."

I do not think I will ever again be able to be neutral or careful while people with whom I share community struggle for empowerment or connection. I am not saying that these two truths, these two touchstones of empowerment and connection, are the usual, or *a* usual, reaction to a natural disaster. This is just what happened with us and with me. I *will* say that some things can be so enormous or be experienced so enormously that people have no choice but to fight to break off a piece of understanding to carry with them. I suspect this happens more normally with chaplains than with some other groups of people. Every one of us must *look to the rock from which [we] were hewn* (Isaiah 51:1, RSV). The name of our rock is God's Katrina, and our understanding is a work in progress.

A MUSLIM CHAPLAIN
ON FINDING HIS WAY

Sohaib N. Sultan
Princeton University, Princeton, New Jersey

Recently, I was sitting in my office with a student who was lamenting the fact that when he was younger, it was so much easier for him to pray. Now when he prays, he doesn't feel the same sense of calm—it's more anxiety, less satisfaction. I remember just sitting there and thinking, *What do I say to that?* I was really at a loss for words. Usually when I'm in this sort of mentorship or counseling situation, I have a question, an insight, a story, but this time I just remember thinking, *I don't know what to say. I quite literally don't know what to say.*

I was completely stuck because the story I was hearing could have come from my own mouth. I could have been sitting exactly where that student was sitting and saying exactly the same words. Ever since I entered the field of chaplaincy and undertook the role that I have, not only at this university but also in my wider Muslim community, it's been difficult for me now to go to the mosque as a simple worshiper.

Sohaib N. Sultan is director of the Muslim Life Program at Princeton University in Princeton, New Jersey. He was formerly Muslim chaplain at Trinity College and Wesleyan University in Connecticut. His work has appeared in *The Koran for Dummies* and in *The Qur'an and Sayings of Prophet Muhammad: Selections Annotated and Explained* (SkyLight Paths). He enjoys watching his favorite soccer teams, hanging out and sharing laughs with students, and spending quality time with his wife—his one true love.

My role as a public religious figure has complicated the ease and comfort I used to feel in my personal spiritual life.

I'm sure every public religious figure struggles with this issue in one way or another during their career. But for me, as one of the first Muslim college chaplains in the country, the complications and trade-offs of my public role seem especially intense and high-stakes. For me, "public" includes my role as a leader of Princeton's Muslim community, but it also means considering issues beyond just my own campus. Because our positions are so new, Muslim chaplains are taking on some important questions for the first time: What should the role of a Muslim chaplain be on a secular campus? What does the word "chaplain" even connote in the context of Islam? The newness of these questions puts a focus on the public elements of my role that I'm still grappling with, professionally and personally.

MY JOURNEY INTO CHAPLAINCY

My journey into chaplaincy began before I even knew such a role existed, when I myself was in college. I went to Indiana University, where I had a really good experience. But in my junior year, I experienced the loss of two very dear people to whom I was very close: my uncle, who died suddenly and unexpectedly of a heart attack at the age of seventy; and just one week later, my aunt, who had been battling cancer for many years. None of my family was able to go to the funerals because it was such an expensive trip to Pakistan.

All of the deaths that I had experienced before that were when I was much younger. I had seen my family struggle through it, but I myself was too young to quite understand what was going on. The deaths of my aunt and uncle impacted me quite a bit. I experienced a crisis of depression, grief, and sadness. All previous trials of life paled in comparison. I had to sit with that grief. I didn't know how to process it. And of course it was an academic semester, so I still had to keep up with my studies and go to class and remain involved in my organizations, and I still had to put on a smile. But I didn't know how to do that.

I didn't feel like there was any real support system for me, and that was particularly true because my religious community was a group of undergraduate and graduate students who were all in the same boat, trying to work hard and graduate. And so despite the fact that everybody in the community was very kind to me, I felt lonely in my sadness.

There was, however, one graduate student who, despite working on a PhD and having a family, took the time to lend me a compassionate ear and offer supportive advice. He was several years older than I was, but he became truly one of the best friends I've ever had. He was there just to listen. And since he was much older, I think it helped me confide in him. It was like having an older brother.

One of the things he told me was that grieving is a process, that it's nothing to rush over. And that was very comforting because a month or two later, I still felt like, *Why am I not able to get over this? Why is this so difficult for me?* I thought that maybe within a week, if I had strong enough faith, the grief should be over. It helped to hear him say that what I was experiencing was normal. I don't even know if he realizes how helpful he was. After that experience I wanted to be that type of person for others, but I never knew that I could connect it to a vocation.

Another transformative experience happened a year later, in my senior year, when I was the outgoing president of the Muslim Students Association. We were a group of students with no chaplain, no administrator, no advisor, nothing. And it was a huge group: in 2001, there were about five hundred Muslim students in the MSA at Indiana University. Usually, being president of the MSA meant putting events together now and then. But then 9/11 happened. People had a lot of anger, they had a lot of questions, and they had a lot of suspicions about the Muslim community. Suddenly, as outgoing MSA president, I was expected to play a real leadership role: speaking at a church, at a synagogue, in a classroom, just anywhere that you can imagine, on an almost daily basis. At the same time I had to be a source of support for my own Muslim community. People were hungry for information, and they were eager to have their questions answered.

In Bloomington, the Muslim community experienced a full range of responses. On the one hand, we experienced insults and threats outside our local mosque. But we also experienced a lot of neighborliness, a lot of compassion, a lot of kindness. People left flowers at the door of the mosque, showing their support for the community. People called and said, "You know, if anyone is afraid to go out, we can buy their groceries for them." People were just enormously helpful. As difficult as the experience of 9/11 was, I think I've never felt more proud to be an American, because the responses could have been so negative and so violent. But the positive responses, responses of kindness, were overwhelming.

Right after 9/11, the Muslim community in Bloomington got together and we asked ourselves, "What should our response be? How can we be a source of reconciliation, and how can we build bridges at this difficult moment in the nation's history?" One of the things we decided to do was to put together an open house at the mosque. We invited everyone in Bloomington to come and see our mosque, eat with us, ask us questions, and just talk. The mayor of the city came and offered comforting words. We pulled this major event together maybe a week after 9/11, working day and night. I remember a moment at the open house when I stepped back and saw all that was happening—just seeing everybody come together and so many people talking to one another, all the bridges that were being built—and I said to myself, "This is something amazing." I stumbled through my new leadership role, but it was a learning experience. At the end of the day I realized that I had a real passion, a real interest, and a real love for working with community at the grassroots level.

After graduating, I did freelance journalism in Chicago for about three years, covering the religion beat for various newspapers, Chicago NPR, and PBS. I enjoyed learning how different religious communities worked, but in the back of my mind I couldn't leave behind the experiences I'd had as a student at IU and in community organizing. As a reporter I could explore how religious leaders served their faith communities, but I wanted to do more than explore. I wanted to dedicate my life to serving the Muslim community in America.

I also had a deeply intellectual interest in Islamic studies and for a while considered earning a PhD and becoming a university professor. But in the middle of this thought process, I met Dr. Ingrid Mattson at the Islamic Society of North America's annual convention and told her what I was thinking. She said, "It sounds like you would make a perfect chaplain." I said I couldn't imagine myself working in the prison system. Those were the only Muslim chaplains I was aware of. Muslim chaplains in other spheres of life—college chaplains, hospital chaplains—are a more recent development. I had literally never heard of a Muslim chaplain in any context other than prison. So Dr. Mattson introduced me to the wider field and told me about the Hartford Theological Seminary, which trains Muslim chaplains. And so my journey to chaplaincy began.

BUILDING BRIDGES, INSTITUTIONS, AND RELATIONSHIPS

One important element of the public role I've undertaken in my own institution is that of bridge builder. I think a lot about how to create programs that will be inclusive and welcoming and give people an opportunity to explore and address even the most difficult questions. I take great pleasure in putting on those programs, events, and study circles. I've initiated a program at Princeton that I call the "Islam in Conversation" series. Even though Islam is often treated as being the "other," as something very distinct from other religions and from American society, I want to emphasize that Islam is in conversation. We're inviting the best of Muslim thinkers, artists, and activists, and when they come, we don't just have an event with them, but we actually put them in conversation with somebody from another faith tradition or cultural perspective. By doing so, we hope that people understand Islam as part of the broader dialogue. We hope that they integrate Islam into their own discovery of self, meaning, and social ethics and see its relevance to their lives, thinking, spirituality, and their own society.

As I work through the challenges of my own public role, I have in mind not only my voice but the voices of others. As the first generation of Muslim university chaplains, we're thrust into this idea of institution building at the same time as we consider the question, *What exactly does institution building mean?* As a group, we find ourselves looking at what other faith communities have done. We think of Catholic Newman Centers and Centers for Jewish Life such as Hillel, and how both groups have been able to create powerful institutions throughout American college campuses. They have directors, staff, programs, classes, and huge budgets. Maybe we need to do our own version of that—people sometimes half-jokingly say, "We need a Muslim Hillel." For some people, that's the obvious direction for us to go. I don't disagree completely, but I think it's a wonderful blessing that in these early phases of our own institution building we can really think about it—"Is Hillel the model? Is that what we're really seeking to do? Is that what is going to be of greatest benefit to Muslim students today, tomorrow, and a hundred years from now?" Every decision we're making feels historic. It's exciting—and intense.

There is much for Muslim chaplains to learn from the experiences of Protestant Christian chaplains, particularly from their emphasis on pastoral care. I find there to be a lot of wisdom in the idea that people deep down have answers to their own questions and that our role is to facilitate their journey of self-discovery. While I see a lot of parallels to this model in the Islamic tradition, it is not what Muslims generally expect when they come seeking counsel. When they come to an imam-like figure they expect an expert in religious moral law: "I have this problem. What does the law say I should do?" I remember one student who came to me with a real ethical dilemma on his hands. I asked him, "What do *you* think?" and he said, "I think that Islam is not about what I think." So I asked, "Well, what do you think the prophet Muhammad meant when he advised his companions, 'Consult your own heart'?" For the first time this student began to see answers as coming from within and not only from books and teachers. Part of what I see as my role as chaplain is gently introducing new models of counseling and thinking about religious uncertainties to my community.

I frequently find myself in settings in which I don't even use the term "chaplain" because I know it's just going to go over people's heads. People often refer to me as "Imam Sohaib." I'm not fully comfortable with that title, but I recognize that it's a title the community is comfortable with. It sounds familiar to them. But at the same time there are all sorts of preconceived notions of the imam—some positive, some maybe not so positive. People are always saying, "I have to call you something. So I'll call you 'Brother' or 'Imam.'" They're not comfortable just calling me by my name. I've noticed that recently more and more students have started calling me "Imam." It just happened organically; I'm not sure how.

For me, the term "chaplain" makes sense. I relate to it, and I find meaning in it. I think it's primarily because of my training at the Hartford Seminary, where we were able to take classes that allowed us to tease out what a chaplain is in terms of being a personal caregiver, offering spiritual direction, being a mentor, teaching, and preaching. That is the work I feel most called to, more than being a program manager. What satisfies me most is building individual relationships with students. Which is why I was so surprised to realize recently how far I've moved from that calling.

This is my fifth year at Princeton, and my first class graduated last spring. I don't have a large role at baccalaureate—students do most of the reading of passages—which left me plenty of time to reflect. It turned out to be a really moving moment for me. I was brought to tears on several occasions through the festivities, just from seeing these faces, now with their black robes and their hats. I was constantly having flashbacks to conversations in my office, or taking a walk around campus, sometimes talking over ice cream, sometimes over lunch or dinner; spending two or three hours discussing, "What does it mean to be a Muslim? What does it mean to be a spiritually rooted person?" or some other deep aspect of life, sometimes one-on-one, sometimes with a group. This feeling continued after graduation, into the next weeks, as I received letters and testimonials, sometimes written and sometimes oral, from students expressing how important it was for them to have me as part of their college experience. I also heard from parents who were genuinely grateful for the meaningful contribution I had made in their children's lives.

While part of my emotion was from seeing these young people reach the point where they're getting ready to leave our community, there was for me a more profound revelation as well: that these students, the students I'd known in my first years at Princeton, had a totally different experience with me than the students who have met me since. I realized that I do not have the same connection with the current freshmen or sophomores that I do with the juniors and seniors. The first two years I was here my program was small, my budget was small, and my focus was on being a chaplain. In more recent years, establishing programming has taken up a much larger share of my time and attention. When I started to ask myself what had changed, the answer surprised me. I realized that my move away from personal mentorship and toward institution building and programming was tied to the way I was struggling with the private and public elements of my own spiritual life.

SEEKING A BALANCE

Very often as I'm on my way to worship at the mosque or the Muslim prayer room at the university, someone stops me with a question or a request. I'm sure the same thing happens to many community religious leaders. People come up, and they want to talk. They want to talk about life's challenges and questions they have and concerns about friends or family members. Or I'm asked to lead the prayer, or to give a short talk, or something else that takes me away from just being a simple worshiper.

On campus, there's an even more interesting dynamic: the space that Princeton designated for prayer is right above my office, in the same building. What happens when I climb one flight of stairs? Does my work continue? Can I ever be just a worshiper upstairs without being in my chaplain role? Students are physically and metaphorically lined up between my office and the prayer space, so that on my way up there I find myself trying to figure out where my chaplain role can end and where my spiritual being can begin. Constantly practicing faith in such a public way can be exhausting, and sometimes it is difficult to have that alone time with God.

Part of the way I hid that struggle from myself was to become increasingly more a program and events manager than a chaplain. I basically went into institution-building mode to avoid internal conflicts and turmoil. Instead of working toward a greater sense of inner clarity, I jumped into the world of "Let's program everything. Let's have an event around everything. Let's bring in the best speakers. Let's go out into the community and do as much fund-raising as possible so we have tons of money to work with." I went from being a present pastoral caregiver to a program director and events coordinator. While those efforts have won me a lot of accolades and they've been important to the broader community in other ways, I realize now that I made that shift as a way to hide my struggle from myself and from my students and my community.

As I stood at graduation last spring, watching my students walk across the stage, I noticed that every single flashback was about the human connection I'd had with each of them. It made me realize that, while programs and events have their place and their benefit, ultimately it's that human connection, that relationship, that is the most meaningful thing you can give to a student—far more so than any program. I spent the whole week of graduation with an overwhelming feeling of "Oh my God" and "Oh my God, how beautiful," of "Oh my God, how great" and "Oh my God, how far I've drifted from that."

I think that I've always known theologically that one has to be rooted and grounded and have a sense of peace in order to be able to help others. But I've noticed it more and more since struggling with my own spirituality. For me it's still about figuring out how to be a devotee of God and a worshiper of God in this very public way. As much as I know I need that private time, it's hard for me to say no to people. It's hard for me to turn away from commitments, especially when it involves meeting the urgent needs of other people or my community as a whole. Though it's hard for me to place limits on the time I give others, I've seen over the past year or so that constant activity is not a sustainable way of being, for myself, for my family, for my students, or for my community.

Even as I struggle to establish a balance, the process itself has been illuminating. More than I might have a few years ago, when a student comes to me and tells me, "I feel like I can't pray," or says, "I lost that connection to God that I used to have," I can feel it. I have a much deeper appreciation for the struggle they're going through.

The day that student came in asking for advice about his loss of religious focus, it was such a powerful moment for me to sit there and realize I didn't know what to tell him. I think I even started saying, "I don't know what to say"—but then I realized I *did* know. I told him, "You are not alone." I don't know how he took it. Maybe he thought I was talking about other people, but I was really talking about myself. I don't know if he understood that. Probably not. But it seemed to offer some relief.

I think everything we experience in life is a blessing from God. Even my current struggle of figuring out how to worship God is a blessing. If and when I ever do emerge with confidence and achieve a comfortable-enough balance between my public roles and the private religious life that sustains me, it will help me help others through their own struggles. Which is exactly why I chose to become a chaplain in the first place.

IN COFFIN'S PULPIT
Re-envisioning Protestant Religious Culture

Rev. Ian B. Oliver
Yale University, New Haven, Connecticut

Very often at an alumni reception or after worship in Battell Chapel, someone will approach me and say something to the effect of: "So you're in William Sloane Coffin's pulpit?" I never quite know what response is expected. Often, it is just an opening gambit to share experiences of the legendary Yale chaplain (1958–75), who rode the buses in the Freedom Rides, led protests against the military draft and the Vietnam War, and is remembered as a legendary preacher and mentor to a generation of students. What they probably don't want to hear is that I hadn't yet been born when Coffin became Yale's chaplain and that, back in El Paso, Texas, where I grew up, people who used three names besides "Javier Jose" or "Billy Ray" got beat up. I have come to know well who William Sloane Coffin was and how much he accomplished, but the relevance of that history today is for me a more open question than the direct connection my alumni interlocutors seem to expect.

The very fact that a kid from El Paso, Texas—a kid from immigrant and poor southern roots—now stands in the pulpit at Yale in

Rev. Ian B. Oliver is Pastor of the University Church and senior associate chaplain for Protestant life at Yale University in New Haven, Connecticut. He was formerly university chaplain at Bucknell University. He notes that at each of the institutions he's served, he's been in a pastoral and preaching role in the campus chapel.

itself shows how places like Yale—and even chaplaincy itself—have changed. It is also a story of the symbolic power of college and university chaplaincy and my own struggles with the legacy of the "Greatest Generation." My story is not representative of all chaplains—anything but. But my engagement with the myths and mythic figures of chaplaincy and the irony of my eventual arrival at Yale does, I think, say something important about what chaplaincy was, is, and may yet become.

It seems important to note that the literal answer to the alum's question of whether I now occupy Coffin's pulpit is "no." Except perhaps for Easter Sunday or state funerals, I'm not in the Battell Chapel pulpit, because our university church doesn't use that pulpit anymore. It's still there, eight feet above the chapel floor; not too grand, but made of beautiful, scarred wood stained a dark brown and with a wonderful old wind-up clock mounted inside where the preacher can see it. The old pulpit is like the prow of a ship, jutting out into the nave of the chapel. But now I preach from a simple portable wooden lectern that we place on the floor at the head of the center aisle at sermon time. Among many symbols of how chaplaincy at Yale has changed, this is an elegant one. There is still preaching in the Yale chapel, but it is from a different place, to a different student body, and meeting different needs.

One lesson I have learned in twenty-five years as an educational chaplain is that all chaplaincy is personal. No matter how hard chaplains seek to share leadership with students, faculty, and colleagues, a chaplaincy is defined by the personal style and philosophy of the head chaplain. Unlike a local church or synagogue, there is little structure inherent in the position. Except perhaps in novels or films about English boarding schools, there is no stereotype of a college chaplain. Often a chaplain is just a single individual, sometimes with a part-time administrative assistant, struggling to engage religion, ethics, and spirituality in all the myriad forms they take on a college campus. It can be a lonely job, but it is also a job where one often has the freedom to define what is right and worthy, what is good religion and bad religion, which causes or groups get encouragement and which do not.

As a result of this personality-driven job description, when a new chaplain arrives there are often ghosts of chaplains past still haunting the campus. The history of chaplaincy is all local. A new chaplain soon learns who the previous chaplain offended, how she defined good religion and bad religion, and who idolized her.

In the case of William Sloan Coffin Jr., I had a predecessor who was nationally famous (and infamous), but whose legacy was not totally clear. Many saw him as one of the greatest prophetic voices of his century—a pivotal religious figure of his day. Others said he used his position to draw attention to himself and to force a political agenda that had no place in the chapel. He was loved and hated.

Some of my colleagues encouraged me to just stay away from Coffin and the past. "What do those dead white men have to do with you or your students today?" one volunteered. Another said, "This history is irrelevant to chaplaincy today—we are in a different world with a different set of challenges." Other colleagues still invoke Coffin at every opportunity, yearning for the intensity and purpose of their own student days under his mentoring. So I had a choice: to declare the present so discontinuous with the past that looking back is a waste of time, or to maintain that the present is the same as the past and thus that the tasks remain unchanged— or a third option, on which I have ultimately settled: to critically engage this heritage and do my best to discern what lessons apply to today and which do not.

THE GHOSTS OF CHAPLAINS PAST:
THE POSTWAR GENERATION

I am not a historian. I do not claim to be telling William Sloan Coffin's story or that of his generation of college chaplains or of his postwar generation more generally. My mentors in chaplaincy, however, were part of this remarkable and distinctive group of men (and it *was* men) who changed the nature of chaplaincy. The children of every generation must look back at their parents and claim their legacy for the future, while at the same time recognizing and acknowledging their very human errors and blind spots. I doubt my ability to ever tell a fully objective truth about my parents and mentors, but I can say what I noticed and how I think it has influenced me.

Yale's past interests me, in part, because I am, believe it or not, the first-ever specifically "Protestant" chaplain at Yale. *Hold on*, you say, *Yale has been Protestant (and not just Protestant, but Congregational) since 1701*. But Yale has had a chaplain only since the 1920s, when compulsory chapel ended and voluntary Sunday services began. The "university chaplain" at Yale was both pastor of the college chapel and administrator for all religious life. "Protestant" was never specified, because, of course, the vast majority of students and faculty at that time were Protestant, and Protestantism was the default, the norm, the establishment. To be chaplain was to be Protestant.

Like many other American liberal arts institutions, Yale has seen a remarkable shift in religious identity over the last fifty years, from the historical default of a generic Protestant identity (even for Catholics and Jews, who were expected to act like Protestants); to a full-scale revolt against and rejection of the Protestant establishment in the 1960s; to an embracing of religious pluralism in the 1980s and '90s; and now, to an interesting moment when our society has become largely secular, in the sense that there is no "established" religion, but where religious diversity is seen as a persistent reality, if not a social asset. In fifty years, the context for being "Protestant" at Yale has changed radically. WASPs were once almost all there was, and they guarded their majority with care. But today, Protestants are a minority, and a divided one at that. Who my Protestant students are is defined, in many ways, by unspoken presumptions about the old establishment. If we are to both understand our history and set ourselves free from its presumptions, we must retell our own story.

Any backward look should begin, however, with appreciation. Coffin, and others like him at liberal arts colleges around the country, helped motivate a generation of students to see Christian faith as a living force for social justice and peace. They saw it as their job to startle complacent students, a complacent university, and a complacent America awake. As young men who had gone off to right the wrongs of the world in World War II, they returned and found themselves resisting the 1950s' cultural climate of prosperity and uniformity. They returned to find that bigotry, warmongering, injustice, and poverty were evils not just in foreign lands, but also at home, and they brought the same relentless energy to defeating them. In the process, they helped free Christian faith from its "suburban captivity"[1]—its unbiblical identification with American culture, capitalism, individualism, and even patriotism. As historian and journalist James Carroll wrote, "[They] changed both how colleges think of themselves and what chaplains dare to undertake."[2] They took great risks, sometimes jeopardizing their personal safety or continued employment, to force connections between the university, the church, and compelling movements for social change. They jumped over generational divides to listen to the voices of students distraught over the moral contradictions of their own society and worked both to channel that anger into effective protest and to make those voices heard in the corridors of power.

Of course, some chaplains did get fired for their activism. And some were not activists at all. But at highly visible universities and important regional liberal arts colleges, there was a core group who seemed to become, for a historical moment, the public voice and face of American Protestantism. What set the chaplains of the 1960s apart was that they stepped into that familiar, established role of chaplain and then used it against itself. They used the power and trust built up in those pulpits to preach against the contradictions of the establishment itself: its complacency, its racism, and its acquiescence to violence and war. They challenged the long-established rules that had restricted access to higher education to their own kind—white, privileged, Protestant males. Protestant presumptions about the absolute freedom of individual conscience led to assertions of the inherent equality and dignity of each individual and pushed these chaplains to be among the first white religious leaders to support the civil rights movement. You couldn't get more

Protestant than this—always examining established authority for feet of clay, even when it included their own feet.

When I worked under these men, the fire of their devotion to equality in American society burned hot. On issues of desegregating the South, ending the war in Vietnam, and opening up leadership in the church and the university not only to African Americans and women but also to Jews and Catholics, they were warriors. But they were also sons of their own times, sometimes cringe-inducing in their patronizing, sexist, I-know-what's-right-for-you attitudes. They were opening doors that only they could open, but many had never experienced or even imagined working for a woman, or a Jew, or an African American, and they still spoke out of an experience defined by white, male, Protestant privilege. To their credit, they worked—theologically and personally—to adjust to a world where new voices would be heard, but the tone of their own arguments for equality assumed that everyone else shared their Protestant worldview. For them, the great Protestant voices spoke for the whole society, in a language the whole society could understand.

I remember a meeting I attended about the legacy of a university's 1960s-era movement to engage and support a nearby poor, black neighborhood. The programs had been visionary and exciting and participatory, but somehow energy faded and the movement died. Up front in the large meeting room, four or five distinguished faculty and other activists from the era spoke. After an hour of wistful reflections from the panel about why the programs failed, the discussion began. A young black man spoke up from the back of the room. He said, "I think I know why this project failed. Look at who was talking and leading—and look at who was supposedly being helped." He pointed to the speakers, all of whom were white and privileged (and male), and then to the audience members, mostly black and poor.

Movements for the social liberation of women, African Americans, and the poor would eventually require powerful white men like these chaplains, who had opened the doors, to step aside. The tall pulpit served for a time as a place from which to exhort, challenge, and liberate, but it ultimately revealed its limitations as a vantage point from which to understand the experience of others.

DISMANTLING THE OLD PROTESTANT ESTABLISHMENT

One of the things that was exciting to me as a divinity school student considering college chaplaincy was how unreligious it looked as practiced by this postwar generation. College chaplains were cool. They had shared dramatic experiences with Dr. King at Selma and in demonstrations after Kent State. Many were spellbinding storytellers and wonderful singers and musicians. They drank. They smoked. They laughed at accepted pieties. I remember my mentor, Rev. Robert D. Dewey, longtime chaplain at Kalamazoo College, stepping down from the pulpit in Stetson Chapel, perching on a front-row pew, and saying every swear word he could think of. It was in service of a point, I'm sure, but what remained in my memory was the congregation's shock—and the delight in the shock. This was the furthest thing you could find from traditional, moralistic, narrow Christianity while still remaining Christian.

The chaplains of the 1960s were deeply Christian themselves, but they set their faith against itself. They imagined religion without the stiffness, as an eternally radical prophetic movement always challenging authority, tradition, and puritanical morality. Whether they fully realized it or not, they themselves helped set in motion the dismantling of their own privilege. Partly due to urging from Protestant chaplains, universities lowered longtime barriers to or quotas on the admission of women, African Americans, Jews, and Catholics. By working toward equality and multiplicity, they helped demolish the long-assumed homogeneity of the university. But the pulpits from which these chaplains thundered were built on that historical privilege and exclusivity. The idea that one Protestant voice could somehow speak for everyone would soon disappear as new populations looked to other traditions and authorities. Radical 1960s-era chaplains destroyed their own role as the sole public moral voice of the university in order to end that role's moral self-contradictions.

And in helping dismantle the old establishment, radical chaplains left a vacuum in which Protestant Christians lost their identity. Iconoclasm loses its purpose once all the icons are gone. The unforeseen consequence of this loosening of tradition was that the next generation, raised on protest and endless questioning, simply wandered away from religion. In a cartoon in the *Yale Daily News* last year, a white, preppy young man is commenting to a friend about the amazing Kwanzaa and Hanukkah social events on campus and then wonders where the Christmas social event is. He concludes by sheepishly admitting, "I have no culture." His conversation partner responds, "Nice sweater vest, though," to which he responds, "Thanks, it's Lacoste."[3]

It's into this context, where Protestant students (Lacoste-clad or otherwise) often feel an absence of meaningful culture, that I arrived at Yale in 2008 and was assigned the unwieldy title of "Pastor of the University Church and Senior Associate Chaplain for Protestant Life." Protestant life? An awkward concept at best, probably borrowed from the generic "religious and spiritual life" used to describe many chaplaincy programs. "Jewish life" I can imagine—or "Muslim life"—cultural and religious elements combined to define a minority experience. But what is "Protestant life"? By its nature, Protestantism has always resisted becoming a "culture"—having been formed, in part, in reaction to the enculturation of medieval Catholicism. Classically, Protestantism is about belief, not practice—just the believer and the Bible—and whatever culture it has should be minimal and is always suspect.

My Catholic and Jewish colleagues, however, regularly remind me that no matter how much Protestants protest that they have no culture, outsiders who have felt the pressure to "act Protestant" know the rules of that culture well. As the *Yale Daily News* cartoonist winkingly acknowledged, no matter how much the religion itself tries to shrug off cultural practices, it's impossible to completely disassociate the faith itself from the subcultures that practice it.

But one of the great joys of my work is that partly because of the demolition work done in the 1960s and '70s, and even more during the culture wars of the 1980s and '90s, the presumption that "Protestant" equals "normal" is quickly disappearing. Demographics are hard to argue. Today, Yale is roughly 30 percent Protestant (though you could cut up that pie many different ways), 30 percent Catholic, 20 percent Jewish, 5 percent other religions, and 15 percent none, other, and combinations. Yale's head university chaplain is a Roman Catholic laywoman (and my strongest supporter). Alongside us in the chaplain's office are an associate chaplain who is a Presbyterian clergywoman, a Muslim coordinator, and a Hindu advisor. Around us, serving the university, are remarkable centers for Jewish and Catholic life, with their own buildings, clergy, and staff. I can't help but think that this diversity is a realization of our predecessors' dreams—though they probably couldn't have imagined what it would actually be like for their Protestant voice to be simply one among a chorus of equals.

INHERITING THE WRECKAGE OF THE OLD PROTESTANT ESTABLISHMENT

Luckily for me, growing up in Texas, my path to Yale was not one that set me up for disappointment over the loss of the old establishment. My fellow Texans were, at best, on the edge of American culture, and our "old traditions" were Spanish, not New England Puritan. Yes, I watched too many old movies about New England colleges and went to Amherst College with a romantic idea of stepping back into the Edwardian era; but Amherst in the late 1970s was newly coeducational and wrestling with its own old traditions, in part because children of the middle class like me were arriving from places like El Paso.

Though I didn't in any way feel like a member of the establishment, I soon realized that I carried its privileges and perspectives with me, consciously or not. My first full chaplaincy job was at a multireligious boarding school in southern India (with its own missionary history to wrestle). There, I was surprised to encounter Hindus who assumed that any good Christian would eventually understand that they too were really Hindu. While divinity school had somehow left my cultural biases unexamined, in the real world of chaplaincy, I discovered that I had the same kind of assumptions as the Hindus who so startled me—that all religious people, if they were honest and true, would admit that they should act like Protestants.

It was at Bucknell University, where I helped build a multireligious chaplaincy, that I received my greatest lessons in the importance of separating Protestant from universal. I served as university chaplain and, in that role, was both overall head of religious life and leader of the Protestant Sunday service. With the support of a courageous administration, the first full-time Jewish chaplain was hired, and the first formal connection to the local Catholic diocese was hammered out. My Catholic and Jewish colleagues became great personal friends, but we also battled each other over our religious differences. It was the rabbi and the priest who made sure I understood that being Protestant did not mean that I understood all forms of religion in order to speak for them. They taught me that no matter however wonderful my University of Chicago education in the Hebrew and Christian Scriptures, it did not allow me to speak for or second-guess the Jews and the Catholics about their own faith or practice. I expected them to allow me to define my own faith and likewise had to let them define their own. After that, we could argue. But I could not presume that I knew their religion better than they did, which was what my Protestant upbringing had taught me.

What it had not taught me, but which I soon learned, was that the American Protestant experience was not somehow ordained by God. It was a remarkable, but local, phenomenon—powerful and compelling, tragic and self-destructive—as culturally bound and as foreign to others as their faith was to me. At its best, American Protestantism is at the core of liberal arts education and the stubbornest ideas of liberty and individual rights; at its worst, it is as arrogant and cruel in its good intentions as any imperial power.

From postwar chaplains like Coffin, I have inherited the wreckage of the old Protestant establishment. But rather than experiencing this seismic shift as chaotic or disorienting, I find myself increasingly aware of and eager to embrace the opportunities it offers. By dis-establishing Protestant Christianity, my forebears have set me free to be a Protestant Christian in ways they themselves never would have imagined. We are experiencing a shocking but remarkable moment in our history. For the first time perhaps since the Reformation, we have the chance to begin seeing ourselves clearly and to discern what our way of thinking and our living faith might have to offer to the interreligious communities in which we now live.

ANSWERING A NEW SET OF QUESTIONS

In my divinity school days, we fought about politics. I trained for ministry with an image of my mentors in mind, assuming that I too might become a charismatic leader with a ready-made congregation confident in its beliefs but ready to be "shaken up" and sent out to change the world. I never imagined that students would be asking me, "Well, what do Christians really believe?" I'm not sure it ever would have occurred to Coffin that a Protestant congregant of his might need a clarification of this basic question—and indeed, they might not have.

But the joy of my work today is that the doctrines and practices that were thought to be unquestionable back then are all on the table now. My students ask me everything without prejudice. Coming out of mixed Christian backgrounds—mother in one church, father in another (maybe), attending an evangelical youth group, but going to Catholic Mass with a friend—they ask the most basic questions and expect me to know the answers. They want to know where ideas like "original sin" came from, not because they're burdened by them, but because they only have a vague impression of them, and wonder what they should believe. They want to know how the idea of the Trinity originated or why we strip the church on Passion Sunday, and they do not seem to feel any guilt that they do not know or to have such a strong liberal or conservative bias that they think they already know the answer. I sometimes feel like this is Day One of Christian life, and I have the incredible joy and the burden of opening up to them what is now a global, ecumenical tradition.

The challenge of responding to students' questions about Protestant identity has forced me back to the sources in a kind of post-denominational scan of the whole landscape. I find myself pedaling very fast just trying to keep up. A wonderful part of the legacy of the past, however, is the great history of preaching and teaching left behind by Coffin and so many of his colleagues. They reminded Christians that the deep moral sense of their faith required them to challenge the self-contradictions of a society that presumed it was homogenous, unitary, fair, and right. Today, I retell and reteach Christianity now that Christians have lost their privileged place and their illusion that their way is the right and only way. We are now a religious minority with a majority history and must, as Lincoln said, "disenthrall ourselves" of the past.

The challenges I face are, in some ways, the opposite of those faced by my mentors. They helped break down a racist and exclusive order that maintained power by reliance on tradition and morality. They succeeded, in some ways, in breaking down tradition but, in its wake, left moral meaninglessness. What do I say when I ask a young person how students feel about the deep beliefs or faith of other students, and he replies, "We're numb to that"? I find students who are so overloaded by expectations, by information, by the complexities of this world's problems that they are shutting down. Looking from outside, one might say they don't care, but the problem is that they care too much and don't know how to care about everything. So students respond by choosing a few things to care about and become numb to the rest.

What I hear from my students is that they are looking for a safe place in a chaotic world where they can construct a moral and religious identity for themselves that will allow them to withstand the whirlwind of our times: *How do I choose between making the most money I can in an economically insecure time and doing all I can to ease the pain of others? What do I do when my supervisor asks me to cook the books? Is it right to tell someone I love them just to get them to do what I want? Does it matter if you cheat if you don't get caught?*

As I try to live out the legacy of my mentors, I find unanticipated end results of some of their revolutions. I find a hypersexualized campus where sex has often become a transaction with no moral meaning and sexual assault is often perceived by students as the price women pay for sexual liberation. I find a level of alcohol and drug use that is frightening in its deliberate quest for near unconsciousness. What do I do with the African Christian student who comes to my office shocked and offended by the drinking and hook-up culture on campus that I myself often find dehumanizing? Perhaps what I can do is articulate a basic Christian morality that doesn't preach to all but says to those listening, Because of Christ, this is the way we act when we have sex, when we choose our careers, when we exercise our privilege.

In this new context, one of the most exciting parts of my role is to help students articulate a morality for themselves in the absence of a universal social script for right and wrong. Students may come from villages in Pakistan or from elite international schools in Geneva or London, and each has to negotiate a campus where the moral universes they know—extremely traditional or morally freewheeling—have to somehow coexist, not only in terms of choosing how to negotiate sex, drugs, and alcohol, but also in terms of defining a good life, a good society, or a good relationship. The chaplain has a privileged role connecting the deep and ancient roots of religious teaching on morality with the complexities of a globalized institution.

BUILDING A COMMUNITY OF FAITH OUT OF DISPARATE PARTS

I look out on my congregation in Battell Chapel now and see students from around the world—black, white, Hispanic, and Asian. I see many full-scholarship students and first-generation college students. Only five or ten new students each year come from homes where both parents belong to the same church. I have gay and lesbian refugees from conservative Christian homes. I have conservatives who don't like praise and worship music and so they come to hear hymns and the pipe organ. I have many students with absolutely no religious background who come just because they like our community.

While William Sloane Coffin assumed a monolithic unity in his congregation, my chaplaincy requires me to build a community of faith out of all these disparate parts and to have it be genuinely holy, human, fun, and free. Many Protestant churches will die in the coming years of demographic starvation, so part of my challenge is to show that Protestant Christianity can be full, joyous, diverse, meaningful, and yet serious and of service to the poor and disenfranchised. My mentors wanted to jolt students and society out of complacency, and they were good at it. I follow in their steps and ask, Now that the old order has been brought down by those jolts, what do we want to build here?

The least complicated legacy of the 1960s-era chaplains and the one I most freely embrace is that chaplaincy means a commitment to peace and justice. More than ten years ago, when I was chaplain at Bucknell University, a student came in and said she wanted to lead a group to Nicaragua in the wake of the destruction caused by Hurricane Mitch. She had studied abroad there and was desperate to help the people she had grown to love. She had been referred to me because the chaplaincy had some resources and was a place where people went when they wanted to do something good. And so, on my fortieth birthday, I joined an unwieldy group of thirty-six pilgrims on their way to Central America to "help."

In addition to the many eye-opening, life-changing encounters we had—similar in many ways, no doubt, to the experiences of other groups on other service trips in other times and other places—the group returned home and said, "We can't just *stop.*" We formed a partnership, created a structure, raised funds, recruited more groups. Over ten years later, hundreds of thousands of dollars have been raised and medical, employment, and engineering projects completed. Not only did the project have an impact, though small, on the poverty and suffering of a refugee community in Nicaragua, it changed the nature of a parochial university community in rural central Pennsylvania. Unexpected people—faculty, students, staff, townspeople, even a former university president—got excited, got involved, and started asking deep questions about justice, policy, economics, and even religion.

My students long to serve. They fight for positions with Teach for America. They hope for integrity in a world where all political speech seems duplicitous. They are eager to learn from people who have experienced something, not just people with opinions or lots of research (they will only rarely come out to hear an expert speak). One of the joys of my work is finding people of integrity for them to meet. They might be American development workers in Nicaragua or poor Nicaraguans themselves. They might be people working with the homeless or mentally ill in New Haven or our neighbors who suffer from the same.

Another of my tasks is to work with the many evangelical Christian groups that serve Yale's students. Some might see this as a betrayal of Coffin's legacy. After all, this means occasionally supporting people whose religious forebears fought tooth and nail to preserve segregation and those who still today oppose equal rights for the LGBTQ community. But when no one religious group is in charge or one voice authoritative, the right of each group to exist and speak as citizens of the university depends on the right of all groups to do the same. What my work has allowed me to see is how many students are cared for and served by these groups and how many evangelical Yale students would never be comfortable at Battell Chapel. That doesn't mean I don't invite them, but it does mean that I don't presume my liberal Protestant voice is the only one on campus and that if students don't like it, they should have no other options.

And too, if a student were to come to Yale and graduate without some clear sense of how to have a civil conversation about religion with both atheists and religious conservatives, what use is a Yale education? I disagree with my evangelical friends and colleagues often, but I haven't given up hope that we might find some common ground in this protected setting devoted to education—common ground that might not be found on the cultural battlefields outside. The chaplain's role as mediator and translator between the secular university itself and the religious people it has invited to campus to teach and study feels especially crucial at a time when both secularists and religious people feel embattled and misunderstood.

To some of my colleagues the tasks of chaplaincy today feel small. They mourn the decline of those days when the Protestant chaplain was the conscience of the university and could walk into the president's office and state his demands, speaking with universal moral authority. But those days are gone, and as Coffin himself was fond of quoting from the old hymn, "New occasions teach new duties; time makes ancient good uncouth."

Coffin and others like him left a remarkable legacy of prophetic preaching, creative activism, and conviction that religious vision can change the world. But to enshrine the particular means, the peculiar style, or the personal attributes of specific leaders is to disrespect the creative genius they brought to their own historical moment. And after all, isn't our present state exactly what those great postwar chaplains fought for? That the unearned privilege of the Protestants should end, and that we should all be thrown into a chaotic, egalitarian marketplace of ideas, where beliefs would sink or swim on their merit and meaning? That the clubby elitism of the old days should disappear and the doors be thrown open to everyone from agnostics to Pentecostalists to Zoroastrians, in all their diverse styles and ways? The narrative of the last fifty years as I read it is a narrative not of decline, but of remarkable freedom.

I will admit, sometimes I do yearn to climb up into that pulpit and thunder from on high about the issues of the day. But I don't. I preach from a portable lectern, which is down on the floor among the congregants. I am not chaplain to Protestant culture as a whole. I am not chaplain to America as a whole. I serve a particular community, and I can discover from my Catholic, Jewish, Hindu, Buddhist, and Muslim colleagues what that vocation looks like. I can help the students entrusted to my care to learn our particular virtues and our particular weaknesses. I can go back to my books and figure out how to articulate a common faith in the midst of our incredible internal diversity. I can take students out into New Haven or into the wider world and show them what poverty and injustice look like, and explore with them how Christ might have us respond. I can look to the deep wounds that divide Christians from each other and ask what it would take to bring us together. It is an adventure deeply rooted in the past and yet excitingly, radically new.

MULTIFAITH CHAPLAINS,

MULTIFAITH CAMPUSES

UNCOVERING GOD
A Global Chaplaincy
on a Secular Campus

Rev. Deanna L. Shorb
Grinnell College, Grinnell, Iowa

E arly in my chaplaincy at Grinnell, a prospective student's parent asked a question at a forum sponsored by our admissions office. He had just read a national report ranking colleges in a number of areas. He wanted to know how I felt about being the chaplain at the "second-most godless campus" in the country. I had not heard of this ranking and was surprised and taken aback. I don't remember what answer I gave him, but I'm sure it was unsatisfying to both of us and probably slightly defensive given how junior and green I was at the time. I do know that soon thereafter, this experience was retold in one of my sermons in weekly chapel. By then I had "done the research"—found the national survey and discovered which one of my colleagues had the distinction of being *first*, working at the "most godless" of campuses. And, while from the pulpit I lightheartedly thanked God that we weren't *that* college, privately I recognized that I had a lot to learn and that there was work to be done around campus climate and religious practice.

Rev. Deanna L. Shorb serves as chaplain and dean of religious life at Grinnell College in Grinnell, Iowa. She is a past president of the National Association of College and University Chaplains (NACUC). Off-campus, she enjoys gardening and carpentry projects (most recently a multiphasic tree house) and spending time at home and at play with her partner and children.

I have given a lot of thought to that admissions moment in the years since. In posing this question to me, the student's father seemed to be imagining a traditional Christian chaplain: one who conducts Sunday chapel services, presides over weddings and memorial services, and cares for the souls of the Christian students. It's not an unreasonable assumption: I am Christian, and I am Grinnell's first and only full-time chaplain. As such, I am the institution's official and unapologetic God-person. What does that role mean in a place where the student body is largely nonpracticing?

Occasionally a faculty member or a colleague from town asks me what time the Sunday service is held on campus. I tell them, as gently and neutrally as I can, that I haven't held chapel regularly on Sunday morning for twelve years. I was trained to give sermons and I truly loved to plan chapel worship and preach on Sunday mornings, but I soon realized that since I was the only full-time religious life leader on campus, it simply wasn't the best use of my time. On increasingly religiously diverse campuses like Grinnell's, a weekly Christian worship service is simply no longer the primary charge for religious and spiritual leadership, especially at our colleges and universities with limited staffing.

Before discontinuing weekly chapel, I polled a number of chaplain colleagues whom I had come to respect who were also more seasoned. I remember discussing the growing list of religious life needs on our campuses and how we also felt as though they were situated in "God's alley" (I would say "God's Christian alley," as there are seven churches within a two- to three-block distance from the perimeter of the college). My greater concern as I came to know my campus in those first two years was that each year I had ended my annual report with this sentence: "Next year, I hope to connect with the Buddhist and Hindu students." I knew that if I wrote that sentence one more time the following year, even *I* would no longer believe me.

While it is true that Grinnell is secular and has many people who proudly profess secular humanism as their tradition, Grinnell also has many undergraduates who are religiously and spiritually active.

There has been a shift in the last forty years, since mandatory chapel on our campuses, toward greater diversity. We no longer assume a Christian identity in our creed or our mission, and so as chaplain, I cannot simply meet the needs of the few Christians who are still interested in Bible study, worship, or prayer. Hearing and witnessing the diversity—cultural and religious (which for many are inextricably linked)—on our secular campuses, we modern chaplains must find a way to respond to *those* needs.

The face of college chaplaincy has changed. The increase in religious and cultural diversity on our campuses has not diminished the importance of Christian history (institutional or individual), current practice, or foundational roots, but for chaplains today, the charge is different, broader. The quest of the global chaplain is to be respected in your own tradition while being respectful and humble toward students from traditions other than yours. Encouraging and supporting the open practice of religions and "spiritualities" *equally* is central to today's college chaplaincy. I must provide flexible, globally and culturally sensitive, ethical leadership. My connection with students, and my work as a chaplain, is far more intimate, inclusive, and diverse than someone assuming a traditional Christian chaplaincy (including many college and university administrations) might imagine.

IT'S ABOUT THE PEOPLE, NOT THE INSTITUTION

When I felt what I perceived as a call to ordained ministry—specifically college chaplaincy—I had no idea what the journey might look like. I had finished my BA and was in my second year of work at Williams College, a small liberal arts college in Western Massachusetts. I was a member of the professional staff in the department of theater, a job I was passionate about. As the months passed, I began to spend free time—weekends and spring breaks—working with the college chaplain, who had become a friend and, I would realize later, a mentor. I assisted her in leading undergraduates in service near and far. Ironically for me, it was after college, during these years at Williams, when I could turn back to being more engaged with God beyond Sunday mornings, that I realized it was time to "give up my day job." What resulted was a six-year journey of discernment—the kind that we chaplains, and not a few college administrators and faculty, now realize can be terribly important as a stage of (hopefully mentored) development.

As I had been a first-generation college student, this was also a time of important cultural education for me. At this time, in the late 1980s and early '90s, "diversity" and the discussion around diverse practice or issues in religion was limited to an intentional inclusion "at the table" or in the dialogue of Protestant Christian, Roman Catholic, and Jewish traditions. My understanding of diversity in religion was narrow, and my knowledge of any particularities within these traditions was even more limited. I had been raised by former Mennonites and current LCA Lutherans (now the Evangelical Lutheran Church in America) in a semirural town in Pennsylvania, and the first Jewish person I had ever knowingly met was my theater professor during my first year of college—so for me, any non–mainline Protestant tradition was still quite diverse and unique.

Working with the chaplain at Williams was my introduction, personally and professionally, into a community of religious practitioners and leaders in a competitive and largely secular academic setting. This meant that for the first time, I understood the importance of diversity in religious leadership—not simply the need for awareness about others' beliefs, but the goal of respect among and between the traditions. That post-undergraduate college community, both on campus and in several of the local churches, gave me the freedom and the permission to think, to discern where God was calling me—to imagine what was possible in campus religious leadership and to prepare for the training and the leadership that would be required of me during my next and future steps. This period was also the beginning of my journey toward an even greater interest in, support of, and commitment to the inclusion and engagement of students from diverse religious traditions.

Eight years after my undergraduate commencement, I began my seminary career at a fine and very Christian divinity school, where I was very happy. During my second year of seminary, I served as an intern at the Church of Christ at Yale. At the time, it was affiliated with the United Church of Christ (my denomination) and held weekly worship services. My supervisor was the associate chaplain of the university. She convened Yale Religious Ministries, a consortium of religious professionals hailing from twenty-seven denominations and traditions representing many world religions that were serving Yale students. It was through that group that I learned more about the potential for interreligious and intra-religious dialogue and became aware of the necessity for chaplains to create an environment where this was possible.

In 1996, I was called as the first full-time (and female) chaplain at Grinnell, which had not perceived the need to have a full position previously. It was a bold move, determined by a presidential task force from all the campus constituencies—faculty, staff, and students—because at the time, nationally, many liberal arts institutions were retiring the position along with the men who had filled them for thirty-plus years.

In my first week as the new chaplain, I met with the president privately. She welcomed me and then informed me that Grinnell no longer had an official relationship with the United Church of Christ. She wanted me to know that we were only historically a religiously affiliated college. "The board," she said, "decided, some time ago, to sever those ties. They felt it was a good admissions move." As I reflected on that afterwards, the messages felt mixed to me. *Hire your first full-time chaplain and then make certain she understands that the institution is not religious.* But what at the time felt contradictory now feels accurate as an "institutional" perspective.

Grinnell is not a specifically or intentionally Christian place. It is not an overtly religious place. In order to appear to be open to any and all religions, it is important to be clear that none is being privileged (or oppressed). So, whether we serve at a religiously affiliated school or one that is perceived as "godless," what we do as chaplains is not, largely, about the institution—in fact, the work that we do as chaplains *cannot* be about the institution. It is about the people.

LISTENING IN A GLOBAL RELIGIOUS CONTEXT

People who think that my role is to talk only about Jesus might be stunned by some of the conversations I have in the privacy of my office. While it's true that historical measures of religious participation, like church attendance, have fallen off in recent years, I would argue that students are actually practicing more. They're often practicing the religion of their parents in their own generational way. Their approach seems to be, *I'm doing it in my way, but I'm not leaving religion behind.* That's why the religious leader's role is vital on college campuses: someone needs to be there for them to be able to speak their truths and their reality and to understand them in the complexity of their identities and in their various developmental stages.

Grinnell's student population is moderately international, with students from over fifty countries, representing approximately twelve world religions. This diversity is clearly a strength, and combined with our domestic diversity, it creates a richer community and learning environment for everyone. But even when recognized as an educational benefit or asset, exposure to others' religious and traditional cultures can pose problems or personal dilemmas for students trying to navigate their life choices. In this twenty-first-century context of unprecedented campus diversity, chaplains in particular need to be prepared for the unique ways we can provide important support.

For example, at different times students have come to see me to discuss dating someone who is very dedicated to a world religion different from their own—the Muslim woman in love with a nonpracticing man of Christian heritage; the American Jewish woman in love with a Bosnian Muslim man who doesn't understand that she is as committed to her religion as he is to his. Some people in our largely liberal and progressive community, if put in the position of offering advice in these situations might think, "In 2013, these women should do what they please." As much as I, too, might personally (or politically) believe that the postfeminist millennial woman should embrace the historically hard-fought and progressively won privilege of personal autonomy and power and choice to practice her own tradition and respect that of her chosen love, my role as a religious figure suggests a different response.

I know these students to be *practicing* religious women who are hurting, weighing a love against a love. My role is to find a way to hear all the sides and then sit with them in that pain. They want their heartbreak fixed, but they know it can't be fixed. I can't, nor will I act as though I can fix it for them. They come to me because a secular counselor may not understand from a religious perspective the pressure between commitment to tradition or to individual choice that the student feels so acutely.

Even though my religious tradition and theirs may seem light years apart, because I'm hearing their worries in the context of religious practices, we have an underlying common ground. I can't say, "We can work this out." They know and I know how little room there is for a cross-religious relationship in their tradition. When they express the fear that marriage outside their culture would mean a life of tolerance (at best) but not acceptance among their family members and fellow practitioners, they know I understand that they are not exaggerating the sacrifice they would be making. They know that I can also hear their loss-of-religion fear—that a departure from cultural expectation might represent a less than pure engagement in their tradition, a less authentic or respectable way for them to practice, which would itself be a deeply felt loss, since they long for the bond with religious tradition in their primary relating, too.

Whether or not the students who come to me ultimately decide to break with tradition is entirely up to them. But in their moment of anguish, and in parsing their options, someone needs to hear them in a *religious* context. They come to me, not for solutions, but because they know I understand the deep conflict they are feeling and they know that I hear them. This is a place where they can freely talk and wrestle with their personal conflict and mourn. We cannot solve the problem, because we both know it's unsolvable. But I'm sending them off caring about them and hurting for them.

This is a unique role that can, I believe, only be played by the chaplain, the global chaplain. By this, I mean someone who is willing to think and process outside of their (his/her/hir) own personal practice (and, perhaps, belief system) and allow for and respect the possibilities, the limitations, theology, doctrine, of another. Conflicts between personal choice and religious tradition are not, at base, a mental health or a physical health concern. Solutions will not be found in the lecture hall, the library, or the research lab. They are not solvable after enough beer or shots on the weekend with friends in the residence halls to numb the pain. These are matters of the heart, "troublings" of the soul. The chaplain, the religious life leader, can hear and accept this spiritual or religious predicament, walk with the student, and support the student through this emotion-laden decision-making process.

AN INTERRELIGIOUS "ETHICAL BAROMETER"

Several times over the years, I have heard a faculty member or administrator say that the role of the chaplain is to serve as the moral compass for the college. I think chaplains of an earlier era were, for better or worse, viewed and often respected in that light. They were relied on for regular ethical pulse taking by everyone from student to president. There are still some instances (very private) where ethical questioning and input are sought or accepted by a college president or an administrator. However, this assumes a shared moral code, and for many colleges the tides of shared theological understanding (or moral code) have shifted in recent decades. Codes of civility and decency are still central for most, and there remains a basic respect for working toward the common good. At Grinnell, I have taken the "ethical barometer" role seriously, even when it moves me beyond the "Judeo-Christian" model of leadership that the administration might have had in mind. Part of my role as chaplain is to make sure all students have a voice with the administration—and that their voice is actually *heard.*

One fall, the college installed a statue of Ganesha as a memorial for a student who was killed while studying abroad in India. We had a great celebration on campus as a sri blessed the god and performed the appropriate ceremonial rite. The next year, a new religious studies professor of Eastern traditions came to my office to introduce herself. She was reaching out to let me know that she wanted to be supportive of our Hindu community in any way that she could. She also wanted to gently push for the statue of Ganesha (installed before she came to campus) to be covered by the same type of structure that was used in holy places in India, a *mandap*—essentially a multitiered roof with pillars. She said that leaving the statue in the open air wasn't appropriate, especially since it had been ritually installed by a high priest. This meant the memorial site was now a sanctuary and regularly being used by our students for worship.

I had not known of the requirement for having this structure to respectfully shelter the god. In my Christian framework, however, it made sense that a worship site with a religious symbol as important as this one might, at the very least, be protected. I asked that she work with me to help our facilities staff understand the design of the uniquely Eastern architecture. She and her husband drew a mock-up of a small *mandap* tailored for our campus and included a picture of a larger one in India. A work order for the construction was submitted to the facilities department. The carpenters at our college are very skilled at their work—they had built several pieces for us in the previous few years, including a beautiful *aron* (Torah ark), now used in Jewish High Holy Day services on campus. I knew that this new structure would not be difficult for them to build.

I was therefore quite surprised when I was told, "There will be no *mandap*," because the administration felt that when the decision had been made to purchase and install the god, they had received different guidelines for installation and site requirements from other knowledgeable campus leaders and the sri who had conducted the original ritual, and they were not interested in amending their original plan. Positions hardened. Eventually, I was told that if the god had to be covered, then it "had to go." I knew I needed to back off for a bit, because removal would have been horrendous—painful for the Hindu community and for the interreligious community and an institutional "black eye."

This was among my first and most profound lessons regarding the role of the campus religious life leader today. My responsibility was to do the right thing as I understood it not just through Christian principles, but through a much broader set of religious and spiritual lenses—those of the world's religions. In this work, some knowledge can be gained through the study of world religions, but much can be observed and absorbed by openness to learning from students, faculty, and staff who are practicing these traditions. Our campuses are educational environments, and our role as chaplains is supporting the religious and cultural lives of students. The chaplain should be present, reminding the institution of students' needs and, when necessary, the inequities and injustice particularly for underrepresented groups.

But, as I learned with the *mandap* request, this is not always easy. The religious leader is still paid by the institution, even as they are tasked with the job of being the institution's ethical barometer. The same institution that sets the rules and policies for the campus also invites the chaplain to speak to their ethics. When the institution's policies move outside of its own articulated morality, or when a chaplain's counselee (particularly a student) is treated in a way that is not in keeping with the institution's ethics, the chaplain is invited to come forward and name the injustice, while at the same time risking, at the very least, relationship with a colleague or even employment. Clearly, this can sometimes make it difficult to fully serve students (and faculty and staff) while remaining a member in good standing of the institution. In a context where secular academic institutions no longer express morality in terms of religious tradition, the chaplain is no longer an automatic mouthpiece for institutional ethics. In fact, if the chaplain were to overtly call upon her religious tradition as a source of ethical authority, this would likely be met with suspicion by the secular institution. In the chaplain's role as ethical barometer, therefore, she must rely on her own, internal sense of justice to know when, where, and how to push the institution to meet the diverse needs of its members—be those needs personal, social, or religious.

In the case of the *mandap*, I decided to steadily push. I was joined by another faculty member and, over the years, several cycles of students. In the end, it took a decade and a new administration for Grinnell's Hindu community to have their god covered. For me, this experience was also a reminder that the chaplain must continue to find ways to gently educate and garner support from the entire campus. Whether observant or not, the majority of Grinnell's employees are still Christian in knowledge, if not practice, but the chaplain must be sensitive to the community as a whole. The *mandap* seemed to serve as a metaphor for this interreligious chaplaincy at a secular institution—working quietly, in many ways, to cover and uncover God.

RECOGNIZING AND EMBRACING DIVERSITY AND SEEKING INCLUSION FOR ALL

Our work is in no way limited to matters of religion, but often extends to race and culture as they relate to religion as well. During my interview process at Grinnell, I was taken to dinner by two faculty members who asked me, "How might you help to make the college a more 'comfortable' place to be openly religious?" There were many other questions, of course, but this one and the story that follows stuck with me and helped me to formulate what would become the basic framework of my chaplaincy and eventually religious and spiritual leadership on our campus—a chaplaincy recognizing and embracing diversity and seeking inclusion for all.

At that interview dinner, one of the professors told me about an African American student who, he said, had been regularly attending a local church. The student had joined the choir and felt he had found a church home in the town of Grinnell. One Sunday during worship, he was physically overcome by the Spirit. The members of this white mainline Protestant church standing near him were so shocked, to the point of mortification, by his involuntary falling down and speaking in tongues that their response was to immediately carry him out of the church. In one day, one single Sunday morning, he lost his worshiping community and his spiritual home.

There are over twenty churches in Grinnell—and all but one are Protestant, all are white. "If you were the chaplain," asked the professor, "what would you do?" I thought for some time after that evening about how this student and others like him might be better served by the community—might have a greater "sanctuary" for worship.

I had an idea. While in seminary, I had heard a young choir sing at our chapel service one morning. It turned out that they were from the most underserved African American elementary school in New Haven. They were spirited and talented—their musical offering had been a gift, and I wanted to know more about them. I contacted their director to inquire about the children and their school and then asked if she would be interested in a collaborative mentoring concert with the students from the Yale Gospel Choir, who sang weekly, I was told, at Yale's Black Church service. We worked together to plan that event. I knew that both choirs were very gifted and that each had something to offer to the other. When I discovered that Grinnell had a gospel choir, I thought that it might be possible to try to engage them in on-campus Sunday worship that might better serve students whose Christian religious practice included ecstatic worship.

Finding some students on campus who were interested in leadership led me to believe that we could start a new worship service with the choir as an anchor—one that was planned with students in a liturgical style that was closer to worship in the African American traditions with which they were more familiar and comfortable. I did not know how to begin creating a worship service in a black tradition, but I took a cue from Yale undergrads in naming the service and moved forward with hope. I soon found interested African American students on Grinnell's campus, and we started offering a monthly service that first fall. Students helped to plan the service, and we invited guest ministers from African American churches in nearby cities.

As modern chaplains, we need to listen to our students and think creatively with them about religious and spiritual needs on our campuses and in our local communities. My role as a religious leader on a "godless campus" in this case required me to help facilitate diversity *within* Christianity, because our college campus is a diverse island in not-too-diverse Iowa. Offering a service in black traditions in response to the faculty member's concern for his student was, finally, a simple and appropriate thing to do. Fifteen years later, we still hold worship services once each month, and the great debate over diversity and inclusion continues in our worship and planning.

Even the name of the service regularly comes under scrutiny as new students and faculty cycle through our academic community. Often, those raising questions about our use of the term "black" hear it as dated and offensive and are concerned that this white chaplain and her students don't understand its implications. In fact, we've chosen the name very carefully as an acceptably inclusive term for the very diverse group of African American, Afro-Caribbean, and African students who regularly plan and lead this worship. One of the questions we wrestle with these days is how to best represent the diversity *within* the "black church." This year, for Black History Month, we struggled with the question of how to truly respect and represent a history that was not shared by everyone on the planning committee, many of whom were African and Afro-Caribbean. Though these conflicts are sometimes painful, this kind of work is the meat, the heart of what we do as chaplains today. We provide a space for conversation about tradition, where students can wrestle over why a hymn matters, is more authentic, or is more powerful. We raise the questions and give the space and time for others to formulate answers in community—as a wonderfully multireligious, or in this case ecumenical intra-religious, community. These are the conversations and this is the education that will rarely happen outside the academy. These are the reflections that have the potential to make a difference after these students leave our campus and enter the communities of their lives.

DISCOVERING GOD IN REMARKABLE
AND UNFAMILIAR PLACES

I have learned that as a chaplain, I can truly serve as an advocate to all who are interested in support, collaboration, and counseling. I am able to be present for those who are committed to their tradition, recently discovering or considering a new one, questioning or rejecting the tradition of their youth, just taking time off, or trying to find their way as one of or even the only practitioner of a religious tradition within hundreds of miles. What we are able to offer as a nondenominational or secular campus is the freedom for all to practice their religion openly or privately or to choose not to practice a religion at all.

I attended a national event at the college recently. As I entered the facility where it was to be held, there were others arriving from many different colleges and universities. I welcomed those who were around me in line as we all waited to enter the main room. As we talked, one of the men said, "I would guess that you might be speaking this evening." I was carrying a portfolio and was dressed in a way that might have signaled an "official" purpose. We introduced ourselves, and I told him that I was there to pray. It turned out that he worked at a religiously affiliated institution. He paused for a moment and then, with some odd combination of humility and mischief said, "I know a bit about Grinnell ... what is it that you *do* as the chaplain?" I couldn't help but think back to the time I was first asked a version of this question by a prospective student's parent, fifteen years earlier.

This time, I was ready with the answer (or at least, *an* answer). "It is true," I said, "that Grinnell is religiously diverse and that we have our fair share of secular humanists as well as Christians. However, there are students from a variety of world religions who wish to practice their traditions while at Grinnell. I work closely with all of them." After that icebreaker, we walked into the hall where the special event was to be held, and we parted with well wishes to each other for a good evening.

I have learned to remain open to the question "What does it mean to be the God-person on a godless campus?" and to embrace and advance the new perspectives that make the work possible. I have learned that it is important to hear the need and think creatively or dream collectively *with* each generation of students that joins our campus community. I have learned to do this without allowing the opinions or actions of others to be an obstacle in my work or, hopefully, in their practice. I have learned to remain open, and this has meant that on this seemingly godless campus, I continue to discover God and God's work in remarkable and unfamiliar places.

"¡SI, SE PUEDE!" (YES, WE CAN!)
Student Ministry in a Multicultural Context

Fr. Daniel Reim, SJ
University of Michigan, Ann Arbor, Michigan

From the rear of the church, people began lighting candles, passing the light forward until the entire church was awash in candlelight. It was Friday night. Over two hundred people had gathered on this November evening, some having journeyed a great distance, physically and spiritually, to be there. The spirit of the moment was somber and yet also hopeful. In the center, surrounded by the glow and the warmth, and the inspiration for the evening, stood Lourdes and her three children.

The community—made up of students and resident parishioners, Anglos and Hispanics/Latinos—had come together that night to join in prayer that Lourdes would not be deported and separated from her children. That night, Lourdes and her children felt the support of their parish in a moment of crisis. For the students participating in the vigil, they experienced the best of what church can be: faith expressed in action.

Fr. Daniel Reim, SJ, is campus minister for Hispanic/Latino ministry and social justice at St. Mary Student Parish and Catholic Newman Center in Ann Arbor, Michigan. In his work as campus minister, he has the opportunity to interact with students on fire for God and making a difference in the world. He says, "We are supported by an amazing parish community invested in the faith formation of our students. And we have a lot of fun. Praise God!"

In our parish, the faith formation of our student parishioners is significantly enhanced through the interactions with our Hispanic/Latino parish community. Students are introduced to a culture and language different from their own. They are inspired by the witness of faith of a community struggling to find welcome in this country and thus enter into the justice demands of our faith. They are developing skills that will prepare them for a Catholic Church in the United States that will soon comprise a significant number of Hispanics/Latinos. Through their participation in various ministries offered by our church to our Hispanic/Latino community, our students have the opportunity to put into action the faith that does justice, the faith that builds community, the faith that leads to finding God on a daily basis through developing relationships with one another.

ALL WELCOME: STUDENTS AND PARISHONERS, HISPANIC/LATINO AND ANGLOS

St. Mary Student Parish is located near the central campus of the University of Michigan in Ann Arbor (U of M). It is part of the Lansing Diocese, and since 2004, the parish has been staffed by priests of the Society of Jesus (Jesuits). While the church has no formal relationship with the university, it is the mission of the parish to serve the Catholic population there: students, faculty, staff, and administrators. Our church hosts a Newman Center (the third oldest in the country), a Catholic campus ministry for students, undergraduates, and graduate students at U of M.

Over the years, since the founding of St. Mary's in 1924, the parish has shifted in its relationship between students and the local resident Catholics. In its beginning, St. Mary's was established as a student center. When the region was transferred from the Detroit to the Lansing Diocese, the parish became identified as a parish like any other. That is, if you were a student, you were welcomed as you would be by your home parish, but the church had no particular student-oriented mission. In 1997, with the arrival of diocesan pastor Fr. Tom Firestone, the current identity of the parish was established—a student parish that relies on the resident parishioners to participate in the mission of forming future leaders of our church.

In doing so, he formed an interaction between the two populations that is mutually beneficial. The resident parishioners enjoy the students' energy and the fact that young church members inspire their own children to participate in church. And the students are supported, financially and experientially, in a way that would not be possible without the resident parishioners.

Significant to the vibrancy of the parish and formation of our students is the growing presence of our Hispanic/Latino community. The first Mass in Spanish was offered in the late 1990s. It was a start, but the pastor soon began to feel that the needs of the Hispanic/Latino community were not being adequately met. The greater Ann Arbor area (Washtenaw County) has a Hispanic/Latino population of roughly ten thousand people, but the next closest Catholic church offering Mass in Spanish was over thirty miles away. In 1997, the pastor decided to start an intentional ministry for Hispanics/Latinos that would offer more ministries than Mass alone. St. Mary's began to offer other sacraments in Spanish, including baptisms, weddings, and funerals. Sacramental preparation (First Communion and confirmation classes) for both children and adults was introduced. Other ministries for this community continued to expand. Inclusion of the Hispanic/Latino community into full participation in the life of the parish has been a priority of the current pastor, Fr. Ben Hawley, SJ.

At its inception, there was not the intention to connect the presence of the Hispanic/Latino community to the faith development of our university students. There was simply a pastoral need calling for attention. This has, however, in fact become the blessed result. For many non-Hispanic/Latino students, interactions with their fellow Hispanic/Latino parishioners represent a rich cross-cultural experience that has a tremendous impact on their own faith development.

The majority of students participating in St. Mary's campus ministry programs are non-Hispanic or "Anglo." Many Hispanic/Latino students at the University of Michigan attend the

English-speaking masses and are involved in non-Hispanic student organizations and activities. While they may feel at home with the Spanish church when with their families, many seem to prefer spending time with their Anglo friends while at school. There are notable exceptions however. Luz Mesa has been very involved in St. Mary's ministry to Hispanics/Latinos during her undergraduate years. St. Mary's served to help her become acclimated to a very new environment and supported her faith development during her four years here:

> Working with the Latino community at St. Mary's was both a method of growth and a method of survival during my four years at the University of Michigan. Immediately upon my arrival, I was completely culture shocked and uncomfortable in my new environment. Having grown up around people who were mostly of my same race, ethnicity, and more importantly, socioeconomic status, I felt lost. I was able to find a home away from home at St. Mary's, and the community helped me stay grounded and aware of the issues my people face.
>
> Looking to the St. Mary's community for comfort also reminded me that there was a reason why I was uncomfortable outside of that environment. Being involved in church activities has always been important to me and has given me peace, strength, and closeness to God, yet seeing this involvement as a way to cope with problems outside of it was not ideal. I was reminded that there was a reason why I could only find people like me at church, instead of in the classroom. Realizing the oppression we face as people of color within U.S. social systems strengthened my conviction to social justice. Being part of the Latino community at St. Mary's gave me the strength to continue working toward equality.
>
> As a contributing member to the Latino ministry and of the St. Mary's Latino community, I no longer felt like a lost Latina on campus. I felt like part of a

> loving and faithful community that I knew would always
> be there to support me, regardless of where I went. I
> have grown up in a faith that was largely family-based,
> strengthened by cultural traditions and a shared love
> for God. Finding a family away from home to share
> my traditions with gave me strength in my faith and
> reminded me that I have a calling to use my time and
> talent for the work of God.

St. Mary's attempts to make everyone feel welcome and included. That is foundational to this ministry. Through our various ministries to the local Hispanic/Latino community, including students like Luz, we hope to share our faith across the language and cultural barriers. For our Anglo students, the opportunities to connect with our Hispanic/Latino parishioners provides a rich cross-cultural experience that makes possible a deepening of their own faith life.

St. Mary's offers an increasing array of ministries for our Hispanic/Latino parish members, many of which involve the assistance of our students. Our sacramental preparation program, for example, is coordinated by two student co-leaders who, with the assistance of a staff member, organize the faith formation of our Hispanic/Latino children. Our English as a second language (ESL) program, new this year, is also coordinated by several students, under the direction of an ESL instructor. This direct ministry on the part of the students provides the skill development for future ministry in the church.

Many of our students participate in advocacy on behalf of those treated unjustly or who, for other reasons, are held back from living life to the fullest. This work has proved essential to their faith formation. In cooperation with the parish's social justice ministry, students are able to integrate principles of Catholic social teaching including that of solidarity and defense of human dignity. Students recently participated in events advocating on behalf of those affected by our country's immigration system, including those of our own Hispanic/Latino parish community.

SACRAMENTAL PREPARATION PROGRAM

It was an undergraduate student named Mike Brown in 2002 who first proposed a sacramental preparation program for the children of Hispanic/Latino families. The students at U of M would be the catechists. Since most of these children are already fluent in English, the classes would be taught primarily in English. Over fifty children are enrolled in the program each year. Seven to ten U of M students serve as the catechists meeting with the children on Sundays eight times per semester. While the children are in their classes, their parents meet with an adult catechist, who provides adult faith formation that parallels the material introduced to their children.

As is often true, the experience of teaching young children has been tremendously rewarding for the young adults who have become catechists through this program. Explaining elements of faith practice to someone else, especially someone younger, draws them toward a deeper understanding of that faith. For the students, it is an opportunity to grow in their own faith as they wrestle with thinking how to teach the faith to children. This was the experience of Ben Tift, who has been serving as a catechist for the Hispanic/ Latino families for the past two years:

> This experience has definitely deepened my relationship with God in several ways. When I am lesson planning for my class of middle schoolers, who often have what seems like a million questions, I have to do a good bit of research on the topic that I am teaching. This has led me to read the Bible more than I have previously and has also given me a much deeper knowledge of my faith. I have also been able to see God working through the families that we serve, and through the kids in particular. Despite whatever may be going on in their lives, when we see the families and kids on Sunday afternoons, they are always happy, smiling, and enjoying each other's company. Through God, these families are able to get away from whatever may be going on in their lives and

> are able to find peace and joy. Through this experience,
> my awareness and faith in God have definitely increased.

The experience of learning as you teach isn't specific to our community (the student catechists of Anglo families gain much the same benefit), but the cross-cultural nature of our community adds another avenue for discovery for student teachers. In addition to the sacramental traditions shared by all Catholics, the Hispanic/Latino parents in our parish want their children to share their religious and cultural traditions. The instruction in our program then includes the learning of various prayers, Mass parts in Spanish, and various Latin American feasts, most notably the feast of Our Lady of Guadalupe. Learning more of the Catholic faith, from a Hispanic/Latino perspective, broadens the Anglo students' perspective and enriches it. Even colloquial expressions in Spanish can express a spirituality that expands a student's understanding of the faith. The phrase *si Dios quiere* (if God wants), often placed at the end of a wish or a hope, teaches the value of placing one's trust in God and desiring God's will over our own. As the students, mostly Anglos, come to know the children and their families, they are able to see and reflect on the cultural differences within Catholicism and come to a deeper appreciation of its richness.

One important element of student teachers' faith formation in this program is the fact that they are experiencing in a real way the future of the Catholic Church in America, which is to say, increasingly Hispanic and Latino. According to a recent *Time* article, Hispanics/Latinos currently make up 17 percent of the U.S. population, and it is estimated that by 2050 that number will rise to 29 percent.[1] Nearly 70 percent of all Latinos are Catholic. In my own ministry, I preside at Spanish baptisms nearly every other week. In most cases, I baptize three at a time! This is easily three times the number of Anglo baptisms in the same time period. The future of the Catholic Church in America, for which we are preparing our student parishioners, will be greatly influenced by this reality.

In encountering and coming to understand how Hispanic/Latino Catholic traditions may differ from their own, Anglo students develop another important element of faith formation. Catholic sacramental traditions look to concrete images or objects to point us toward the unseen mysteries of our faith. Anglo students may be familiar with the way that water, the Easter candle, the Stations of the Cross, and stained-glass windows all serve as sacramentals to help us connect with God. But they may be surprised by how Hispanic/Latino Catholics take this value even further by, for example, having a table in their home reserved for statues, photographs, and prayers, all to serve as reminders of God's presence and their commitment as believers. Hispanic/Latino parishioners often seek to have many items blessed by a priest: rosaries, statues, their car, their home. God, then, isn't to be found only in church on Sundays, but rather every day and in all places. What a tremendous lesson learned by our students! When Anglo students are exposed to the way their own religion is practiced differently by different cultures, it deepens and expands their understanding of the spiritual values underlying Catholicism.

ESL PROGRAM

Limited in the resources available, St. Mary's normally restricts its ministry to faith-based services, rather than social services. We do not, for example, provide a soup kitchen or other direct services for the poor of our parish or neighborhood. Yet, at the request of members of the Hispanic/Latino community and with the offer of help from an ESL instructor, we created a pilot program intended for ten adults wishing to improve their English speaking skills. Several students who are minoring in Spanish or who participated in a service-immersion trip to the Dominican Republic or El Salvador in the previous two years volunteered to assist with the program.

As soon as the program was announced, we had twenty adults wishing to be admitted to the program. With the requirement of English proficiency as a prerequisite to the possibility of U.S. citizenship, more and more Hispanics/Latinos are looking for such classes. More immediately, many parents wish to keep up with their children's English language ability. As with the catechism classes, though this time with adults rather than with their children, our students enter into an important cultural dialogue within a church context.

By working in this program, students are participating in the church's effort to assist a minority group and to welcome an immigrant population into our community. In *Strangers No Longer: Together on the Journey of Hope*, a statement issued jointly by the Catholic bishops of Mexico and the United States in January 2003, the bishops call for the recognition of the inherent dignity of human persons, regardless of their legal status. And they call for a Christlike compassion that seeks the good of others, especially those most in need:

> We speak to migrants who are forced to leave their lands to provide for their families or to escape persecution. We stand in solidarity with you. We commit ourselves to your pastoral care and to work towards changes in church and societal structures that impede your exercising your dignity and living as children of God.[2]

Providing an ESL program is one way of helping our brothers and sisters to become more acclimated into life in the United States. It also helps our students to put into practice this social teaching of our church.

While only meeting with the ESL class for about an hour each Sunday over a ten-week period, the students serving as facilitators were able to establish a close connection with the adult ESL students. And though both groups struggled with the language, still a communication of compassion and mutual understanding was clearly achieved. Julia Conley, a graduating senior, offered her reflections on the perspective on life gained through these exchanges:

> I have heard stories week after week about the struggles of having a strong accent. I have heard stories about employers not understanding them because they use the wrong tense. I have heard stories about the embarrassment of being in a store and struggling with a store employee because they cannot produce the words to ask the questions they have. In light of these struggles, I

would have expected these ESL participants to be more bitter. They could resent the United States or question why they are struggling more than others, but they do not. They are all such deeply faithful and happy people. We have fun in each and every class. They also have such a strong desire to learn and improve. They are helping me grow as a person in my faith and in my outlook on life. They help me grow in my faith by just spending time with them and seeing how loving and faithful they are despite everything. I have gone to class before feeling truly overwhelmed by things in my life, but without fail I always walk away from the class with a smile on my face and bounce in my step.

Entering the world of those from another culture, even in such a limited way as this ESL program, provides students with the opportunity to increase their perspectives on life and faith.

Because these classes are offered in the context of the church, the learners and student teachers have their shared faith in common. Often, the lessons focus on practicing in English a passage from scripture or other faith-related materials. This lesson structure leads to conversation. Talking about a common text with someone coming from a different cultural background and understanding deepens Anglo students' understanding of the text and enlightens their view of God. Megan Steffes, also a student assisting with the ESL program, learned more about her Catholic faith through struggling with other parishioners trying to learn each other's language:

Typically we discuss current events, life experiences, or just about anything that is requested by the class members. A large part of those requests are the Mass responses, the Ten Commandments, and religious holiday vocabulary. Though not always scriptural, faith plays an integral role in our conversations. During one of our class discussions, we focused on marriage and relationships. This led to a conversation about the role of faith in relationships. Besides conversations like this in class, I personally feel more connected to the Hispanic ministry and have learned a lot about the religious traditions of Catholics in Mexico, Costa Rica, and Equatorial Guinea. Additionally, conversation circles have formed outside of the class in order to allow for more practice!

We hope to expand the ESL program in the coming years to provide more assistance to members of our Hispanic/Latino community in acclimating themselves to the United States. For our students, this program also serves as a means of introducing them to Catholics from other countries, expanding their cultural and religious horizons, and providing them with an experience of ministry that hopefully will prepare them for leadership in the church.

INVOLVEMENT IN SOCIAL JUSTICE

"Faith in Action" is a slogan we often use to emphasize one aspect of our ministry with students. Attending Mass on Sundays, living a good personal moral life, as important as this is, is not enough to fulfill our calling as disciples of Jesus Christ. Jesus's teaching of the "Judgment of the Nations" (Matthew 25:31–46) calls us to reach out to those in need, not only when it is convenient, but as a requirement for entrance into God's Kingdom. We need then to care for the sick, the homeless, the imprisoned, and so on. We are called to speak for the voiceless and to work toward change for those whose lives are unjustly diminished by structures in society. This response to Christ's call to care for others requires both works of charity, meeting the immediate needs of individuals, as well as works of justice, to change those social structures that continue leading people to need works of charity.

March for Immigration Reform, April 2013

Many in our Hispanic/Latino community are of the eleven million or so in this country without proper documentation. For many reasons, they have come here illegally or have overstayed their visas. They have come with great sadness in leaving their home country, their families, their way of life, their native language. And now they are striving to make a life here in Ann Arbor. They work in our hotels, restaurants, and farms. And they are actively involved in our parish community.

And yet our nation's immigration policies give a mixed message: "We want your work," they are told, "but if we catch you, we'll deport you." Many in our community, then, live in constant fear. Or worse, members of families get separated through deportation. Our Catholic social teaching emphasizes the dignity of the human person and solidarity with our brothers and sisters. Our students are given the opportunity to apply these principles to the real and present issue of immigration lived out among our own parishioners.

In April 2013, members of our parish participated in the national march for immigration reform in Washington, D.C. Twenty-eight students and resident parishioners boarded a bus on a Tuesday evening and traveled through the night to D.C. Some from our group participated in the morning liturgy for immigration reform sponsored by the U.S. Conference of Catholic Bishops. Others met with Michigan state senators and congressmen to voice their views. In the afternoon we all attended a rally of over one hundred thousand supporters of comprehensive immigration reform. We then boarded the bus and returned to Ann Arbor early the next morning.

One of our students, Megan McGuire, offered this reflection on participating in this event:

> Immigration reform was never a personal issue for me, but as I became friends with these people my own age whose entire lives are affected by our country's poorly organized immigration system, I started to feel empathy and a sense of solidarity with them. Suddenly, their problems became my problems. It didn't matter that none of my family were immigrants because the dignity of the human person had consumed me. This is a Catholic social teaching that no one should have taken away from them. So in that sense, solidarity was a huge part of the day.

So much of ministry is about providing students the opportunities to learn life lessons. We can't make them happen; we can only encourage the students to open themselves to encounter something new. It is also through opportunities such as this that students are most likely to have transformative experiences. It's possible to be moved by reading about immigration, for example. One can feel strongly about the injustice of families separated after watching a documentary. But there's nothing more powerful than actually meeting real people, learning their stories, and entering into their world, which will result in significant personal change.

Maggie Kuznia, one of our students who'd had little interaction with our Hispanic/Latino community, decided to take part in the Washington, D.C., march for comprehensive immigration reform. The experience introduced her to the social issue of immigration but also to the relationship between her faith and the call to serve others:

> Throughout this day, I have never been so proud to be wearing my "Michigan Catholic" tee shirt. I feel so grateful to belong to a church where everyone in the parish not only values education, but also values service and beneficial action. I feel closest to God, personally, through meeting and exploring the lives of others. The Hispanic ministry who came along with us had plenty of stories to share that definitely broadened my world. It is humbling to hear about how blessed I am to grow up on a certain side of a line. At the same time, however, it hurts that people who are not as lucky as I am are practically punished for pursing this "American Dream" that I was born into. God gives us all obstacles in life; however, I find it my calling to make other people's obstacles a little easier to get through.
>
> What I take away most from this trip is noting the call to serve. Going on this D.C. trip meant leaving my comfort zone of Ann Arbor, missing school, and learning about a topic that is controversial among most

Americans. Part of me was a little nervous, but in the end I felt excited that I was presented with the opportunity. I grew up learning that God created a world that welcomes all, and I plan on following through with this belief by learning as much as I can about all of God's people. Overall, I am so grateful to have a diverse parish that brings in a completely new perspective to my world.

University ministry makes no sense whatsoever if it does not lead the student to take what they've learned, what they've experienced, and then find ways to bring that into the world. Maggie experienced greater compassion for the people she met during the trip to Washington, D.C., and, more generally, for "God's people" in need whomever they might be. She came to a deeper conviction of the necessity of putting her faith into action.

Cait Hanley, a graduate student in social work, also participated in the march in D.C:

As a teacher at two low-income elementary schools in California, immigration reform became a personal issue for me. I saw families torn apart by our immigration system. My star fourth grader became a depressed fifth grader as she waited for news about her father after he was deported. Her mom suddenly became a single parent who struggled to provide for her three children.

Since moving back to Michigan and starting grad school, I have felt somewhat disconnected from the issue of immigration reform. The trip to D.C. with St. Mary's was a powerful reminder that there are many other people—both in Ann Arbor and from across the country—who are committed to fixing our broken system. I felt reenergized seeing people of all different ages, races, SES statuses, and faiths coming together to work for change.

The large presence of faith-based groups at the immigration reform events was especially striking to me. Our St. Mary's group was one of many groups who came to D.C. to put their faith in action. I felt God's presence as I walked alongside my brothers and sisters who were also hoping, praying, and trusting that there will be justice very soon.

In *Communities of Salt and Light: Reflections on the Social Mission of the Parish* (1993) the U.S. bishops extol the importance of legislative advocacy:

> Parishes need to promote a revived sense of political responsibility calling Catholics to be informed and active citizens, participating in the debate over the values and vision that guide our communities and nation. Parishes as local institutions have special opportunities to develop leaders, to promote citizenship, and to provide forums for discussion and action on public issues. Parishioners are called to use their talents, the resources of our faith, and the opportunities of this democracy to shape a society more respectful of the life, dignity, and rights of the human person. Parishes can help lift up the moral and human dimension of public issues, calling people to informed participation in the political process.[3]

Participation in the march for comprehensive immigration reform was an opportunity for our students, along with our resident parishioners, to advocate not only for the "issue" of immigration, but for the real people of our parish directly affected by our nation's policies. Students put into action their faith that calls them to show compassion, in deeds more than words, for those who suffer from indignity and injustice. This march also provided the opportunity to participate in the challenging legislative process and to see that their voice does count, their actions do matter.

Vigil and Rally for Lourdes Bautista Salazar

In October 2011, a member of our parish informed me that she was scheduled to be deported. Lourdes Bautista Salazar, mother of three

U.S.-born children, and living in the United States for fourteen years, would have to return to Mexico. She asked me if our parish would be able and willing to help cover the travel costs for her return, as required by Immigration and Customs Enforcement. This was not the first time our parish had been asked to fulfill such a request. And yes, we would be willing to provide this help once again.

But several days later, I asked Lourdes if she would permit me to share her circumstances with our parish. Her plight is the same as that of an estimated eleven million in this country without proper documentation. Lourdes, like many others, overstayed her visa. The national debate over our immigration system is not an academic one for us. It is one affecting our own parishioners. This issue is front and center not only for our Hispanic/Latino parishioners, but for students and others of many countries who, for various reasons, are in the country illegally.

In August 2011, Secretary of Homeland Security Janet Napolitano announced the administration's policy of "prosecutorial discretion." Immigration and Customs Enforcement was to suspend the prosecution of non-criminal immigrants with long-standing ties to the United States, especially in cases involving children.

In Lourdes's case, her husband had already been deported in 2010, leaving her the sole parent of her three children. She had started her own cleaning business, owned her own home in Ann Arbor, and was an active member of our parish community. She has no criminal record. The most stress-inducing factor of all this was that her U.S.-born, American children, including a thirteen-year-old, had established their lives here and had no connections in Mexico.

At first, our intention was to offer a prayer vigil for her, allowing her to share her story with those interested and for us to pray for her and for a change in our nation's immigration policies. But then we received an offer from a local immigrant rights advocacy group to help us petition for prosecutorial discretion on Lourdes's behalf. Soon, students, resident parishioners, and other supporters of Lourdes began an online petition and letter-writing campaign to Janet Napolitano and to John Morton, the director of Immigration and Customs Enforcement. Our request was that Lourdes be shown prosecutorial discretion and be granted a deferment of her deportation.

In November, we held our prayer vigil and rally for Lourdes. Over two hundred members of our congregation, Hispanic/Latino and Anglo, came together to show our support for Lourdes and her family and to speak out in favor of comprehensive immigration reform. We chose scripture passages from Leviticus, "When a foreigner resides among you in your land, do not mistreat him" (Leviticus 19:33–34); and from the Gospel of Luke, "Who is my neighbor?" (Luke 10:29). We invited Lourdes to share her story with us. We then prayed with Lourdes in our candlelight service, praying the Lord's Prayer in both Spanish and English.

When the solemn moment concluded, a soft, but growing drumbeat began from the back of the church. Students carrying signs and banners in English and Spanish reading *Fe* (Faith), *Esperanza* (Hope), and *Amor* (Love) began dancing toward the front of the church singing, "We can make a difference!" Once the group reached the front, they turned around and led the entire congregation in song and chant, out of the church, down the steps, around the corner, and two blocks around the church. Along the way, people chanted, "*Si, se puede!*" ("Yes, we can!") and "*Familias unidas jamas seran vencidas!*" ("Families united will never be defeated!") At the end, the marchers reentered the church and signed petitions to be sent on to Washington, D.C.

This was church at its best, providing the students who were present an example of faith and justice coming together in concrete form. While our parish's annual Good Friday bilingual Stations of the Cross is a wonderful opportunity for our Hispanic/Latino and Anglo communities to worship together, this prayer service and rally resulted in a deep bonding that has changed how both communities see each other. One member of the Hispanic/Latino community said afterward, "This no longer feels like the Anglo church that allows us to have Spanish Mass here. It now feels like it's my parish too!"

Amy Ketner, a junior at the time of the vigil, was profoundly moved by the vigil and rally:

> The vigil for Lourdes was more than an attempt to keep a family together here in the States. It was deeper than a cry out against unjust immigration policies. For me, as a then junior at the University of Michigan and active member of St. Mary Student Parish, this vigil was a crucial moment in my understanding of my Catholic faith. As we gathered around the altar, just before marching the streets of Ann Arbor, I looked around the church and realized the incredible beauty and remarkable reality of our faith. There it was clear that we were a diverse people of all ages, speaking many languages, hailing from hometowns around the globe, embracing different cultures, and carrying unique background stories. A diverse people, yes, but we were a unified people. In that moment, and always, we are united by our universal faith. That we could celebrate our unity through our rich diversity was astounding to me, and that we could do so in order to raise the voices of the marginalized and rally for justice moved me. Never before have I been more awed by the greatness of our God, nor had more trust and pride in our Catholic Church.

On December 13, the day after the great Mexican feast of Our Lady of Guadalupe, Lourdes received word that her request for deferment of her deportation had been granted.

LIVING LIFE TO THE FULL

"I came so that you might have life, life to the full" (John 10:10). These words of Jesus ground much of what I try to do as a campus minister. The question for me and for what we at St Mary's pose to our students is "What makes life full, really full?" While we live in a world that emphasizes the accumulation of goods, power, and security for oneself as the means to happiness, the Gospel of Jesus Christ offers a counter-message of self-sacrificing love of others, modeled after the life and teaching of Jesus. Participating in ministry to and with our Hispanic/Latino community members, our students experience more deeply this truth of our faith. They experience, through their interactions, what makes life really full.

Students participating in programs for and with the Hispanic/Latino members of our community come away with a deeper knowledge of the cultural world of our parishioners, many recently immigrated, from Central and South America. They learn new perspectives on their own faith through the stories and experiences of these community members. They are introduced to an array of social justice issues affecting the lives of this segment of our parish. And they are given the opportunity to develop skills for future church ministry, ministry in which Hispanics/Latinos will play a large part.

Now a graduating senior, Amy Ketner sums up well the faith formation possible through student participation in our Hispanic/Latino ministry:

> The immigrant community at St. Mary's has demonstrated to me the diversity, strength, and universality of the Catholic Church. The community members have showed me how our faith can manifest itself in unique ways and that we are all connected by our Catholic identity when we gather at the altar, whether for an immigration vigil or in the Eucharist. This has shaped the way I understood and thought about my faith during my time in college and will continue to do so as I leave St. Mary's and U of M. It gave me strength in my time working abroad in Peru for a summer, and it will continue to do so as I move to Chile for the next two years as a Jesuit Volunteer. Thanks to my experience with Catholics from around the world at St. Mary's, I know that not only is God with me wherever I end up, but so too is my church and a community of Catholics who will love and support me as their sister. Whether working for justice or sharing the Body of Christ, regardless of

our location, culture, or language, I now rest in the confidence that I will always have a community of brothers and sisters. For me, this is one of the most incredible and beautiful blessings of our Catholic faith.

While our ministry to Hispanics/Latinos was never intended as a means of faith formation for our university students, it has become an excellent avenue guiding our students to understand our world more deeply and the place of faith and service within it.

"NOT SO RELIGIOUS"
Jewish Chaplaincy
in the Twenty-First Century

Rabbi Rena S. Blumenthal
Vassar College, Poughkeepsie, New York

A number of years ago, the purchasing department, which supervises my college credit card charges, questioned why I had ordered a package of large, colorful feathers for use in the Bayit, Vassar's center for Jewish campus life. Our office administrator explained, as best she could, that before Passover the Jewish students enact a ritual hunt for pre-hidden bread crumbs using candles and feathers. I was sorry not to be able to listen in on this discussion and could only imagine how peculiar the ritual must have sounded to bureaucratic ears.

Though the purchasing department has never again, to my knowledge, questioned any of my equally odd credit card charges, I know I am not the only college chaplain whose work remains mysterious to other campus professionals. But confusion around the question "What exactly does a Jewish chaplain *do*?" doesn't end with administrators. Even to my chaplain colleagues, there is often a lack of clarity about the distinctions between their roles and mine. In

Rabbi Rena S. Blumenthal is assistant director of the Office of Religious and Spiritual Life and Irving Rachlin Advisor to Jewish Students at Vassar College in Poughkeepsie, New York. Prior to becoming a rabbi in 2003, she worked as a psychologist for fifteen years in New York City and Jerusalem.

my ten years as Vassar's Jewish chaplain, I've become aware of how chaplaincy—a job invented and in many ways still defined by liberal Protestant tradition—is embedded with cultural assumptions about how campus religious leaders should care for their students. The default assumption is that Jewish chaplains and Christian chaplains do the same work, but with a different set of texts and rituals—that the way my Protestant colleagues care for the emotional and spiritual well-being of the young people in their charge is exactly the same way I care for the Jewish students I work with. But, it seems almost too obvious to state, the differences between Judaism and Christianity go much deeper than a difference in texts and ritual. Because the cultural context of Jewish life is fundamentally distinct from that of the Protestant majority, my role as a Jewish chaplain is equally distinct from that of my Protestant colleagues. As a Jewish chaplain, I am charged with helping students negotiate the complexities of Jewish history, ritual, liturgy, law, cultural developments, and identity formation in a setting that, despite all good intentions, can be profoundly unaware of Jewish cultural norms.

What does Jewish life on a campus consist of? A short list would have to include weekly Shabbat (Sabbath) services and meals; a multitude of holiday services, meals, celebrations, and programs; educational, cultural, and social events; text study; and a kaleidoscope of sometimes esoteric ritual. Jewish life on campus explores theology and values; the relationship of Israel to contemporary Jewish life; the quandaries of fixed liturgy; the obligation toward social justice; the tension between *halakha* (Jewish law) and spiritual innovation; Jewish music, film, and arts; and the complex nuances of Jewish history and identity. The territory is so vast, it is often challenging for Jewish student leaders on a small campus such as Vassar to know where to begin to focus their energies.

Perhaps the most common thing I hear from students new to the Bayit ("house" in Hebrew) is one form or another of the phrase "I'm not a very good Jew." Given the complexities of Jewish identity in modern American life, it is hardly surprising that so many Jewish youngsters feel that they are not living up to an idealized sense of what a "good" Jew is. They arrive at college for what may be their first moment of choice about how to actuate their Jewish lives, and many of them discover that they don't know how to do that. The questions they face—Can I be Jewish if I am not "religious"? Can I belong to a Jewish community if I speak no Hebrew and don't know the customs? Are the Jewish people powerful or vulnerable?—are complicated and urgent. The Jewish chaplain has not only to help clarify some of the complex dynamics that underlie these questions, but also to reframe the question from "Am I a 'good' Jew?" to "Why should I live a Jewishly infused life?" It is my job to provide students with multiple opportunities and entry points for exploring the ways in which integrating Jewish experiences into their lives can be meaningful, joyful, and life enhancing.

THE RELIGIOUS-CULTURAL DIVIDE

About a year ago, I overheard a student leader of the Vassar Jewish Union (VJU), a young woman who had been attending Shabbat and holiday services regularly for three years, say that she was "not so religious." I said to her, "Really? If you knew of a student who chose to spend every Friday night at the Bayit, despite all the distractions available to her on campus, and despite her heavy workload, who sometimes even led services, and who, on top of all that, came to every holiday observance that we offer—would you consider that student 'not so religious'?" She looked puzzled at first, then smiled broadly. I asked her this question not because I wanted to convince her that she really was "religious," but because complicating the often simplistic ways in which words like "religious" and "secular" are used by Jewish students is a key part of my chaplaincy.

The confusion that Jewish students manifest around the word "religious" is certainly understandable. It is tied to the very essence of Jewish identity—a complicated mix of religion, culture, and ethnicity—that can only be understood within a historical perspective.

Before the modern era, Jews primarily understood themselves as *am Yisrael*, "the people Israel." *Am Yisrael* engaged in certain characteristic behaviors—they observed Shabbat, kept kosher, studied

Torah, and perpetuated a host of liturgies and rituals related to holidays, life-cycle events, and daily life. There were rules that determined who was part of the Jewish people, including matrilineal descent and conversion according to certain guidelines. There were beliefs that the Jewish people held, including the existence of one deity and the sanctity of Torah. There were foods that the Jewish people ate, and languages that the Jewish people spoke. These behaviors and beliefs were not static, and what *am Yisrael* did and believed could differ across time periods and geographical locations. But the basic identification as a people was fairly constant. There was no word for "religion," or even "Judaism" in premodern Hebrew, no concept equivalent to race or ethnicity, and for the most part, no particular interest in systematic theological dogma. Within these historical conditions, being Jewish primarily meant belonging to the Jewish people and engaging, broadly speaking, in Jewish practices; there was no perceived difference between Jewish "culture" and Jewish "religion."

The distinction between religion and culture in European Jewish life only became relevant after the political emancipation of the Jews, a process that began in the eighteenth century. Through emancipation, the Jews gained a great deal—including all the rights and responsibilities of citizenship—but there were also costs. In order to become citizens of their respective nation-states, Jews had to accept a shift in their self-identity—becoming, for example, "Frenchmen of the Jewish faith"—thus taking on an externally imposed distinction between their religious and cultural identities. This artificial split in identity served to privatize and partially eclipse their primary self-identification as a people.

Although this brief summary is necessarily oversimplified, a historical perspective is essential in depicting the ways that Jewish students today are navigating between different assumptions of what it means to be "religious." Vassar's Jewish student body comes from a wide range of backgrounds, from families with no religious affiliation to families with traditional (but rarely Orthodox) halakhic observance. But the vast majority of these students, like my VJU leader, would not describe themselves as "religious." Even those who grew up within a religious denomination will frequently refer to themselves as "cultural" or "secular" Jews. What they mean by this is either that they are not halakhically observant—a practice-based definition perpetuated by the norms of the Orthodox community—and/or that they don't believe in God—a faith-based definition primarily drawn out of Christian culture. The word "religious" in contemporary Jewish life is therefore complicated from two directions. It is no easy feat for young, liberal Jews to situate themselves in the narrow channel that runs between Orthodox norms and Christian cultural assumptions.

The result is often a Jewish self-definition that is based primarily on the negative. Most Jewish students at Vassar can tell you what they are not—"religious"—more easily than defining what they are. Although there is a strong secularist Jewish tradition, very few young Jews are immersed in it, or even familiar with it, and can give no clear, affirmative definition of what a "cultural" or "secular" Jew is. When students describe themselves as "not religious," they sometimes mean "not kosher"; sometimes, "I don't believe in God"; sometimes both; sometimes neither. Although we have many Shabbat-attending Jewish atheists at a school like Vassar, this phenomenon tends to puzzle people who have been raised in Christian culture. One frequently hears reference to "students of the Jewish faith," a phrase that is discordant to many Jewish ears and betrays a profound lack of awareness of lived Jewish experience. What is even more problematic is that many young Jews who have grown up in a Christian environment will adopt similar language and attitudes and will avoid Jewish events that would otherwise draw them in because "I am not so religious."

An incident from my first semester at Vassar exemplifies how this dynamic plays out. Still learning my way around the college, I decided to take a campus tour to see how Vassar presents itself to prospective students. The Bayit is a small, two-story house situated just outside Vassar's north gate. As we passed along the northern periphery of the campus, the tour guide gestured in its direction and said, "Behind that building is the Bayit, which is used by our religious Jewish community." This categorization of the Bayit as a space for "religious" Jewish students, as if it were the Vassar "synagogue," would have made the students who attend Bayit programs acutely uncomfortable, but it would have hardly surprised them. Few of them identify as "religious," and none of them believe that the Bayit is meant to serve such a distinct, and minute, subset of the Vassar Jewish community—but they are fully aware that that is how it is frequently perceived.

This perception is reinforced by the fact that at Vassar, as at many small colleges, Jewish life is defined as part of the Office of Religious and Spiritual Life and advised by a rabbi. Although Hillel, the national organization for Jewish campus life, only rarely employs rabbis as directors, the model of rabbi-as-director largely persists at small liberal arts campuses, primarily because Jewish life functions under the rubric of the chaplaincy or religious life office. This has many advantages, especially for interreligious work, but it also has the disadvantage of reinforcing the primacy of "religion" as a category for a student population that is overwhelmingly nonreligious in its self-understanding.

Shortly prior to my arrival on campus in 2003, Vassar students were rated by the Princeton Review as "most likely to ignore God on a regular basis." Although I have never understood exactly what that means—doesn't almost everyone "ignore God on a regular basis"?—this distinction was cited frequently in my early years at Vassar, and the pride that the campus took in it was palpable.

The identity formation of Vassar's Jewish community is playing out, then, in a social context that is uncomfortable with overt manifestations of religious identity. Religion is often treated on campus as an idiosyncratic, private, extracurricular activity. At best, it is viewed as an object of tolerant curiosity; at worst, as a sign of peculiarity or limited intellectual rigor. This religious stigma impacts all Vassar students but impacts the Jewish community in its own unique way. On the one hand, for members of an intensely communal religious culture, in which there is an inherent lack of religious-cultural distinction, the assumptions about what a student "believes" when he or she attends a Shabbat or holiday service, and the stigma attached to these projected beliefs, can be particularly challenging. As stated above, Jews attend Passover Seders and High Holy Day services, not to mention Jewish films and bagel brunches, regardless of their level of practice or their theological convictions. But in a campus culture in which Judaism is subsumed under religious life and in which religion in general is privatized, presumed to be faith based, and generally suspect, it is hard for Jewish students to reconcile the collective Jewish cultural norms with the surrounding, often antireligious, ethos of the campus.

But the flip side of this coin is equally problematic. As a result of the perceived stigma of religion on campus, all students, including Jews, are unaccustomed to spiritual language and particularly uncomfortable talking about God—jokingly referred to, in our office, as the "G-word." Since Judaism tends to focus more on practice than on faith, the discomfort with spiritual language is already internally socialized and then reinforced by the secularism of the larger campus culture. The research our office has conducted as part of the "Secularity in the Liberal Arts" project has confirmed what I see on a day-to-day basis—that our students often feel inhibited or self-conscious in talking about questions related to meaning, purpose, mystery, and transcendence. Accessing Jewish wisdom to address these kinds of "big question" issues can be particularly problematic for those students who have subliminally incorporated the religious/cultural divide—either as a way of distancing themselves from active Jewish life and practice or, inversely, as a way of holding on to Jewish identity while keeping their distance from the stigmatized religious identification.

Confusion about what is meant by "religious" creates both opportunities and challenges. On the one hand, it is quite common in the Jewish community to think of oneself as a "secular" Jew and nonetheless participate in seemingly "religious" events such as Shabbat and holiday services, or even maintain some semblance of a kosher diet. I sometimes ask students whether they think of a

Passover Seder as a religious or cultural event—a question that is, of course, impossible to answer. Jewish students instinctively understand this, which provides me an opportunity for challenging the problematic religious/secular binary that pervades the larger societal discourse. The challenge I encounter is that students have no language or historical perspective to assimilate this odd religious/cultural mix into their developing Jewish identity. Gently drawing their attention to the ways that cultural assumptions and language based in Protestant traditions can be at odds with Jewish cultural norms helps them see their own struggles to articulate their Jewishness in a new light.

My primary role at the Bayit is to try to create the conditions that can help students, despite these obstacles, be more securely grounded in their Jewish identity. I do this, in part, by ensuring that everything that the VJU sponsors is student directed and student led. As an example, every week a different student leads Shabbat services, which includes prayers, singing, and a short discussion on a topic of their choice. All but the most experienced student leaders meet with me ahead of time, sometimes more than once, to make sure that the service reflects their commitments, aesthetics, and vision; that they feel confident in their service-leading skills; and that they have thought through their discussion questions well. These skills are often new to them, and their service leading and discussion facilitation are often rough around the edges. But I am deeply committed to this model of student empowerment, not only for Shabbat services but for all of their programming. By making room for them to develop their own voices—rough edges and all—I am enabling them to more fully own their Jewish lives.

Students who are securely grounded in their Jewish identity can play an exciting role in complicating the larger discourse in which the terms of "religious" and "secular" life are so rigidly employed. More importantly, understanding the complexity of Jewish identity can help these students be fully engaged as Jews and have their lives enriched by Jewish tradition in ways that are not inhibited by identifications external to the Jewish experience.

JEWISH PARTICULARISM
AND THE YEARNING TO BELONG

"Freshman Shabbat," which occurs during orientation week and appears on the orientation schedule, usually draws a huge crowd by Vassar standards—about seventy-five students. By the following Shabbat the number dips to about forty, and it then settles in at around thirty for the rest of the year. Although I find this trending to be perfectly natural, students are perpetually disturbed by it. Where did all those enthusiastic freshmen go? Every few years, the VJU leadership decides to conduct a survey assessing why students do or do not participate in their programming. The question of Shabbat attendance is always on the survey, and the top-billing answer has remained remarkably consistent.

The biggest reason that students give for not returning to the Bayit after Freshman Shabbat is that they didn't know the tunes. I was surprised and somewhat bemused the first time they got this response and decided that every year I would encourage the student leader of the Freshman Shabbat service to make a big deal of this in the introduction—to tell the freshmen that most of them will not know all the tunes; that the tunes will vary from week to week depending on who leads the service; that if you come for a few weeks in a row, you will start to know many of the tunes; that the leaders themselves had the same experience their first time at the Bayit. Nonetheless, after many years of this introduction, both the falloff after Freshman Shabbat and the response to the survey question haven't changed at all.

I am beginning to understand the reasons that an unfamiliar tune can be so off-putting for a young freshman's first experience at the Bayit. On the simplest level, this is related to the diversity of the Jewish community we serve. It has never even occurred to many young Jews, who may have grown up in a particular community, that other synagogues have different melodies or practices. But this is hardly a sufficient explanation. After all, college is full of often radically new experiences. Why the extreme sensitivity to something as simple as a new melody?

The vast majority of students, when asked why they get involved in Jewish life, will tell you that they do so for "the community," and there is nothing that makes student leaders prouder than when the Bayit is described as a warm and welcoming space. Judaism is an intensely communal culture, and in the age of what Robert Putnam describes as "Bowling Alone" America, this is undoubtedly its greatest strength and attraction. Most Jews instinctively understand that one can "belong" to the Jewish people regardless of one's level of halakhic observance or theological convictions. But aside from the essential confusion about "religion" outlined above, the challenge of Jewish particularism is an additional obstacle to students' often powerful wish to engage with Jewish life. This too can only be understood through a brief examination of its historical roots.

Prior to their political emancipation, Jews often lived in relative cultural isolation. Although there were often extensive economic ties with the wider society, Jews generally had their own schools, courts, welfare systems, languages, and, of course, places of worship. Raised from early childhood within this cultural hothouse, children easily mastered the complex ritual and textual traditions that compose a rich Jewish life. Moreover, the boundaries of Jewish life were not very fluid—it was a culture difficult, though never impossible, to join or to leave.

Post-emancipation, the issue of Jewish particularism has become more complex and conflicted. Jews no longer live in a distinct cultural framework, and there are, of course, a multitude of advantages to the access Jews now have to the larger American culture. But the flip side of this access is that most young Jews, outside of the Orthodox world, cannot possibly master the complex tangle of rituals, customs, texts, and halakhic norms that comprise Jewish life, not to mention the Hebrew language, which forms the foundation for much of this knowledge. Supplementary Jewish schools, and even Jewish day schools, work hard to teach Jewish children the basics of Hebrew language, liturgy, *halakha*, holiday customs, Jewish music, literature, and arts and to foster a connection to Israel and Jewish communal history. But these schools are often limited in their effectiveness because of the complexities of Jewish life, the constricted time they have to devote to Jewish subjects, and the attenuation of Jewish family life. The Jewish community is struggling to resolve the question of what it means to be an educated liberal Jew in contemporary America.

The generally sophisticated and accomplished young Jews who arrive at a competitive school like Vassar are well aware of their lack of basic Jewish knowledge, some despite many years of frustrating and unsatisfying Jewish schooling. These newly arrived college students are also at precisely the point in life when Jewish involvement becomes a choice, and not a parental dictate. For many, a feeling of inadequacy weighs heavily against the impulse toward joining Jewish life on campus—the realization that Jewish "belonging" may come at the price of facing one's Jewish ignorance.

Several years ago, the VJU held a parlor discussion entitled "Healing the Trauma of Hebrew School." The program drew a wide range of students, not because Hebrew schools are abusive places— the students readily understood the humor of the title—but because these schools are often either unclear or unrealistic as to what their mission should be under the current cultural conditions of Jewish life. The first half of the program consisted of students telling their "horror stories"—the impossibility of mastering Hebrew in once-a-week sessions; the inability of the often nonprofessional teachers to control their uninterested students; the traumatic narratives of the Holocaust and one-dimensional depictions of Israel; the ahistorical teaching of biblical and Rabbinic stories. When they had gotten enough of this out of their system, I gave them some historical perspective—it is not, after all, for lack of trying or caring that Hebrew schools so often fail. I then asked them how they would design a Hebrew school for their own children and they bubbled with ideas and excitement. It had never occurred to them that there were real historical circumstances that could explain the inadequate educational environment that they had encountered.

Just naming the fact that most American Jews have, at best, a second grade Jewish education—and that this is inevitable, given the challenges of Jewish education in the modern era—can relieve students' feelings of inadequacy. I often tell students that I myself, despite an Orthodox upbringing and four intensive years of rabbinical training, don't know a fraction of what a rabbi would have known one hundred years ago, never mind what many Orthodox laymen know today. For example, because I was a girl, I did not study Talmud as a child and only encountered a Talmudic text for the first time in my forties, too late to master Rabbinic literature in as comprehensive a way as I would have wished. It is because I understand some of the historical and social circumstances that determined my Jewish education that I am able to accept my own limitations and to help my students normalize their own.

The sensitivity evoked by an unfamiliar tune is not unrelated to these dynamics. Students who already feel insecure about their level of Jewish knowledge or practice can be knocked right out of the game by a new melody—the one part of the service they may have thought they had mastered, and that most poignantly represents "home." While they have no choice but to take on the many new concepts and experiences that college offers, they can easily say no to this one additional affront to life's certainties. Too often, that one unknown song is enough to make them feel they will never know what they need to know to be active, engaged members of the Jewish community.

But lack of Jewish knowledge is not the only hindrance to Jewish students' yearning to belong. I have found that students are often equally attracted to and disquieted by the tribal nature of Jewish culture. On the one hand, there is great comfort in the "home away from home" feeling of a place like the Bayit (reinforced, of course, by the very "house-ness" of our building, never mind the Jewish "mom" who runs it). On the other hand, there is much anxiety lest anyone feel excluded and a hypersensitivity to any hint that they themselves might not fully belong.

The Bayit strives to be radically welcoming to all who enter its doors, but it is also, clearly and emphatically, a Jewish space. Although there are always many non-Jews attending Bayit events, including our Shabbat services and dinners, students perennially worry that their non-Jewish friends are even less able to "belong" than they are, and in a way, they are right. This idea is unsettling, and sometimes off-putting, to students who want to participate in Jewish life but not to the exclusion of other important affiliations. There is an unspoken fear that particularism equates with a sense of superiority and exclusiveness. Boundaries, however fluid they may be, are a challenge inherent to a powerful communal sensibility.

The existence of powerful, but not fully visible, cultural boundaries can be an awkward fit with the implicitly universalist ideology that pervades the surrounding campus culture. This universalist strain is tied, in part, to the faith-based ethos of Christianity, with its intentionally fluid boundaries. Although there is much rhetoric around "diversity" on the contemporary American campus, there remains concern about deeply articulated cultural and religious difference and the feeling of exclusion it can inevitably cause. Jewish students' sensitivity to this possibility of felt exclusion can sometimes impact how fully they want to participate in Jewish campus life.

Part of my task is to help Jewish students understand that deep difference need not be associated with hierarchies of superiority and exclusion. To explain this, I often employ the metaphor of language. I can certainly hear the beauty of French, and I know that there are things you can say more elegantly in French than in English, but acknowledging its distinct gifts doesn't mean that French is therefore a "better" language than English. For me, there will never be a language in which I can express myself more fluently and joyfully than in English, my mother tongue. It is to the benefit of all humans that there are thousands of languages, each of them with its own strengths, weaknesses, and quirks, and the same is true, I believe, for religions and cultures. Judaism is my spiritual and cultural mother tongue, and I am a firm believer in the idea that cultural diversity is as beneficial to the global human community as biodiversity is to the biome. As an inheritor of an exceptionally ancient and rich cultural tradition, I feel a responsibility to tend my tiny Jewish corner of the human biome and nurture precisely those parts of it that are most idiosyncratic and distinct, resisting the common impulse to suggest that "we are all the same." We are the same in some ways, but not in others, and this is a good thing. I share this perspective with students often, but it can be a hard sell in a culture that declares a great interest in diversity but often tiptoes around deep difference for fear of the conflict, hierarchies, and exclusion it might spawn.

Student leadership can be very rattled by the Freshman Shabbat survey results and everything the "unfamiliar tune" issue implies. They often want nothing more from Jewish community than to belong and to have others feel that they also belong. Sometimes I think they want it too much—more than wisdom; more than spiritual grounding; more than critical perspective or new knowledge. And for some of the students they most wish to serve, they will fail—even fail spectacularly. No matter how hard the Bayit attempts to be pluralistic and welcoming of all levels of practice, some students' expectations will be rudely challenged. There will be too much Hebrew for some and too much English for others; the service will be too long for some and too abbreviated for others; too traditional for some and too innovative for others—all happening in a setting that is fueled by insecurity, nostalgia, and the yearning to "belong." It is part of my job to normalize and contextualize the sensitivities evoked by these strong feelings so that the joy and depth of Jewish practice can carry equal weight to the comfort of belonging.

NAVIGATING THE RHETORIC OF RACE

At a recent parlor discussion on Judaism and feminism, sponsored by the VJU, a Jewish student I had never met before declared, "I never identify myself as Jewish because people would interpret it as distancing myself from my white privilege." No one challenged her statement, and several students nodded in agreement.

As if things were not complicated enough, questions of religion and culture, belonging and exclusion, particularity and universalism, play out against the background of the fraught rhetoric of racial politics in contemporary America. Jews, of course, come in many skin tones. But the majority of Jews in America are of Ashkenazi origin, have relatively light skin tone, and are understood by the general culture to be "white." This was not always so clearly the case; until the latter half of the twentieth century, Jews, as well as many other immigrant groups, were not seen as fully "white," and the category of "whiteness"—so tied, as it is, to the long and conflicted story of black-white relations in America—is experienced by some Jews as another externally imposed identification. Ethnicity was one factor (although hardly the dominant factor) in the historical definition of Jewish peoplehood, which was thought to be an irrevocably inherited status. Needless to say, "whiteness" affords light-toned Jews considerable privileges in American culture, but it also serves to erase the particularity of Jewish identity in a highly race-focused culture.

The discourse on identity on the contemporary liberal arts campus is so heavily color based that it is sometimes hard to see beyond it. The peculiarities of Jewish identity, which has an ethnic component but is not primarily ethnic in nature, can challenge the simple binaries of racial discourse in a constructive way, just as the religious-cultural fusion can challenge the binaries of the religious and secular. But so charged is the racial discourse in contemporary America that this is not an easy role to inhabit. The result is an even further inclination to confine Jewishness into a "religious" box, with that term's Protestant assumption of something inherently separate from culture or ethnicity, thereby eliminating it from the identity-based conversation. The double standard applied to racial and Jewish cultural particularism is fascinating to observe. It is hard not to challenge students to consider, for example, why it feels acceptable to create "safe spaces" for race-based identity groups but not for the exploration of Jewish identity.

The erasure of Jewish identity that can result from this brand of identity politics can be startling. A women's studies major, who was not in any way involved in Jewish life, recently told me that in four years of women's studies classes she had never heard a feminist scholar's Judaism being referenced, never mind explored for its impact on her experience or scholarship. According to that same student, a campus memorial program for the poet Adrienne Rich, for whom Judaism was a major influence and focus of her work, never directly referenced her Jewish background or interests. In my experience, it is not at all uncommon for exhibits of Jewish artists or lectures about Jewish thinkers to similarly ignore the impact of their Jewish heritage. Perhaps more surprisingly, an employee informed me that an administrator, in the context of a hiring process, told her, "Judaism is not part of diversity at Vassar."

In some ways, it is highly advantageous to Jews to be invisible in these ways, just as it is advantageous to be perceived as "white." Jews have not forgotten the quotas that long kept them out of elite college campuses. Today, schools like Vassar have large numbers of Jewish students and faculty and experience few overt signs of anti-Semitism. Vassar is not at all exceptional in its tendency to "not see" Jewishness as an identity marker, and many Jews welcome the absorption into "whiteness" and the exclusively religious definition of Judaism that is current in liberal America. But as a Jewish chaplain, I cannot help but see the ways in which the erasure of Jewish cultural identity as a category of inquiry can be harmful to the identity formation of young Jews. It is part of my work to highlight the dissonance as it occurs.

Several years ago, I was on a college committee that decided to do a "multicultural audit" of the campus. There was much anguished discussion on the committee on how to parse the different cultural categories. Early on, I suggested a category of "religiously identified" students, which would almost certainly not have made its way into the audit without me, but was readily accepted. But further into the process, when I suggested a category for "cultural Jews," there was greater resistance. Although the category was eventually included— mainly, I suspect, because I was one of only a few people actively working on the audit—there was clear discomfort with the idea. Not surprisingly, large numbers of students checked the "cultural Jewish" box; but, also not surprisingly, there were a few overt expressions of hostility from students questioning why there wasn't a "cultural Muslim" or "cultural Christian" box. By inserting cultural Judaism so visibly into a public dissection of identity categories, I had shaken some unspoken norms. But I like to think that I had also provided an opportunity for the many students who checked that box, most of whom I would probably never meet, to have their primary identity made visible in an unexpected context. I understand it to be part of my role, as a Jewish chaplain, to gently push at the edges of what are considered legitimate categories of identity.

JEWISH POWER AND VULNERABILITY

One of the most moving programs that VJU students sponsor is the annual Holocaust Day Commemoration. A tiny group of students—never more than twenty—gathers on the chapel lawn at dusk for about twenty minutes of song, poetry, and personal reflections, most of the latter by grandchildren of Holocaust survivors. The program is followed by a walking meditation through candle-lit luminaria. Although I am moved to tears every year by the sweetness and sincerity of the program, I am also saddened, as the daughter of a survivor myself, by the inability to draw more widely from the Jewish student body and the larger campus community. I suspect that the small turnout for this exceptionally beautiful, student-developed, and student-run program is partially due to a deep ambivalence among young Jews about issues related to Jewish victimhood and power.

Many of our students have never experienced overt anti-Semitic speech or actions, though all of them are acutely aware of the Holocaust and the long history of persecution that preceded it. But one anomaly of modern Jewish life is that despite being only two generations away from attempted genocide, Jews have been extraordinarily successful establishing themselves in America—socially, politically, and financially. As a result, Jews are emerging as a powerful presence in contemporary America, with all the opportunities and dangers the exercise of power holds. This juxtaposition within the Jewish community of a long history of vulnerability and newly acquired opportunities for the exercise of power can engender considerable discomfort in a campus culture that is highly suspicious of political and economic power. The complexities of the conflict in the Middle East, involving the first expression of Jewish military power in two thousand years, makes this issue a tinderbox. Are Jews a minority or part of the majority, powerless or powerful, victims or oppressors? The question, which intersects uncomfortably with race-based rhetoric, provokes much confusion for young students attempting to define their identity as Jews and situate that identity within the larger campus discourse.

The virulence that accompanies the debate about Middle East politics is partly rooted in this acute ambivalence about power. Lingering Holocaust trauma runs deep in the Jewish community, and every Jewish student, no matter how Jewishly disaffiliated their background, has absorbed the Holocaust-to-Israel narrative arc of victimhood to redemption. Unhelpfully, this narrative is sometimes spiced with a glorification of political and military power, and rarely accompanied by an in-depth study of the complex history of the Middle East conflict. As a result, the relationship with Israel is similar in some ways to many Vassar students' relationship to the Bayit. There is a sense of "home-ness" that the Jewish State offers, fueled by both the popularity of Birthright trips and students' often strong familial connections, which can be both attractive and empowering. But the critique of the Israeli use of power that students discover on campus, sometimes for the first time, makes this sense of "home-ness" suspect and conflict ridden, resulting in aversion to the entire subject. At almost every end-of-the-year recap, I find our student leadership self-critical of their own avoidance of Israel programming—a stance that is readily understandable given the political and psychosocial dynamics of the issue.

Helping students navigate questions related to Jewish power and vulnerability is one of the most complicated and vexing roles I have to play. To the extent that anti-Semitism occurs on campus at all, it is usually of a type so nuanced and subtle that one can hardly pin it down. Is ignoring Adrienne Rich's Judaism or a reluctance to include "cultural Judaism" as an identity category a neutral sociological phenomenon or a subtle form of anti-Semitism? What about the disproportionate attention that Israeli violence receives compared to other instances of state-sponsored aggression? Does a swastika on a wall, not an uncommon occurrence on college campuses, have anything to do with Jews and the Holocaust, or has it become a generalized symbol of rage? It is difficult for me to parse these delicate issues—how much more so for college-age students who may be confronting these phenomena for the first time.

This year, Yom Ha'atzma'ut (Israel Independence Day) fell earlier than usual in the Gregorian calendar, during peak campus programming season. I pointed this out to the students a couple of months ahead of time and asked them if they wanted to mark it in some way. There was a brief discussion, and a committee was formed to think about the question, but the committee kept forgetting to meet or report back. Not surprisingly, Yom Ha'atzma'ut came and went with no program of any kind. At the end-of-year recap, I pointed out to students that not doing any programming on Yom Ha'atzma'ut was as much a statement as throwing a party or sponsoring a probing lecture—but that instead of actively deciding to make that statement, they had passively let it happen. The discussion that followed was hesitant, but a step in the right direction—fully revealing the deep ambivalence about issues related to Jewish power and vulnerability that pervades Jewish life. I am undoubtedly as conflicted about these issues as my students are, but I try, as gently as I can, to raise their consciousness about these questions as I see them playing out, both in their own behavior and on the campus at large.

JEWS AND INTERRELIGIOUS PROGRAMMING

Like many campus chaplaincies, Vassar has seen an exciting increase in interreligious programming over the past ten years. This programming has ranged from large, all-campus events, such as our annual interreligious coffee house, to intimate gathering spaces, like our Religious Spiritual and Secular Forum (RSSF), which meets weekly throughout the year.

At the end-of-year evaluations, students from all our religious groups express a strong desire to engage in more interreligious programming, and they often evince a hunger to learn about other religious traditions. It has been fascinating to note, however, that students' expressed interest in interreligious experiences far out-paces the number of initiatives they take in this area, and even their participation in such programs when organized by others. Some of this is natural shyness about reaching out to unfamiliar traditions and fear of offending others through ignorance. But for the Jewish community, which expresses as much desire for this kind of pro-gramming as any other group on campus, there seem to be particu-lar concerns that inhibit their natural curiosity and desire to reach out to members of other religious communities.

There are a number of dynamics at work in this apparent ambiv-alence. First, of course, is their own unease about being included in the "religious" category. But putting this issue aside, there is also considerable anxiety that Jewish students experience around the prospect of Christian evangelizing, understandable in light of the long and discomfiting history of Jewish-Christian relations.

At one year's Religious and Spiritual Life (RSL) Coffee House, a student from the Vassar Christian Fellowship, the evangelical group on campus, offered readings quite overtly aimed at proselytizing the audience—something that rarely happens on campus and was not approved by the other members of his group. I watched, with some humor, as one Jewish student after another went to the bath-room, walked out of the room to make a phone call, or suddenly realized they were too busy to stay to the end of the program. When I explored the incident with them afterward, they all insisted that they had good reasons for leaving at that moment; only when prod-ded a bit did they also acknowledge their deep discomfort and sense of vulnerability. Jewish students' confusion about the different types of Christian groups on campus and their extreme sensitivity to any hint of Christian proselytizing can lead to a generalized discomfort in programming with Christian groups.

And then there is the problem of the Muslim-Jewish encounter. Jewish students are particularly fascinated by Islam but are often wor-ried that they will encounter anti-Israel sentiments that they will not know how to respond to. The VJU's two collaborations over the past years with the Vassar Islamic Society are enlightening. Both events were initiated by the much larger VJU, took place in Jewish spaces, and were carefully controlled events—a discussion held on Yom Kippur afternoon that focused on fasting in Jewish and Muslim traditions, and a Shabbat service that focused on the idea of Sabbath in Jewish and Muslim traditions. The success of these two events was predicated on tight thematic control that excluded the possibility of uncomfortable political tensions emerging.

The understandable discomfort with Christian and Muslim encounters feeds the general reluctance among Jewish students to engage, despite much interest, in meaningful interreligious dialogue. The conviction on the part of Jewish students that they are insufficiently grounded in their own complex religious tradition, a feeling they often share with other students but that can be more acute due to the textual and ritualistic complexity of Jewish life, is the final nail in the coffin of good interreligious intentions. The general challenges of moving beyond the often superficial interreligious models that we tend to fall back on—either the "bring a text from your tradition" model or the "let's all feed the hungry together" model—is beyond the scope of this discussion. Suffice it to say that the Jewish community, though confronting its own specific challenges, is not alone in not knowing how to engage in the kind of substantive interreligious encounters that our students so clearly crave.

In helping students think through this issue, the fact that I wear two hats—I am both the assistant director of RSL and advisor to Jewish students—provides me with a unique opportunity to serve as a bridge between RSL and Jewish life. In this capacity, I can translate Jewish sensitivities—many of which also apply to other minority religious traditions—for RSL and can also alleviate the "religion" anxieties that Jewish students bring to their participation in RSL programming. Jewish students see the close, collaborative relationship that I have with the Protestant minister who directs RSL, as well as the warm relationships I have fostered with other religious student group leaders. I try to provide a model for them of how to be committed to interreligious conversation without losing one's own deeply articulated religious and cultural integrity. Strong

Jewish participation in the interreligious life of the campus not only benefits the Jewish community, it can also contribute to campus chaplaincy by unsettling and broadening its understanding of the religious. Ideally, it can also help empower other minority religious traditions to more boldly question Protestant assumptions that can, in subliminal and unarticulated ways, inhibit their own groups' development on campus.

CONCLUSION: MAKING AN ANCIENT TRADITION NEW

The VJU leadership rightly prides itself on creating a warm and welcoming environment at the Bayit, something that involves a great deal of work and intention. Students put much thought into planning interesting and varied Shabbat dinner menus that take into account the needs of vegans, the gluten intolerant, and the chocolate obsessed. Service leaders are careful to mention where the songs are transliterated and to translate Hebrew words and phrases. Through this level of commitment and attention to detail, every week they create a powerful Shabbat experience—a respite from the over-busyness of a secular liberal arts campus. Friday nights at the Bayit are a moving and powerful experience of Shabbat as it should be—a time out for communal contemplation and bonding, an entrance into sacred time.

I am delighted that students from a wide range of Jewish and non-Jewish backgrounds have made themselves at home in the Bayit, relishing the chocolate chip challah that inaugurates their weekly Shabbat dinner. But I can't help hoping that "belonging" is only an entry point, not an end point. Jewish students have inherited an ancient and multifaceted tradition full of wisdom and resonance. Once they are assured that they "belong" inside the Jewish tent, they can use that sense of belonging to plumb its depths for meaning and joy—marking the seasons of the year and the cycles of life with powerful and complex ritual practices, exploring their responsibilities to others and to the grand prophetic project of making the world a better place, and opening themselves to the great mystery of the human condition. By helping them securely inhabit their Jewish communal world, I hope that they will feel enough ownership to experiment with those raw materials and create rich and inspiring Jewish lives.

The quandary of inheriting an ancient tradition is that the sheer antiquity of it can have powerful resonance, but it can just as easily feel stale and out-of-date. Working on a college campus, I have considerable freedom to bring the rituals, texts, and traditions of Jewish life into the modern age. A couple of months ago, I led an *upshirin* ceremony for this year's RSL interreligious fellow. *Upshirin* is a fairly obscure haircutting ritual that is generally held for three-year-old boys who, in some Jewish circles, do not get their first haircut until that age. The ceremony also represents their initiation into a life of study. Joey had decided to dedicate his summer to Torah study—and besides, his hair had gotten very long. About fifteen students came to sing, eat cake in the shape of Jewish letters, share readings about the significance of the ceremony, help cut little snippets of Joey's hair, and tell him how much we had appreciated him over the course of the year. No one in the room, including me, had ever experienced a ceremony quite like this, but it was joyful and innovative, yet deeply rooted in Jewish text and tradition. It was certainly educational—everyone who was there will remember what an *upshirin* is—but also radically playful. No one complained that an *upshirin* should only be for three-year-old boys, in part because almost no one had ever heard of it before. It takes a level of chutzpah to translate ancient rituals into a contemporary idiom. But if we can be spiritually courageous anywhere, it should be on a college campus, where this kind of experimentation and exploration should be commonplace.

What would it mean to infuse all our liturgy, ritual and text study with that same combination of tradition, meaning, and fun? Where better, for example, to do intellectually rigorous text study that fuses historical criticism with spiritual exploration than on a college campus? As we discard outmoded binaries of "religious" and "secular," we can find meaning in text without obfuscating its history and origins. Finding the balance, in an ancient tradition such as Judaism, between tradition and innovation is a constant balancing act, and sometimes we totter too far to one side or the other. But when the balance is right—when the resonance of the ancient is melded with the immediacy of the present moment—the result can be exhilarating.

The same year the purchasing department questioned my need to purchase feathers for my work, about ten students joined me on the Sunday before Passover to clean the Bayit kitchen for the holiday. I printed out three pages of complex dietary rules—which foods are permitted and which prohibited, which are permitted when purchased new and which can never be permitted—and we emptied the pantry and refrigerator of all prohibited foods. We moved all the pots and pans upstairs, turned the music on loud, and scrubbed every hidden corner of the room. One student took apart the oven into so many pieces, I wondered if he would ever manage to reassemble it. We filled pots with boiling water and immersed some of our ritual objects, covered the pantries and counters with contact paper, poured boiling water over the sinks, and turned on the ovens and burners to high heat. Several days later, after I had hidden five bread crumbs in various locales around the Bayit—on a windowsill, inside a bookshelf, on the lower shelf of the coffee table—a group of students said a blessing together, then took candles in hand and searched the house. When a bread crumb was found, we all gathered around excitedly as the student who had found it took a large, colored feather and swept it out of its hiding place. When all the bread crumbs had been disposed of, we gathered together in a circle to do a few readings about what it means to banish from our lives all the leavening—the pride, greed, and arrogance that puffs us up and distances us from that which is true. Most of the students had never participated in the ritual of *bedikat chametz* before, but there it all was before us: the peculiar, idiosyncratic, moving drama of a Jewishly infused life.

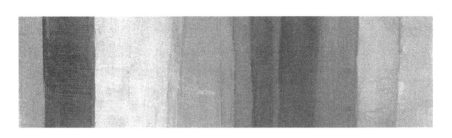

A HEART
FOR THE
COMMUNITY

"GOD IS IN THIS PLACE"
Mentoring, Ministering, and Making Meaning at Stanford University

Rabbi Patricia Karlin-Neumann
Stanford University, Stanford, California

It was in the spring when I found myself sitting across from one of Stanford University's "golden boys." Attractive, athletic, "wicked smart" as the students would say, he hailed from a small, rural, impoverished community. His whole town celebrated when he was admitted to Stanford. Now a junior, he needed a recommendation for a staff position in the dorms, but he didn't feel that he knew any professors well enough to ask. While we weren't close, our paths had crossed a few times, so he sheepishly asked me if I would be willing to write on his behalf. We arranged a time to talk so he could update me on what he was thinking and engaged in. I was happy to learn what I could about him—and see what would be honest and fair to say in a recommendation.

He had a full load, studying in the sciences and engineering. He was in a fraternity and enjoyed socializing but kept his focus on academics. His GPA was impressive. We discussed why he wanted to

Rabbi Patricia Karlin-Neumann is senior associate dean for religious life at Stanford University in Stanford, California. Her work has appeared in the books *I Am Jewish: Personal Reflections Inspired by the Last Words of Daniel Pearl; Encountering* Disgrace*: Reading and Teaching Coetzee's Novel;* and *Reading Ruth: Contemporary Women Reclaim a Sacred Story;* and in the *Journal of College and Character.* Patricia enjoys swimming, reading, knitting, hiking, and sharing time with friends and family.

be on dorm staff, what he hoped to contribute, and how he understood the role he was seeking. After some give and take, I asked, "Tell me about a time when you've failed at something." His relaxed demeanor disappeared. His face grew dark and disturbed. His shoulders squared and his hands clenched. "That's not a fair question!" he blurted out.

"Why not?" I countered. "If you are going to work with younger students who may be facing their first disappointing grades, or their relationships hitting troubled waters, or the loneliness and uncertainty of being in a new, highly charged environment, wouldn't it be important to know what they may be experiencing? Would you be able to empathize with their disappointments?" Slowly, he allowed that failure might be worth discussing. "College is a safe place to experiment," I argued. "Student affairs staff, friends, and even faculty are here to support you as you learn how to get up after being knocked down." Undoubtedly sounding like the mother I am, I preached how valuable it is to discover and build resilience. As I challenged his carefully constructed self-presentation, this capable student began to consider what it would mean if he didn't appear to be supremely successful in everything. Would he still be himself? Could he acknowledge the value of exposing his uncertainties and missteps? Even to himself?

It is no surprise that he was skeptical. In a university overflowing with excellence and accomplishment, could it possibly be safe to allow the perfect image he projected to be seen as tarnished? How many conversations have occurred in bastions of high achievement where people have been schooled to answer questions about their limitations by offering a thinly veiled litany of their successes? Too often, students see and perhaps try to follow the model of their faculty—wildly successful but rarely satisfied or secure, burying uncertainty in bravado.

Rabbi means "teacher," and of all the roles attributed to chaplains—pastor, priest, prophet—it is teacher that calls to me most sweetly. In my own life, I was only able to imagine myself doing holy work because my teachers—people I trusted, admired, and studied with—imagined it for me. Working at the crossroads of education and religion is my tribute to them. Learning itself is, for me, a religious enterprise—participating in a community where learners pursue their interests and discover their abilities is sacred indeed. I view the chaplaincy as a calling—to care for the whole student in a setting that too often regards that care as incidental to its mission.

As a university chaplain, I am often found encouraging students, like my young friend the Golden Boy, to question conventional definitions of success and to consider a wider, richer purpose—what I call "making a living, making a life, making a difference."

Among the many fulfilling relationships the chaplain is privileged to build, one of the most enduring is as a mentor, encouraging dreams, helping students to imagine new possibilities with their many gifts. In both subtle and explicit ways, I hope to help students move from a narrow focus on individual success toward a more expansive civic-mindedness, a more worldly perspective, a more enduring vision. In a university with a long list of accomplished graduates, and in our high-powered, competitive culture where anticipated salaries and external measures offer a ready definition of success and satisfaction, I work to provide students with the time and space, the tools and trust to listen to their own lives, to imagine what may be their singular and irreplaceable offerings to those around them, so that making a difference is not an afterthought and making a living does not mean being deaf to their life.

The chaplain has the opportunity, rare amidst the pace and productivity of the university, to set a table for treasured moments of reflection, for calling in close those who might help us to learn more deeply and intentionally who we are, what is worth doing in our lives, and where we can use our unique insights, influence, and intelligence to repair the world.

My work as a university chaplain is firmly rooted in Jewish soil and in Jewish texts, in the interplay of teachings and experience, in the balance between received tradition and tomorrow's innovation. But even as I treasure my intellectual, spiritual, and ethical Jewish inheritance, I have chosen to study and practice my rabbinate in a diverse religious context, respecting the authenticity and wisdom of many spiritual and religious traditions and the richness gained by listening and learning from each other.

As I read Jewish tradition, I find guidance for learning with others and for weaving learning into action. I aspire to be a *rav l'tikkun olam*, a teacher to repair the social fabric, a teacher for social transformation, one concerned not only with faith but also with actions, not only with ideas but also with well-being, not only with individuals, but also with community. While I care deeply about the well-being and promise of individual students and attend carefully to the rich relationships we develop, I also consider myself called to engage with the educational institution itself. I believe the chaplain can help the university maintain a double allegiance—to remain true to its responsibility to young people at a key moment in their development as well as to remind the institution itself of its sacred purposes.

We look to colleges and universities not simply for information or for a well-trained and educated labor pool, but also for preserving the richness of the past, for ongoing discovery, for wisdom in understanding intractable problems. We look to the university to be reflective, ethical, and responsive stewards of our culture and its democratic and civic values. My ideal educational institution is one in which students and the faculty and administrators who guide them acquire not only knowledge, but also the confidence and commitment to become lifelong learners and engaged citizens, to recognize that learning is not simply a means to a job or a career, but the foundation for a life of purpose. I want to contribute to a learning environment where students learn to think critically, but more, to live connectedly.

Such an education emerges when students and their teachers are loved, valued for the unique gifts that they bring, for the struggles that have shaped them, even for the approximations and failures that are often their most enduring, if painful, lessons. This kind of learning is not only of the head, but also of the heart and of the hands. In their journey through the university, I want students to learn not only how to make a living, but also how to make a life and how to make a difference.

MAKING A LIVING

Every year when I speak to the parents of Stanford sophomores, I acknowledge the pride they feel in their children, one that I share with them as the mother of two Stanford graduates. Then I describe one of my favorite cartoons. A man and his young son are at the door of a classroom. The father turns to his son and says, "Now remember, Zachary. It's not kindergarten. It's pre-pre-pre-pre–medical school!" In the knowing laughter that ensues, we can all recognize ourselves in that father's impulse—to race past the present to the future, to measure worth by achievements, to impose upon others our fantasies of success, and when we do, to ignore the real person before us, with actual talents, interests, and limitations.

Our students, while not quite fitting the cartoon's satire, are awfully close. But along with their gifts, they may pay a steep price for their achievement. Too often I see how they constrict their vision in search of a succession of brass rings—elite schools, excellent grades, athletic championships. In the face of such relentless and pervasive expectations, to whom can they turn? In whom do they trust? Too many parents, teachers, and coaches have accepted a definition of success so narrow, so rigorous that they have unwittingly colluded in dressing those they care for and love in an elegant straitjacket.

Stanford president emeritus Donald Kennedy coined the phrase the "Stanford Duck Syndrome" to describe students like my young friend the Golden Boy. They appear placid on the surface, but they're paddling like hell underneath. Amidst that constant movement, the accumulation of awards and accolades, how do we create an environment that allows for reflection, for reconsideration, for rebooting? What do we teach or model regarding how to discover bedrock—how to determine what is worth basing one's life on? If appearances matter more than reality, if students struggle furtively, fearfully, shamefully, their fears never shared, no matter what the cost, then what have we communicated about human fallibility? How do we befriend and teach those who falter?

Religious traditions are fluent in the language of how to make a life and how to make a difference. On campus, the wisdom of the ages is invoked far less when it comes to making a living, which is, for many, the purpose of a university degree. Yet, regarding decisions about vocation, calling, and livelihood, even in a secular environment, there is a religious or spiritual perspective to impart. As indelible as the "bright college years" may be, our students are with us along the way to somewhere else. They will graduate, make their way in the world, leveraging the lessons of the classroom, of the coffee house, and of the playing fields into their future. Some are eager—the young man who is running for office in his hometown even as he takes his winter-quarter finals or the young woman launching a start-up from her dorm room. Some are bound for graduate school, confident of their destiny and overflowing with enthusiasm. Others are uncertain about what lies ahead, dreading any questions with the words "after graduation" in them.

One February, halfway through winter quarter, halfway through their last year at Stanford, a group of women sank into overstuffed couches, welcomed one another, and caught up from the previous week. They had responded to my invitation for "Heartbeats Away: Listening for Life after Stanford," a series of workshops I conceived, inspired by Parker Palmer's book *Let Your Life Speak: Listening for the Voice of Vocation,* to "think deeply about yourself, your experience at Stanford, your mode of making decisions and ultimately, how to listen for what might be your next step after Stanford." Initially, we read together the biblical story of Jacob's exile from his birthplace.

When Jacob left Beer-sheba, the text reads, he rested his head on a stone and fell asleep. "He dreamed, and lo—a ladder was set on the ground, with its top reaching to heaven, and lo—angels of God going up and coming down on it." And God said, "Here I am, with you; I will watch over you wherever you go." Waking from his sleep, Jacob said, "Truly, God is in this place and I did not know it!" (Genesis 28:10–17).

In silence, choosing construction paper of varying colors, these cerebral, accomplished, and articulate students, from a range of religious backgrounds and none, tore the paper into shapes and constructed a visual representation of their interpretation of Jacob's journey. This exercise, creating a "Handmade Midrash," was developed by art historian Jo Milgrom, to link holy text with inner wisdom. There is much in the biblical story of Jacob's journey, mostly unfamiliar to them, that spoke to their own experience—of leaving home having been lavished with blessings, of preparing now to set out alone to an unknown future, of a glimmer of connection between the holy and the everyday, the gift of a hopeful future, a nostalgic appreciation for the place they were preparing to depart from, while wanting to savor its magical qualities.

Using their hands and eyes rather than their heads created new perceptions. The torn strips glued together depicted sunbursts and ladders, figures holding hands, seas of uncertainty, forms symbolizing family standing close by, dark stretches of color evoking fear, and multiple identical forms suggestive of friends continuing together into the future. All were colorful. Some were three-dimensional. Every visual interpretation was unique. As each young woman explained her artwork, others offered what they saw in the picture—strength or struggle, camaraderie or creativity. In community, they built on one another's insight; they taught one another, helped one another to trust their past and to forge a path ahead. They displayed their artwork, as they had when they were children, but now it served to reveal what they'd uncovered or embraced about this moment of transition and what would accompany them as they prepared to leave.

The next week, returning to the more familiar form of writing, I asked them to bring their academic transcripts, not to reveal their grades but to remind themselves what courses they had taken, to look over their educational journey in order to construct a narrative of their college years. We read poetry and reflected on regret and renewal. We meditated on the wisdom of Rev. Frederick Buechner, seeking for ourselves "the place where your deep gladness and the world's deep hunger meet."[1] I encouraged them to weave a narrative that would inaugurate the story of their adult lives; to identify the coherence, originality, and intelligence behind the account, as well as the academic work they had accomplished. I conveyed that this is one step in a lifelong process of listening to our lives, of attending to the discoveries and insights that emerge from inhabiting our own story and reflecting on its meaning. I invited them to write a graduation document for themselves. I reminded them that it did not have to be definitive; it could change with time and greater reflection. If they chose to share it, I would enjoy it, but it was for their discernment, not my edification.

I never cease to be touched by the courage and confidence the students revealed. One young woman from a family of engineers who had majored in engineering despite being drawn to art made the brave decision to follow her heart and apprentice with a sculptor, knowing that it would disappoint and worry her parents. Another revealed that she knew herself well but was slow to trust and act on her self-knowledge. Her friends gave her strength to accept a position in Alaska with the Jesuit Volunteer Corps and delay entrance into a graduate program in literature. Another unburdened herself concerning the conflict she faced at home. Her immigrant parents believed education to be the ladder to success—until their daughter decided to become a public school teacher, earning too little and engendering too little prestige. That these students could say yes to one another and promised support and strength to one another helped them to trust in their new ventures.

In our materialistic world and in the university's avowedly secular context, students sometimes have to venture far off the beaten path to nourish their hungers and acknowledge their dreams. Beyond declaring majors and taking required courses, identifying the purpose of their education, finding their passions, and knowing their own heart all require more than writing papers, preparing problem sets, and taking exams. It cannot be done by proxy or even by following a popular teacher's path. Yet time for reflection, encouragement from peers, or space created for self-knowledge can go a long way toward helping students learn the direction to take their lives.

These are gifts of religious and spiritual life that chaplains are poised to offer. Who, if not those schooled in the teachings of the sages, can challenge the profound individualism in our society? Who, if not those touched by our civilization's most enduring religious visionaries, can encourage students to make a life built on their dreams?

MAKING A LIFE

From the inception of the university, Jane Stanford believed that it was "the duty of the university authorities to send out into the world students with good physical health as well as with good mental attainments, in order that they may successfully fight the battle of life."[2] Where do the discussions take place that might call the university to this part of its mission?

Evidence of "good physical health" is easy to find in the Stanford sun, as students run, bike, and play ultimate Frisbee nearly every month of the year. But evidence of "good mental attainments" is sometimes fabricated by Stanford ducks trying to out-paddle crippling anxiety, frequent class absences, and plagiarized problem sets. Extreme stress, disengagement, and honor code violations implicate not just the individual; they also call into question the values of the institution. Integrity, educational engagement, and well-being are cornerstones of the university. Yet, raising awareness about their erosion occasions a significant educational task—to make the case that student well-being is not the province of our counseling and psychological services, but rather it involves the entire university community. Student well-being can be influenced not only by the provost and the faculty, not only by student affairs professionals, but also by many members of the university community—from those responsible for attending to the religious, spiritual, and ethical life of our community to the groundskeepers, whose care in making a beautiful environment enhances our students' moods and attitudes.

While everyone who belongs to the university community has a role to play, to the chaplain falls the duty to keep this question before the community: "How do we create an intentional culture on our campuses that reflects the values we claim to hold?" Do we augment or undermine what we proclaim at opening convocation and commencement? As the stereotypical southern preacher thunders, "The only sermons worth giving are the ones that you see, not the ones you say."

Stanford's provost, concerned about student mental health and well-being, asked me to co-chair an initiative of students, faculty, and staff to study our "campus climate." I have no training as a social science researcher, nor as a psychologist, but as a chaplain I could keep the vision of community prominently in the forefront of our efforts. Together with faculty and our colleagues in the counseling center and student affairs, we set about trying to understand what sermons our students saw. What were the values they absorbed at Stanford? We began to ask a series of questions. What creates stress? What mitigates stress? Does the social safety net that we pride ourselves on work as effectively as we hope? What sermons do our students see from the high priests of the laboratory or the lectern? How well is Stanford University carrying out its founder's vision for the health of its students?

As we set about trying to learn more about Stanford's campus culture with students, faculty, and staff—a project that we lovingly referred to as "capturing the fog"—we came to divide campus culture into the categories of emotional health and resilience, academic experiences, and social connectedness and well-being. All three are intertwined.

The university is not a mental health institution. It can't be and it shouldn't be. Yet the reverberations of emotional instability and fragility are profound and echo in every corner of the campus community. The finding from the study that I found most powerful illustrates this. It is both simple and counterintuitive—our students' academic success does not necessarily equate to well-being. Students who have achieved their lifelong dream of admission to a university like Stanford are accustomed to succeeding academically regardless of their emotional health. Their apparent success in this one area of academic achievement may mask a tremendous sense of failure in life. Indeed, when the rest of their world is crashing down around them, pushing themselves to succeed academically is the only thing they believe that they can count on. No matter how high their GPAs, our wildly accomplished students don't get a transcript for emotional well-being.

As our task force tried to raise awareness about the sermons our students see, often as our own children went through the local high schools, one by one, faculty and student affairs professionals came to understand the high cost of achievement; a large number came to realize that the pressure was personal and pernicious, as they witnessed it at home as well as at work among their students.

In the university, students like my friend the Golden Boy have no monopoly on carefully manicuring their image. They are taught how to do so by experts. Yet, even experts sometimes cannot bear their own dissonance. More than once, the university has been stopped in its tracks by suicide. If anything silences the purr of the engine of excellence that is the university, it is the suicide of an apparently accomplished, successful student or professor who succumbed to despair. I have comforted stunned and stricken friends and colleagues at tragic, untimely funerals, as, seemingly out of the blue, gifted scholars or students choose to end their lives. In a culture of achievement and accolades, where the currency is brilliance and distinction, students learn many helpful things, but one of the least helpful is the rarely disputed lesson to hide their doubts and disappointments.

In such moments, chaplains step into the breach, honoring hopes, both dashed and realized, affirming humanness, and embracing uncertainty as well as knowledge. I bring prayers to places they are not often heard—the school of engineering, fraternity houses, administrative offices, locker rooms. Soul searching takes the place of studying as not only individuals but also the institution itself pauses, questions echoing endlessly, as we attempt to understand, to comfort, to prevent, to make sense. In such moments, chaplains are invited into the realm beyond the tidiness of the resume, the books, and the reputations, to acknowledge and respect the messiness of life.

With this in mind, as I travel the campus, as I encounter students, I am on the lookout for moments, by design or by grace, where learning beyond numbers, beyond facts, beyond hard knowledge—where learning about life, about making a life—can arise.

The Hebrew word for "understanding," *binah*, has within it the root *bein*, "between." Understanding—about oneself, about ideas, about the world, about love—comes by attending to what occurs in the between, through relationships. I have often joked that my epitaph will read, "She recommends books and connects people." My fierce desire to yoke head and heart emerges from the Jewish guidance *Ohev et habriot, u'mekarvan l'Torah*, "Love human beings and bring them close to Torah" (*Pirkei Avot* 1:12). The simple meaning of *Torah* is "teaching." But a more far-reaching connotation understands Torah to be the wisdom learned by lived experience. Book learning, heart learning, outstretched-hand learning, loving-arms learning, fixing-the-world learning, all are encompassed for me in Torah. Both a scroll of Torah, when it has deteriorated beyond repair, and a human being, when the soul has left the body, are buried, because they both contain divine teaching.

Along with the often brilliant classroom teaching that faculty offer throughout the university, there are also moments beyond the classroom of divine teaching. These teachers are undergraduates and graduate students with deep ties to home, to losses they have encountered among their family and friends. Researchers suggest that over twenty-five percent of any student body is mourning the loss of a loved one at any given time.[3] Yet students believe that few of their peers bear their singular burden—of being mourners, of knowing loss in their young lives. Students who are mourners are often invisible among their peers. I help those students to become visible to one another, to know that they are not alone.

Along with a residence dean and a therapist, I invite these students to find one another, to talk, comfort, and console, to gather in a quiet room around a table overflowing with food. Our students are Jewish and Christian, Native American and Hindu, Buddhist and Muslim, Shinto and secular. Their common experience of loss binds them. Our ongoing grief and bereavement workshops provide the time and space to cast off the many obligations of being students in a high-powered academic environment and, instead, to be fully the children, grand-children, brothers, sisters, and friends of those they have lost.

A freshman is uncertain when to reveal to potential friends that a parent has died. A young man struggles with how to answer when a housemate innocently asks how many siblings he has. The absence so present in their lives is invisible to others. In their day-to-day lives, they weary of explaining who they are, or they don't want to intro-duce discomfort for others. So they are silent. Until they find one another. Then they cry unself-consciously in one another's presence; they seek one another's counsel; they make plans to be together for Mother's Day, for Parents' Weekend, for the anniversary of the death that so diminished their world. For many students, the grief group is a lifeline. Our gathering is devoid of religious symbols or rituals, yet presiding over this group of mourners is one of the most sanctified acts of my chaplaincy.

But the students and our community still seek ritual as they mourn. Each May, I convene "Honoring Lives, Remembering Losses," to remember those in our family, writ large and small, whom we mourn. Soft violin music fills the air as people are greeted warmly. We offer paper and pen for reflection and eulogy. Candles wait to be lit in the center of a wood-paneled sanctuary, with silk banners painted for peace in many languages of the world's religions. There is meditation and story, as mourners light candles, speak the names, and share the legacies of those who have shaped them. All are welcome and often convey that they find it holy. The wisdom of our respective traditions infuses power into the ritual, but what takes place does not look like a memorial service from any of our traditions. In this, as in other cam-pus rituals, I try to meet the community where they are, to preside over a congregation never envisioned in my rabbinic training.

Yet sometimes, I get to braid what I was educated to do with what I have shaped in my untraditional rabbinate. I came to know a com-passionate young ecologist through the grief group. Jana lost her brother just before her freshman year, and throughout her under-graduate years and her graduate work at Stanford, she never missed a grief gathering. She was an anchor for new mourners, gentle and gracious, strong and sympathetic. Her stories of her brother's life were so vivid that I felt I knew him. One day, she called from the East Coast, where she had made her home, her voice filled with joy. She was engaged to her high school sweetheart, the person she had been with on the summer evening she learned of her brother's death. Having shared her grief, she asked, would I share her joy and officiate at their wedding?

What an honor! What a pleasure to meet her fiancé, to plan a creative ceremony to celebrate. Because she was marrying a man from her close-knit small town, everyone present had known her brother. The guests also thought they knew that neither the bride nor the groom was Jewish, so I reassured them that there were no secrets about to be revealed, that I was before them not because we shared a religious tradition, but because we shared a deep human connection.

My text for the wedding was from Psalms: "You have turned my mourning into dancing" (Psalm 30:12). Everyone gathered on that gorgeous summer day had held one another on a different, heartbreaking, summer day. But this time, they and I got to hold each other to dance.

Whether in weddings or at graduation, on the quad or in their work lives, I want our students to dance. I want them to live with joy and laughter. I want them to know love and compassion. I want them to live life fully, as willing to acknowledge sadness and disappointment as to celebrate success. I want them to experience the fullness of humanity, the relatedness of being a person with responsibilities to others, with a sense of purpose, with a direction that enables individual contributions to the public good.

And beyond that, I want them to make a difference.

MAKING A DIFFERENCE

Stanford University is recognized today for its technological and entrepreneurial innovations, but its founders had a broader vision for its future students. In 1885, the founding grant identified Stanford's purposes—"to promote the public welfare by exercising an influence in behalf of humanity and civilization, teaching the blessings of liberty regulated by law, and inculcating love and reverence for the great principles of government as derived from the inalienable rights of man to life, liberty and the pursuit of happiness."[4]

Whether teaching in the classroom, leading our community service and interfaith engagement initiative on hospitality and immigration, or reflecting on their community partnerships with participants in our summer Spirituality, Service and Social Change Fellowship, I try to help students discover their voice and sustain their conviction to make a difference, to repair the world.

Civic leader, activist, and son of Stanford, John W. Gardner used to instruct the students, "Liberty and duty, freedom and responsibility. That's the deal." I warm to those words, to the reminder that we need one another, that the privilege of a liberal education calls forth a concomitant obligation. It is the deal for me—the ties that bind, the bridge that connects, the community that embraces.

I love the pageantry of opening convocation, of baccalaureate, and of commencement, the ritual moments when, dressed in academic and religious regalia, we honor our aspirations and make visible our values, celebrating professors for being dedicated to teaching or graduating students who will leave Stanford and create in the world beyond the quad a legacy of service. Delighting in the communal ritual and affirmation when we gather to evoke and celebrate the university's purpose, I craft my ninety seconds of invocation or benediction to honor the moment very carefully.

Similarly, issues of community and accountability—from immigration reform to religious violence, from comprehensive health care to the responsibilities of citizenship, from the ethics of sexuality to the effects of gun violence—often make their way into the sermons that I preach in my congregations—whether the predominantly Christian one found on Sundays in Memorial Church, the multifaith gatherings on special weekends of the academic calendar, or the Jewish ones I lead on Rosh Hashanah and Yom Kippur.

I try to bring the words, wisdom, and wonder of religious tradition to inform the complexities of the day. I believe in the power of preaching to speak to both head and heart. I aim to offer a nuanced study of holy texts to illuminate what human issues are at stake in a given conflict, to understand the anxieties and aspirations of both adversaries and advocates. Writing and preaching on controversies that cry out for religious guidance is one of the ways I try be a teacher for social change. I hope that by listening to and discussing the wisdom of the ages, my students and community will be both more effective and more inspired to make a difference.

Stanford students do make a difference. They become social entrepreneurs and teachers in low-income schools. They become senators and Supreme Court justices. They preach and practice the gospel of social change in every corner of this country and in many parts of the world, often returning to campus to share their work and wisdom. Their presence brings the campus community together to learn from and commemorate their contributions.

My experience is not that students are averse to spirituality, to "religion writ large"; rather, they may be suspicious of religious authority and religious institutions and see all too vividly the harm that has been done in the name of religion, whether violence or patriarchy or battling to defend and maintain an unjust status quo. To those critiques, I say, "Amen." But in considering religion writ large—the big questions of life, vocation, purpose, relationships, authenticity, and community—I believe that religion and spirituality have much to teach and to question, and often, students come to appreciate the language, ritual, challenge, and comfort that religion and spirituality offer in addressing these issues and more.

For most of our students, it is not worship in a building, but a challenging course, a conversation in the dorm lounge, a roommate from a vastly different background that occasion midnight questions and a re-evaluation of previously unconsidered assumptions. Some of the most profound and enduring experiences our students know occur beyond the classroom. They seek to create thoughtful and compassionate friendships, to contribute to their communities, not only to enrich their pocketbooks, but also to repair the broken world they have inherited.

But some of the most important teachable moments arise unbidden. When tensions in the Middle East break against the sandstone and tile of the campus, when activists peddling hatred enter our arches to demonstrate and divide, when the dreams of our students are dashed by the defeat of the DREAM Act, when violations of college coaches call into question the honor of athletics, the protected "Stanford bubble" is pierced.

Al tifrosh min hatzibur, "Do not separate yourself from the community" (*Pirkei Avot* 2:4), the Jewish wisdom tradition cautions. Every religious tradition recognizes that communal support, communal prayer, communal embrace can offer solace, comfort, and hope. We know we need to come in close in our sacred spaces in the aftermath of a national or global tragedy—9/11, Hurricane Katrina, tsunami, earthquakes. We need to come together when something has pierced their world. In our role as priests, chaplains, and religious life deans, we are asked to symbolically hold a healing vision of community and community well-being for the university.

One such global moment hit very close to home when a beloved Stanford graduate, living out his dreams and using his education to make a difference, was murdered by those whose values were antithetical to his.

Daniel Pearl graduated a decade before I arrived at Stanford. I didn't know him. But like so many who were riveted by his kidnapping in Pakistan in January 2002, I felt a kinship to him—a *Wall Street Journal* reporter known for traveling the world writing stories emphasizing our common humanity, making distant places seem familiar with his pen, his personality, and his fiddle. He had taken to heart the admonition of Stanford's founders, "to promote the public welfare."

I gathered Muslims and Hindus, Buddhists and Baha'is, Jews and Christians, seekers and secularists for an interfaith vigil, praying for his safe return. It was not to be. In the wake of Daniel Pearl's brutal murder, with his family's blessing, I organized a public memorial in Memorial Church at Stanford.

I needed, indeed, we, as a university, needed, to come together to mourn, to pay our respects to a Stanford graduate, to recognize, through ritual a bond stretching from Stanford University to halfway around the world, a man who believed in humanity, a man who believed in discovering the identity of others and affirming his own identity, literally to his dying breath. Danny Pearl's last words were "I am Jewish." Daniel Pearl was a Jew who had embodied the best of his secular education and his religious tradition, a man who did not separate himself from the community, a man whose writings would be collected in a volume entitled *At Home in the World*.

Speaking in front of a colorful silk screen created by Stanford students, faculty, and staff, a visual interpretation of Rev. Dr. Martin Luther King Jr.'s reminder that "we are tied together in the single garment of destiny," Stanford's president and Danny's professors, colleagues, friends, and classmates evoked his gregariousness, humor, and dedication. I was determined that the horror of Danny's death would not overshadow the grandeur of his life. Quoting the Mishnah, "We need not make monuments for the righteous—their words serve as their memorial" (Jerusalem Talmud, *Shekalim* 2:5), I reminded our heartbroken community that Danny's words—spoken on the radio, printed in the newspaper, conveyed in love to his family and friends—would always testify to his humanity, his humor, his zest for life.

The outpouring of appreciation and affinity for Danny did not end with the shared words of the Mourner's *Kaddish* or with the last strains of Bach as people streamed out of the candlelit church into the sunlight. Shortly after the memorial, a man who had been awarded a Purple Heart while serving as a medic in Vietnam contacted me. He wanted to give his medal to the Pearl family to convey his appreciation for Danny's valor and kindness. In a moment I can only describe as holy, Stanford's President Hennessy, who is himself a professional colleague of Danny's father, and I accepted this generous gift on behalf of the Pearls. The family was touched by this gesture; I was privileged to be the messenger to bring the Purple Heart to them.

Then, in the quiet months of summer, Danny's father Judea called me with a request. The newly formed Daniel Pearl Foundation wanted to hold World Music Day Concerts in honor of Danny's thirty-ninth birthday in all the places he had lived. I turned to our music department faculty, who were honored to plan and perform for this concert. They too had come to Stanford after Danny had graduated. But they knew what values he had encountered in this community as an undergraduate. They embodied those values—reaching across difference, appreciating connections, embracing public service.

Their kindness and generosity were boundless. Indeed, we couldn't accept all the offers from world-class musicians and teachers who wanted to be part of that first "Harmony for Humanity." The Hasidic tradition teaches, "Through music you climb to the highest palace.... Music is Jacob's ladder forgotten on earth by the angels. Sing and you shall defeat death; play and you shall disarm the foe." The music brought hope and promise to a time of darkness and continues to do so each year. Our annual Harmony for Humanity is characterized by greetings from Danny's family, a blessing from me, and sublime music. Each year it grows in creativity, generosity, and communion, planting hope with notes and melodies, inspiring new generations of students. Danny's friendships across the globe, his ability to recognize our common humanity in every language, culture, and religion, continue to teach and inspire. In this, he continues to embody the mission of his alma mater.

As the anthropologist Barbara Myerhoff once taught, "In ritual, it is the doing that is the believing. And the doer, being your own body, is singularly persuasive, because it is your own experience which finally persuades you."[5]

When, as a chaplain, I create rituals such as the memorial and the concert honoring Danny in the university, it is not only for those who knew him or those who want to honor the past. The rituals take place in the present; the affirmation of life is now; the reminder of who we are as a university is alive. In these moments, I aspire for those present to experience a sense of sanctity, to be persuaded by our own bodies as we absorb and perform music, as we laugh and cry with the memorable stories, to carry on the same communal vision that animated Danny. The commitments of the university live on in us.

And sometimes, no matter how many eloquent words may be written or spoken, it is through ritual, with its stories, music, and memory, that we learn more powerfully and profoundly that this legacy belongs to us, if we are willing to weave it into our lives. Yes, Stanford University was secular in its origins. But it is sacred in its purposes. Ritual helps us to know that, to feel that, to transmit that.

If alumni like Danny, even in death, inspire students to make a difference, Stanford University itself is a monument to making a life. After the loss of their only son from typhoid fever at age fifteen, Jane and Leland Stanford famously said, "The children of California shall be our children." Out of loss and death, they created opportunity and hope. They wanted to provide students, now reaching far beyond California, with the chance for a life of purpose. That Jane and Leland Stanford chose to do so through teaching and learning is an inheritance that I never forget.

In Jacob's tale of transition from home into the unknown—the biblical narrative that my students and I recalled in our torn-paper art—the figures that draw my attention are the *melachim*, the messengers or angels who are ascending and descending the ladder. In his evolution from youth to adult, the biblical Jacob is not alone. Messengers accompany him, messengers who help him to know what to strive for and how to cushion a fall; messengers who help him to imagine possibilities and then to witness their development; messengers who guard his dreams. In describing the ladder, the text says that God is standing *alav*. *Alav*, often translated "upon it," can also mean "with him." God is standing with Jacob. God is standing with Jacob by means of spiritual messengers who assist him in moving from youth to adult, spiritual messengers who accompany him on the way, spiritual messengers who help him to become the best he can be.

This interpretation of the biblical text provides the frame that contains my story—that of being a rabbi and a university chaplain. Within that frame is a patchwork quilt lovingly stitched together, with distinct squares composed of a program or a class, a worship service or a sermon, a memorial or a wedding.

This is how I understand the art of the chaplaincy. We are the spiritual messengers in our students' lives, present as they move from youth to adulthood, trusting and encouraging their gifts, guarding their dreams. As an advisor or a pastor, a teacher or a friend, a challenger to students like the Golden Boy or a comforter to those in mourning, I hope to be one who points the way to holiness. I hope to be regarded as a *malacha*, as a spiritual messenger, for our students, for those who teach and mentor them, and for the university in which they grow.

PILGRIM TRANSFORMATIONS
The Chaplain as Traveling Companion

Rev. Dr. Paul H. W. Rohde
Augustana College, Sioux Falls, South Dakota

"The trip changed my life!" Travel is one of the few conversational topics in which people spontaneously make claims of transformation. We claim it eagerly, but it's often difficult for any of us to say exactly what about the travel proved transformative. At Augustana College, providing students with opportunities to venture into wide, diverse, and global contexts is one of our educational priorities. And transformation is one of our hopes. As campus pastor, I often lead students on these trips—and get to participate in these hard-to-define moments of transformation.

In my twelve years in campus ministry, I've given a lot of thought to the transformative role of travel in the lives of young people. I began a study of pilgrimage as a Christian practice, initially to help students reflect more deeply on their experiences. I wondered what pilgrimage could help us understand about what makes travel so compelling, what

Rev. Dr. Paul H. W. Rohde is campus pastor at Augustana College in Sioux Falls, South Dakota. Before campus ministry, he served as pastor of three Evangelical Lutheran Church of America (ELCA) congregations for twenty years. He is the author of *And Grace Will Lead Me Home: A Guide for Pilgrim Journals*. He and his family have made more than twenty pilgrimages to Holden Village, a retreat center in the Cascade Mountains, where they enjoy hiking, homemade bread, stimulating conversations, and contemplative worship.

it could help us know about how faith and learning come together, and what it could clarify about transformation. I hoped that thinking about our trips through the lens of pilgrimage would offer perspective and useful language both for my students and for me.

While I started by traveling to sacred sites, my study quickly moved past a focus on the destination. As I walked with Celtic Christians on Iona and prayed with the monks of Taize, I came to realize that many pilgrims describe not the wonder of arrival but the power of each step. *The Canterbury Tales* are not really about Canterbury. As trite as it sounds, pilgrimage really is about the journey.

Pilgrimage is understood geographically, but its power lies in far more than a departure from place. In the paragraphs that follow, I shall attempt to describe some of the many ways pilgrimage empties us. A pilgrimage is all about being called out of one's expectations and preoccupations and called into attentiveness and surprise. Our daily lives are so crammed and distracted, many of us have a hard time sensing God or meaning in the everyday. Above all, pilgrims walk in the promise that God encounters us in each step, each companion. I seek to give witness to the power of these discoveries.

When something you are not anticipating happens, it bursts your sense of the world. The practice of pilgrimage calls this liminal space—that which lies beyond the known, trusted, familiar, or comfortable. Liminality is a step beyond one's sense of self or world or God into the unknown. Even if they cannot articulate why, people who travel often identify that these steps change their lives. Transformation happens via a departure, a letting go of what is known.

I relish my role in supporting students, logistically and emotionally, as they venture beyond their expectations and preconceptions into new discoveries. On a recent trip, our group of twelve walked the Camino de Santiago in northwest Spain. For ten days we carried all that we needed in compact backpacks. With no room for laptops, electronics, or even cell phones, we traveled with a minimum of clothing and gear. One of the biggest thrills for me on that trip was watching how liberating the students found being unplugged from their devices and unburdened from their stuff. This simplicity was new territory, and though we dreaded leaving behind many things we consider essential—could I do a transatlantic flight without my Kindle?—we discovered a lot of freedom in the lightness.

An essential part of my chaplaincy work is taking students into risky situations as a way to encounter God and world and self. I think of myself more as an accompanist or companion (from the root *compana*, "with bread"). I am present to give support and encourage discoveries of what is about to happen, as opposed to being a shepherd or leader moving students toward a predetermined conclusion. I have discovered that I can best encourage and support students in their own transformational experiences by allowing myself to be open and surprised as well. I cannot be telling students to go on a pilgrimage and not be on one myself. If I ask students to let go, I have to let go as well. In our shared travel experience, we are all learning to be open—genuinely open—to the unexpected and unpredictable.

While this reciprocity in the experience is vital, I still play a distinct role on the trips. In addition to the important work of helping students navigate liminality and trusting transformation to come, I am responsible for their safety and well-being. This tension—between maintaining a vital openness to the unexpected and fulfilling my responsibilities to students and their families who have entrusted me with their safekeeping—is one I constantly seek to better understand.

THE INHERENT RISK OF LIMINALITY

The Sioux Falls airport is nothing if not convenient. Travelers are dropped off no more than forty feet from check-in. The "Gates 1–6" sign promises that even the furthest gate is not very far away. On almost any day, a security wait of five minutes is long—ten minutes is almost unheard of.

Somehow all of this convenience was lost on Carolyn. Her daughter, Angie, a first-year student at Augustana, was going on a spring break service trip to New York City. It had been just six months since the tragic events of September 11, 2001. Even our cheery small-town airport had caught a new tension. More questions about our luggage, slower movement through security, and grim expressions on staff faces made it impossible not to notice the uneasiness.

All of this was on my mind—and probably Carolyn's, too. Carolyn's face was stern, her voice intense. Her stressed demeanor stirred all my insecurities about leading students on such an adventure for the first time. A high school volleyball coach by profession, she aimed her question like a torpedoing spike across the net. "Will you keep them safe?" she asked.

What could I say? A simple "yes" would betray both the risk of the moment and the validity of the question. I wanted to say, "I don't know. I hope so, but I'm plenty worried about that myself." Would that have been too much transparency? My understanding of ministry suggested I offer, "I'll be with them," but I instinctively felt the insufficiency of the simple words. Angie's mother would *not* be with her, and I would be audacious to nominate myself as a surrogate. Furthermore, there were twenty students and only two leaders. We were present, but we could not be omnipresent.

I tried to meet her gaze calmly. I waited to hear if she would say more. But she clearly awaited my return serve. "We'll do our very best," I said finally. "The congregations who are hosting us will instruct us carefully about life in the neighborhood, staying together, and being safe." Her next question came fast: "Have you been there before?" I managed to respond, "Yes. I flew out two months ago to meet our hosts, navigate the subways, and verify our connections." Words are a pastor's most important equipment, but that day I felt empty-handed.

Meanwhile, Angie seemed oblivious to her mother's concerns. She was a tall, very gifted student athlete, already demonstrating that her mind was as agile as her body. Giddy with excitement, she meandered aimlessly between her mother and her friends, floating between these few uncomfortable moments and the independence just a few hours ahead of her. She was more than ready to get on the plane. If she had any anxiety, she hid it well. The word "departure" triggered very different meanings in Angie's energy and her mother's concern. The same trip that stirred so much anxiety in her mother meant excitement, freedom, and thrill for her.

Before she embraced her daughter with a tearful good-bye, Carolyn had one more sentence for me. "I'd yank her right off that plane if she'd let me," she said. I quietly watched the good-byes and then counted the students one more time as they made their way through security and toward the gate. Even though this meant just a few hundred feet in our friendly little airport, I felt the weight of Carolyn's words in every step.

I do not consider New York City the most dangerous place in the world. But in March of 2002 I can easily understand why a parent would see it as an epicenter of fear. And Carolyn's objections notwithstanding, her daughter and I were taking steps toward that fear. Our steps were taking us toward facing poverty at a soup kitchen in Manhattan but also through the Museum of Modern Art and to a Broadway play. We ate soup kitchen food, but pizza and cheesecake were never hard to find. In every step it was clear these young people would help me discover things I would never see on my own. The diversity of their majors informed their understandings of everything from impressionist art to the pulse of the financial district. Their emotional reactions were just as diverse.

I began to learn that joy and apprehension exist in very close proximity. The delight of adventure and threat of peril also live in terrifying proximity. I have never had another job where I laughed so much, but I have also never had work where I grieved so intensely. Being young and fun-loving is no immunity to tragedy or disaster. Transformation is always some combination of dread and delight. I was learning that travel is good practice on both counts.

Carolyn's candor potently pierced my self-understanding as a pastor. Her questions were so clearly valid and the obvious affirmations she sought so clearly rang hollow. I wanted as much as Carolyn did to say I would be in control. Carolyn's anxiety was an important turning point in my awareness of how vital it is to embrace what we cannot know or control. As appealing and valid as a need for safety seems, it undercuts the very purpose of movement or growth. Liminality is inherently risky. If we are always perfectly safe and careful, we function with a domesticated God. The essential importance of a journey is that it involves risk and excitement, requiring trust and openness. Pilgrimage is *about* risk. And so is transformation. I was only beginning to learn to embrace that risk both as leader and participant. On another New York City service trip, I encountered this conflict in a way that troubled me for years.

THE COST OF TRUST

It was January in Manhattan, cold and windy, dark and dank. I'd come to New York City early for a few days of study and had gone to LaGuardia airport to meet a group of students who were coming to work at the soup kitchen hosted by friends on the Upper West Side of Manhattan.

Our plan was for host families to meet the students at the church. But the plane was very late. Our host, Pastor Elise, realized that all the host families lived between the church and LaGuardia. So to spare the families and the students an even later evening, she devised a chart for students to meet their host families at bus stops on the way into Manhattan. As weary students climbed onto the M-60 bus, she methodically seated students and their luggage in the order they would be getting off. She phoned ahead to the host families, who could then simply walk to the bus stops and meet their guest students. It was a brilliant plan and worked beautifully for the first six or eight students along the route.

Then the bus stopped to let off sophomores Darcy and Molly. The door opened routinely. We gazed with anticipation into the dark, cold night. No one was there. Pastor Elise scrambled to dial the expected hosts. I attempted to stand in the door of the bus, lodging it for a few seconds so we could decide what the students should do. The bus driver immediately demanded that I step out of the way of the door. In the impulse of a moment, I complied.

I will never forget Darcy and Molly's body language as they got off the bus at that stop. Their shoulders were heavy, not merely with the weight of their bags. They had never been to New York before. They knew only that they were in New York City and it was very dark and cold. They were bracing themselves against more than the icy

January wind. They knew the names of their hosts, but they had, of course, never met them and had no idea where they lived. Their frames were heavy with the weight of aloneness, uncertainty, and emptiness. I immediately felt that I had failed them.

In the exact instant that the bus pulled away, we saw the host family round the corner and embrace the students. It was a gasp of grace after a breathless moment of uncertainty and indecision. The students were fine. They had a delightful time that week. It took me considerably longer to make peace with my own feelings of responsibility.

I anguished for months that I did not get off the bus with Molly and Darcy. I knew the route; Pastor Elise was with the others. I could easily have gotten off, waited for the hosts and caught the next bus. At the airport with Carolyn and Angie, I had confronted the conflicted feelings of another. This time I confronted my own limitations. I felt like I had let down someone counting on me for safety or at least help. It is one thing to be inarticulate in reassuring someone of one's presence, another to flatly become absent. It is one thing to be between a student and her mother, or a parent and her expectations, another to be suspended between my own expectations and my own actions. I was safely on the bus, and my students walked alone into the night.

In the years since, this story has served as an illustration of habit and the power of habit to resist liminality. I once took an ethics seminar focused on the power of habitual practice, because many of our most important ethical decisions are made in a matter of seconds. When the bus driver was screaming at me to get out of the way of the door, I did not have time to read a book, do an Internet search, or even say a prayer. In a split second, I had to decide which step to take—in or out. As I stepped in, my feet revealed a pattern of compliance I often do not even see. Impulses follow patterns. Patterns are very difficult to break—even when you feel the anguish of your students to your bones.

Pilgrims do not necessarily choose liminality. There is no predicting what circumstances or discoveries will force us from our pattern or undo our sense of ourselves in the world. Within seconds of the door closing, I knew I had violated a value, an understanding of ministry, a sense of myself. At other times liminality arrives uninvited in a person we call "stranger." Or it comes when accidents and mistakes happen. We get lost or sick or lose our valuables. Pilgrimage is practice in being opened and in being vulnerable, often unexpectedly. In these moments, we find ourselves suspended between who we thought we were and what has just occurred. Even if we receive it as a metaphor for some other part of life, it is also a real experience.

I was so caught in regret for not getting off the bus that I failed to notice that Darcy and Molly did not describe the experience as abandonment. When we spoke about it later, they described fear and adventure, but not abandonment. I was so worried about my role, it escaped my notice that Darcy and Molly took the lead in navigating the subway the next day. The next year Darcy led the trip.

Though I shudder at the limits of my own ability to protect my charges, the bus incident helped me discover the importance of students facing uncertainty and learning their own resources. I was learning something of the cost of trust. In this particular case, everything came out well, but it could have gone very differently. Finally, faithful trust is believing that students learn and discover in all kinds of episodes. This incident provoked my thinking about how to support students in ways other than being physically present and assuming all the adult responsibility. The college experience is about releasing students into their own strengths. As campus ministry launches students to larger encounters with God, their neighbors, and the world, my pilgrimage is learning to trust them to undertake those journeys.

This letting go of what and sometimes who we hold dear may begin as a call to openness, but it is also a call to trust what we cannot control or even see. This knocked me off balance at first. But pilgrims well know that the very act of walking is imbalance. All one's weight is on one foot and then another. Single steps require being a little off balance and sometimes lead to stumbles. The vast majority of students survive both imbalance and stumbling. Not a few of them say it changes their lives. It is vital that the leader not get in the way of this experience. Part of my work is to release students into their own experience, even when it scares me to do so.

THE GIFT OF TRANSFORMATION

It's a lesson I learn over and over, especially when it comes closest to my own life. Sarah is the oldest of our daughters and, as it goes for oldest children, had to endure the first departure from her parents. There is no question that letting my own daughter "off the bus" brought me into a whole new level of liminality.

The day Sarah was to leave for college, she dallied. Friends dropped in. She thought of yet another errand. The last thing to pack was her piano music. Since she wasn't getting it sorted, her mother began to do it. (I cleaned. Scrubbing was just the right gesture.) Thankfully the drive to Moorhead was uneventful. In the morning we unloaded all of Sarah's stuff into the tiny dorm room. I assembled the loft; Sarah's sisters helped unpack. We connected the computer, attended the parent meeting, and had ice cream. There was nothing more to do. The moment we had anticipated for months had arrived. Sarah was subtle but clear: "I'll walk down with you."

In the parking lot we exchanged long and tearful hugs. Each of us said, "I love you," "Take care," and "You'll do great!" as many times and with as much intense hope as we could muster. And then it was time. The memory that is forever frozen in my consciousness is Sarah turning to walk toward the dorm alone. Her mother, sisters, and I turned to the van. We had each other ... Sarah was alone. It felt so deeply wrong for her to be alone.

My mentors in prayer have taught me to stay with an image and trust it. In the days and weeks that followed I lingered with that picture of Sarah walking away alone as I ached to know how she was doing. As Edna St. Vincent Millay said, "The presence of that absence is everywhere."

Ever so gradually the image redeemed itself as it became a symbol not of our abandonment of her, but of her strength. There was no denying that she walked away from us, but it helped to see her walking toward what I believed and trusted she could do. If I knew cerebrally that she could never be an adult until she left us, her pilgrimage away from home made it tangible.

In the years since, my daughters often tell me they are glad that I have been a campus pastor while they were in college because they believe it has made me more patient with them. Campus ministry has certainly given me practice in letting go and trusting the power of redemption and transformation. One of the reasons I have found the study of pilgrimage so valuable in my work is that the undergraduate experience is bracketed by departures. Students leave home or some other familiarity to begin their years of study, and then at graduation they depart yet again for even greater unknowns. In between, students explore all kinds of unfamiliar "territory"— new ideas, relationships, identities, and commitments. Pilgrimages, by their very nature, teach us to risk these departures. And then pilgrims, ancient and contemporary, teach us to be attentive with all our senses and intuitions and memories and hopes, with mind and heart and strength and neighbor, to explore what the step may mean. We listen with heightened intensity because in liminality we no longer know where we are, perhaps even who or whose we are.

This is why colleges like Augustana see travel as an essential part of education—in changing your context, you change your whole way of seeing. The learning is of a different and deeper kind than in the classroom. Away from home, in new surroundings, you can't just put down your book and go back to what you were doing.

Some days I think this ministry has even made me more patient with myself and with the church. When I am anxious about what is coming, pictures and stories of people like Carolyn and Molly have helped me learn to trust. When it looks like the shape of the church and academy are changing drastically, I hear myself reminding folks that transformation has always meant letting go of the old. I love to travel for all kinds of reasons, but among them is recognizing that I need practice in letting go.

With a little practice, the feelings that come at the threshold of departure begin to include trust and anticipation of gifts. Pilgrimage opens us to wider attentiveness so that those gifts are as tangible as the risks. My sense is that with both God and travel, people yearn for the magical; we hunger and thirst for wonder, for the breathtaking, to be suspended in an awe-filled moment. It is a sheer gift when it happens. Surely these are God moments. Being transformed has as much to do with noticing things, even and especially miniscule, unlikely things, than an arrival at either a holy place or holiness itself. If life and faith are only new when they are open to surprise, travel is good practice.

ROOM TO BREATHE
Nurturing Community
by Creating Space

Rev. Dr. Susan Henry-Crowe
Emory University, Atlanta, Georgia

Emory University has a beautifully designed and built campus. It is marked by Italian tile roofs, Georgia marble, intentionally planned green spaces with conveniently placed coffee carts. It is far more crowded with modern buildings than it was forty years ago. Gravel paths are now neatly paved walkways. The perimeter of the campus is dedicated to parking edifices that tidily conceal thousands of cars. Though the campus center is pedestrian-friendly, with trees, flowers, and two hundred varieties of native holly, an ob-gyn friend of mine said of a winter walk around campus, "It feels like there is no room to breathe." After years of watching the university implement strategic plans to make the campus beautiful, attractive, green, livable, and a destination for young people from around the world, I was startled. But I was also viscerally mindful of his insight.

Rev. Dr. Susan Henry-Crowe has served as dean of the chapel and religious life at Emory University in Atlanta, Georgia, since 1991. She is the secretary and treasurer of the Association for College and University Religious Affairs. Her work involves overseeing Emory's vibrant Inter-Religious Council, twenty-eight multifaith campus religious organizations, and the hallmark Journeys program. A United Methodist minister, she served on the Judicial Council for sixteen years. She has a long-standing commitment to social justice and interfaith as well as ecumenical relationships.

It was more than the nostalgia of a wise and aging physician and Emory alumnus. It was an observation of some of the losses found in a postmodern, spiritually ill-defined, ever-connected, often lonely, and never quiet world. He remembered the un-coiffed quad, musty buildings, summer afternoons on a blanket outside a residence hall, dusty walkways, random and disorganized parking (for those who did have cars) of four decades earlier. From his perspective, the spacious beauty that planners and architects had intended with these newly tailored grounds, immaculately designed quad, and ever-present coffee carts had instead resulted in a sense of tight and shallow circumscription. Rather than finding a sense of expansiveness, openness, abundance, and richness, he had a sense of limitation, constraint, even loneliness. As I started to think about my friend's observation, I realized that there are few places in the world of higher education that truly create room to breathe.

Between classes and hurried lunches, students check e-mail, text while walking to class, or chat on their smartphones, earbuds shutting out the sounds around them. Every second between scheduled events is obsessively filled with a screen or a sound. But with every moment and space full, how can one reflect on a lecture, or make connections between science and poetry, or think about the person just encountered, or notice the tree in blossom?

For faculty members too, keeping a balance between focusing on research and teaching while serving as a teacher/mentor/citizen to undergraduate and graduate students is desirable, but often increasingly difficult. A passion, intensity, and commitment to one's own work is essential, but on top of that there are departmental meetings, preparations for class, dissertation defenses, research grant submissions, monographs that are a year past the deadline—all of which together leave no space to pause, to remember, to reflect, or to think. Add to this the stress of family obligations and commuting (in many places, junior faculty can no longer afford to live near campus), and it becomes clear that faculty too have lost some essential room to breathe.

As my friend's comment revealed, when every inch of space and every moment of time are tightly defined, we lose an essential freedom and openness to possibility. A campus with little undefined space leaves no place for surprising encounters. A campus culture with no time for reflection leaves no room for growth or deepening of spiritual life. As the dean of the chapel and religious life, part of my work is affirming both particularity and universality on a richly diverse campus. Part of the way I do this is by being a companion and walking with people where they are. Another way is by making sure the community has space, time, and room to breathe. My role in caring for the religious and spiritual life of individuals, groups, and the institution itself is by creating spaces—both literal and metaphorical—that are undefined, open, safe, inclusive, and roomy enough to include everyone and that invite new discovery, insight, understanding, and encounter. The more that people have room to breathe, the more they touch the deeper places in their minds and hearts and engage with one another.

THE CHAPEL

Cannon Chapel is Emory's most religiously identifiable space, where all are welcome and are assured that this is their religious home. I have the good fortune of presiding over a space that was conceived and intended to be multireligious. Cannon Chapel was designed in the late 1970s by Paul Rudolph, a forward-thinking architect in the use of concrete and indigenous natural materials. He is one of the early pioneers of what today is known as green architecture. Often he is aligned with the "brutalists" as well. He, along with the designers, imagined a place where various faith communities could authentically pray, worship, and meditate with integrity, honoring the deepest observances and practices of their own traditions. Rudolph's clean lines, natural light, and cavernous spaces create the illusion of spacious simplicity. The lines, acoustics, height, sparseness, natural light, and poured concrete provide expansive room for breathing. The place welcomes silence. It invites interiority. It is both hugely communal and at the same time warmly intimate. The reality of working in Rudolph's sparse and vast space is that it allows for an astonishing variety of uses.

Among Emory undergrads, no religious group equals more than 35 percent of the population, and therefore every group is a minority. All Christians (Roman Catholics and all Protestants, evangelical and nondenominational) total 34 percent. The Jewish population has been large at Emory for decades but is still a minority. Muslims and Methodists account for an equal percentage, as do Buddhists and Episcopalians. Hindus and those of the Vedic traditions are the fastest growing populace on campus. While Emory has a majority identity and ethos (usually understood as Protestant Christian), it does not have a majority *reality*.

Emory's multifaith reality makes the work of the chaplain both easier and more difficult. It is easier because there are relatively few voices asserting a singular cultural authority ("This is a Methodist school and we must be Methodist"). But working with such diversity requires constant education, cultural sensitivity, respect, and multilingual communication. Part of the chaplain's role is to represent every religious community, especially minority groups, to remember and protect the rights of those on the margins, and to promote understanding between them to represent the interests of each faith family. When there are campus prayer services for tragic events such as the earthquake in Haiti, the tsunami in Japan, the assassination of Yitzhak Rabin, or the bombings in Boston, naming the service is very important. It is not "worship"—the language itself denotes a Protestant identity. We call these "vigils" and "moments," interreligious or multifaith "gatherings" or "prayers." By being sensitive to even the smallest detail, the chaplain makes room in the community for everyone.

In some cases, the "room" is literal. A typical weekend in Cannon Chapel looks something like this:

On Friday at noon, the students, faculty, and staff of Candler School of Theology finish celebrating the last Eucharist of the week. They have held two other worship services during the week for the seminary. The cross is taken down. The prayer space is soon divided laterally by magnificent handcrafted screens made from over one thousand tiny oak strips that echo design elements in the room. Towels and baskets are placed outside the washrooms. By 2 p.m., over 125 members of Emory's Islamic community gather for *Jummah* prayers. All face east toward Mecca. Brothers pray on the outside, sisters on the inside. The service begins with the Call to Prayer (*Adhan*). The movements are rhythmic, the tones prayerful and soothing. The colors are soft—browns and grays for the men and multicolored hijabs for the young women. Someone gives a sermon, and the congregation offers their prayers. Following prayer, the congregation gathers for a community meal in the Commons area.

As Muslim students straighten up the prayer space, an energetic group of Hindu undergraduates prepares for the *Aarti* (prayer). Not needing the screens separating the women and men, they place the handcrafted dividers around the room, enclosing the space and making it more intimate. The young Hindu students bring out their altar, tenderly designed and crafted by Emory's artisan Jack Scheu, who also built the screens for the Muslim community and a case for earth blessed by His Holiness the Dalai Lama. The Hindu *Aarti* is prayer, offerings, a meditation, and a meal following the prayer. The music is rhythmic. Their festively colored cloths, fruits, and clothes brighten the room with reds, oranges, yellows, silver, brass, and gold. Sweet aromas of myrrh, frankincense, and anise fill the space.

On Saturday evening, those who care for the building check for misplaced chairs, dropped cloths, and forgotten shoes before the Roman Catholics gather on Sunday for the first Mass of the day. For this service, the cross is prominent, and the original altar is moved to a central place in the asymmetrical sanctuary. The pulpit is also placed before the congregation, and the sacristy is prepared for the Eucharist, with the vessels, the crucifix, and the altar cloths. The incense and the censor are readily accessible. The smell of incense soon fills the air, and the student-friendly music from the Catholic hymnal *Ritual Song* pours through the vents. The colorful procession with candles, Gospel, and crucifix indicates the beginning of Mass.

Following the morning Mass, Protestants immediately prepare for worship. The pulpit is moved slightly more toward the center, indicating that preaching is central to Protestant Christian worship. The Eucharist, sometimes neglected by Protestants, takes place each week, affirming the identity and historical theology of the ever-changing multireligious world. The preachers are nationally known, inspiring, and well trained in the art of proclamation. The hymns are magnificent, harkening back to the heart of Wesleyan or Lutheran theology. Contemporary music blends into the historical hymnody, acknowledging both the contemporary as well as the historical elements of Christian worship. The colors are more subdued than the colors found in the gathered Catholic community, which reflects the greater cultural and language diversity of a worldwide Roman Catholic church. Yet, the vitality of proclamation from preachers such as Joseph Lowery or Barbara Brown Taylor inspires and expresses the best of Protestant worship.[1]

The Jewish community, which has prayed in the university chapels for sixty years now, holds High Holy Days, Memorial Services, and some Passover gatherings in the university chapel. In 2011, the Jewish community built the Marcus Hillel Center adjacent to campus. Chabad has a house within walking distance of the front gate and welcomes students on a daily and weekly basis. The weekly Shabbat services are held in the nearby Jewish centers. In Cannon Chapel, the High Holy Days of Rosh Hashanah and Yom Kippur bring the Reform communities together for the blessings of the New Year and the Days of Atonement. The prayers are beautifully laced with images that evoke the spirit of the Divine. The Hebrew liturgy is sung or chanted, offering praise and thanksgiving. The rabbis preach sermons, lead prayers, and sing the songs of Israel.

Cannon Chapel is flexible enough that it can provide room to breathe for these many different campus groups. Sharing does not usually create conflict. It requires thinking creatively and adaptively. Sharing space can bring communities together and can welcome and accommodate the needs of all. People and groups do not always need the same things. Making it all work is a matter of the chaplain's listening to needs and figuring out how to make space—literally and metaphorically—available to everyone.

THE COMMONS

Every university has a few hidden places that take shape from the way they are used by the community. The Commons area of Cannon Chapel is one such space. It was often used as a gathering space for theology students and otherwise untouched by the wider community. When it began providing for the dietary needs of several religious communities, students began to discover it.

In this space, people overlap. They sit side by side. Jews, Christian seminarians, Muslim undergraduates, professors of Hinduism, and Tibetan Buddhist monks sit across the room from one another. They can be actively engaged in conversation or simply feel connected to the larger community in a welcome and safe space. A young Jewish undergraduate who often studied there recently commented, "I like this space, where I can think, breathe, read, sit at a table, and overhear graduate students dissect the Hebrew Bible." For this young woman, the Hebrew Bible is her text. She is a religiously observant Jew, though not a religion scholar. Knowing that someone else on campus is taking her texts seriously is an important element of her sense of belonging at Emory. It is a gift to have a place in a chapel that provides hospitality, respite, and intellectual stimulation with those not always encountered. In the heart of the campus, this room provides a place to read, to sit, to overhear, to touch, to think, to wonder, to wander, and simply to be.

A student recently quipped, "The Commons room is a little messy but is a place where I can breathe the best." One of the roles of the chaplain is to help to create, preserve, and protect these undefined and welcoming spaces. In a formal dining room we do not breathe the way we do in a coffee shop. In a coffee shop we do not breathe the same as we do in a chapel or meditation room. It's in these informal sanctuaries, holy corners, rooms of trust and healing, where the *ruach* (in Hebrew, "the breath, life-giving animation") comes. Where breathing, thinking, talking, reading, listening to music, overhearing, staring into thin air can happen, where individuals can be engrossed in a project but surrounded by others. Providing a space that has no clearly defined purpose but invites everyone to share in it is one more way that the chaplain can care for everyone on campus, not just those who are religious or spiritual.

THE DISSECTION LAB

For thirty years the chaplain at Emory has been a part of the medical school's anatomy labs. This is the course where future doctors learn about the human body firsthand by carefully dissecting cadavers. As part of the program, the chaplain participates in the introduction and orientation to the lab and is on hand for many days during the lab. She meets each table of students and accompanies them throughout the human anatomy experience.

On the first day of the dissection lab, students have very different responses. Some are very eager. They have waited their whole lives for this day. Some are tentative. Some afraid. A few are openly sickened. Several are filled with grief in the presence of death, remembering a grandparent, parent, or loved one who has recently passed away. Some have qualms for religious reasons—bodies are to be buried, not dissected. My role as chaplain in this room is not to persuade anyone to feel, or pretend to feel, anything other than their true emotions. I am there to accompany these young people through one of the most intense educational experiences of their lives. Though this lab will move them closer to their future roles, they are not yet doctors or researchers or scientists—in the chaplain's presence, they have permission to just be themselves.

In the beginning, it is an overwhelming adventure (students' breathing in the lab literally presents its own issues because they spend a great deal of time exposed to formaldehyde). There is so very much to see and learn. Very often, students express gratitude to the stranger who has offered them the tremendous gift of their body. The body itself tells the students a story. This silent teacher offers some of the most important lessons of their lives. The students often become attached to "their" body donor. Often, they give him or her a name. As they see the enlarged heart, the silicone breast implant, the arthritic fingers, the tattoos, or the fingernail polish, they receive glimpses into the most intimate life of another. They will come to see the body as a whole and how its many parts are interconnected. For most of them, this is the only time they will have the privilege of seeing the intricacies and mysteries of a whole body. Though they may see hands, eyes, lungs, brains, hearts, and eardrums, depending on how they specialize, even the general practitioners will never interact with the human form in quite this way again. My role is to simply accompany them on this magnificent and mysterious journey of discovery.

After months of stressful and sometimes tedious dissections, students become profoundly grateful to the body donor and her or his family. At the end of the semester, the students from the medical school class (along with classmates from the physical therapy, physician assistant, and anesthesiology programs who have also had human anatomy lab) celebrate this gift. In the Service of Remembrance, the chaplain, students, faculty, and staff offer words of remembrance and gratitude to the families of the body donors.

We compose music, sing songs, offer dance, and write poetry; we gather flowers and light candles in memory and gratitude for the precious offering of these body donors. Students mention the red nail polish, the tattoo from France, the back surgery, the ashy lungs that tell a chapter in the story of one person's life. They come to honor not only this largess but also the process itself, knowing that never again will they have the opportunity to see and hold a whole human body in such a way.

As they are keenly aware, the vocations of these medical students are being formed during these labs. As they move toward defining their future careers, some students seek me out in private to utter their struggles. Most of the others involved with these students' education have defined roles with clear boundaries—academic advisor, professor, admissions officer, parent. My companionship is different. I give no grades. I offer little advice. I do not have a stake, of any kind, in their decisions. I don't even offer myself as denominationally religious, only as a grounded presence in a moment when they need one. My only job is to walk alongside as they find their way.

Because I'm offering a conversation free of any outside expectations, they often feel free to confess things they might keep to themselves elsewhere, where the stakes are higher. One says, "I hate this;

I never want to work with a body again. I want to go into psychiatry."
Another says, "I love the heart; I want to spend my life looking at
hearts." And yet another is so profoundly taken by the experience he
decides to prepare to teach anatomy. In this case, I offer *myself* and
my presence to these young people, to help them find a moment
of room to breathe at a critical juncture in their education—a presence that asks nothing defined of them and from which they can
find a moment to reflect and consider and become.

THE CHAPLAIN'S OFFICE

People often comment on how peaceful they find my office to be.
It is a small space with a high vaulted ceiling. There is a sense of
warm respite, with bookshelves, rugs, a few works of abstract art, and
soft light. There are also gifts from many people and communities
around the world: blessed earth from His Holiness the Dalai Lama;
a chalice and paten crafted by a Muslim artisan in Izmir just for
the Christian community; a singing bowl; the Hindu deity Ganesh;
icons of the Blessed Virgin Mary; several copies and translations of
the Qur'an; photographs; a computer screen saver of four students
(one Tibetan Buddhist, one Muslim, one Christian, and one Jewish)
praying at the World Trade Center Memorial. Despite the clutter,
there is something about the room that lets people feel that they can
breathe. This often seems strange to me because at times I feel like I
cannot breathe here, where every pile of papers begs my attention—
but I know what they're talking about. If asked to imagine peaceful
places in meditation, my heart and mind's eye most often return to
my office.

In my little "holy" space, people talk about the issues closest to
their hearts: a young woman coming out as lesbian; a faculty member grieving the death of his mother; a young professor denied tenure; a couple caught in a quagmire of pain; a Hindu in love with a
Christian whose family is having an impossible time with the idea; a
young Jewish woman at odds with the friendly new Orthodox rabbi
in whose presence she does not feel she has a legitimate voice; a staff
person daring to speak about a supervisor despite fear of retaliation;

a student who has recently learned of his sister's death. My office is there to welcome all of these stories.

As chaplain, part of my vocation is creating a safe space: of trust, of welcome, of respect, of compassion. Part of my role is hospitality, remembering the word's Latin root *hospitalitas*, or hospital, a place for the sick, wounded, and injured. Part of my role is creating a space that cares for and holds the deepest wounds and pain. A place of gentleness. A respite from anxiety. A place for tea. A place to encounter that which is holy. A space to safely say what is in one's heart. A place to grieve. A place of healing. A place to breathe in a weary world.

THE CHAPLAIN

It is odd that I have learned far more about prayer and praying in my time as a university chaplain than I did as a parish minister. I find that within my own Protestant faith community there is sometimes a sloppiness about prayer. At times, a few words mumbled to the Almighty pass for prayer. It's been from traditions other than my own that I have learned the *art* of praying. Breath, intention, reverence, posture, gesture, language, silence, pause, ending, communal response—these are all significant. The Shabbat prayer begins with covering the eyes. Muslims' *Adhan* (the Call to Prayer) invites us to listen; Hindus sit in silence in a meditative posture, breathing intentionally.

Appreciating some practices and habits of non-Protestant and non-Christian traditions, I have integrated some of what I have learned into my own practice. Now when I pray publicly, as I am often called to do as chaplain, I find that it's refreshing to include lines the listeners know by heart, gestures that are part of the prayer, words that evoke praise, spaces that express gratitude, and pauses that invite breathing. Guiding a gathered community to find a space of calm, peace, joy, delight and comfort in a moment of prayer is edifying. At times like these when I am invited to briefly become a guiding presence for a group, I need to be an authentic voice in that moment. While my grounding in my own tradition means that I cannot haphazardly borrow prayers from others and still retain authenticity, I can still find ways to acknowledge the interconnected-ness of all who gather, our relationship with the Divine, and the con-nection with the larger world. I always pray for those who prepare and serve the meal. I try always to name a community far away that is suffering. It is a small way of remembering that we belong to a larger universe and are part of an amazing human family.

I also consider the prayer's time and place. An invocation is dif-ferent from a blessing. A petition is different from a prayer of com-mittal. Whether it's an invocation at a formal lunch, a pastoral prayer for a memorial service, an opening prayer for commencement, a prayer at a graveside, or a benediction, I take care in the preparation of every prayer. I sit and breathe. I think about and remember who will be gathered. I think of the occasion. I conjure up the images of places and the names of those I have and will encounter: from those who have died to students connected to the moment, to the ground-skeepers, to the president. I remember the people, their histories, their hurts and hopes, joys and sorrows. I know the community who will listen may not be attuned to the prayer's finer distinctions, but I also know that they do understand and hear the importance of the occasion and the authenticity of how it fits into this community of scholars. Then I write—as simply as possible, invoking clear imagery and including many pauses to give us room to breathe.

Prayer is a public way to care for and breathe new life into the institution. Very often, no matter the occasion, people have gath-ered hurriedly. Staff and faculty have rushed to finish up a long list of e-mails and then dashed out of their offices. Those coming from off-campus have had to face the trials of finding a parking spot, walk-ing up a steep hill, finding their way through the name-tag line, greeting a few friends before making their way to a seat. Out of this hectic day, my voice will often be the one inviting them to focus on the reasons we've gathered. I take my responsibility seriously at these times. I have the power to offer busy people a moment to sit, to breathe in, to let go. For some people, it may be the first quiet moment of the day; for almost everyone, it will be the only moment they'll gather with a community to sit silently and breathe together.

Quieting the space is important. Most Protestants (with whom I identify fondly) are accustomed to designing their own prayers with ample improvisation. There is a place for this kind of prayer. But in many public university settings, many who gather are neither Protestant nor Christian. For many of those gathered, chants, prescribed prayers, even silence are all forms of prayer, ways to expresses gratitude and thanksgiving. The pastoral role of the chaplain is to include a diverse community in a moment of prayer—offering a pause that people can occupy in their own way is one way to find an authentic voice in that moment. Some of those gathered, especially those undergoing trauma in their own lives or in their community, need a place to breathe the breath of sorrow in a community. In the face of unspeakable tragedy—earthquake, tsunami, terrorism—words are inadequate. Quiet space is what comforts and heals. Offering space that allows deep feelings of loss, pain, and sorrow to be articulated in their own language with their own words is what gives strength and ease for the pain.

When I begin, I try to keep it short, trusting that the spirit will move for each one gathered. I may borrow an image, a phrase, a poem, a word that I think will connect with the whole community. Being clear about the occasion and resisting the temptation to instruct the Divine and Holy about the moment is important. The Holy will find her way without instruction. The occasion and space should be enough—I try not to clutter them with my words. I try to create a sense of calm and solitude in the space and to evoke simple images of gratitude, peace, rest, thanksgiving, attention, and holiness.

Learning to breathe is not easy. Learning to breathe is learning to pay attention to scents and smells, accents and hues, sounds and silence. It is finding a moment to let go of the old and stale and bring in the new and fresh. It is what takes place in the space that belongs to more than one world. It is learning to listen for the spirit of the deep. As chaplain, this is just one of the ways I serve my community: creating room, temporal, physical, and metaphorical, for everyone to breathe.

BLUES SONGS AND LAMENTATIONS
Chaplains on the Crisis Team

Rev. Dr. Charles Lattimore Howard
University of Pennsylvania, Philadelphia, Pennsylvania

Music, I have found, has often served as an apt metaphor for the life of chaplaincy. So much of our work is performed at the conductor's stand as we gently try to guide an orchestra from multifaith cacophony to interfaith harmony. Or often, while playing in the jazz band of higher education, we find ourselves improvising and taking turns riffing with colleagues whose instruments sound very different from our own. Our work allows us to play joyous songs of celebration at graduation, beautiful love songs at weddings, and even passionate marches as we try to move others to lives of service.

But from time to time the music stops and it becomes difficult to form even a single note as the community looks to us to lead sorrowful songs of loss. Songs of lamentation. The blues.

While the most visible aspect of college and university chaplaincy may be our ceremonial role with the invocations and benedictions offered at major university functions, and the most understood and accepted aspect of our work is the service we provide as deans or

Rev. Dr. Charles Lattimore Howard is university chaplain at the University of Pennsylvania in Philadelphia, Pennsylvania, and a former hospital and hospice chaplain. He is the editor of *The Souls of Poor Folk* and author of *The Awe and the Awful.* He deeply enjoys spending time with his wife and two daughters, swimming, and reading a good book with a plate of cookies and a glass of milk.

directors of religious life, in this brief chapter, I want to consider the *pastoral* role of the chaplain—particularly as it pertains to being present during those moments of campus life that may be described as crises.

CALLS FROM SHARON

Over the last decade, more and more colleges and universities have been asking certain designated staff members to serve on crisis response teams. This of course looks different from campus to campus, with variations based on the size of the school, the frequency of events that can be classified as crises, the location of the institution, and other factors. The composition of these teams may also vary based on the nature of the emergency. An incident involving a campus fraternity or sorority would necessitate the director of Greek life being involved. If one of the students involved is an athlete, then it would make sense for the athletic director to be invited. When an incident involves a medical emergency, the student health office is notified and brought into the response team.

Yet there is often a core group that is involved in almost every case. This usually includes the dean of students or a designee, someone from the counseling office, someone from public safety or security, and the chaplain. Some larger schools have a person whose sole job is to coordinate a university's care for those who need intervention. On our campus for the last several years that person has been my dear friend Sharon.

Sharon works with a significant number of cases or situations in which I, as chaplain, am not included. I am called in when there has been a loss of life or the possibility of one, be it a student losing a parent or the situation that everyone on campus dreads and prays for protection from—the loss of one of our own students.

There are only four calls that I always take no matter what. A call from my wife, a call from our provost's office (my direct supervisor), a call from the university president's office (because, well, she's the president), and a call from Sharon, our director of student intervention services, our crisis response team. Sharon is a very close friend of mine; I'd go so far as to say that she is my sister. But my sister Sharon never calls to just say "Hey." When my caller ID reveals that it is Sharon from student intervention services calling, I always answer.

It is difficult to describe what happens next. Sadly, these calls have come far too many times, and each call brings with it a situation unlike any other. We have had to say good-bye to too many young people who never got the opportunity to apply what they studied, to accept the job offers that were coming, to matriculate at the graduate school of their dreams, to play their sport or perform their art professionally, to graduate and return one day with their own children, to show them where mommy or daddy used to live and go to school—looking back on these unrealized dreams is very sad and very painful.

Prior to working in higher education chaplaincy, I served as a hospital and then hospice chaplain. They are very different ministries in some ways (just as prison and military chaplaincy have nuances that make each a distinct form of chaplaincy), yet the long days and weekly overnight shifts were an important season of preparation in my life for the work that I am blessed to do on campus today.

During my years as a hospital chaplain, a week didn't go by without me being asked to offer a prayer of commendation, or to "give the last rites." An overnight shift seemed to always bring multiple car accident victims or an individual injured from violent crimes. And this was profound for me—a twenty-four-year-old chaplain who was probably too young for the job—seeing young black men who looked just like me being wheeled in as the victims of gunshot wounds.

Having to call the victim's loved ones and tell them that their son or daughter was there in the emergency room or having to walk with the doctor and tell the families that "they didn't make it" was deeply challenging and constantly heartbreaking. And while I always felt blessed to be allowed to serve people during the most excruciating moments in their lives, these were difficult times. I flinch at rereading this paragraph, feeling as if I'm reducing hundreds of moments where I bore witness to grief—accompanied by screams, tears, punched walls, cries of "why" and "no"—into just two or three passive sentences. These moments will always be more than words or stories to me.

You'd think that this work at the hospital or in my later role as a hospice chaplain, journeying with numerous patients to the door into the other side, would have prepared me for the far less frequent moments of tragedy that college life brings. Yet the reality is that the various crises that visit the lives of our students move me just as deeply—in many ways more so—as the traumas that came through the hospital door. You never "get good" at this kind of stuff. And I always prayed that I would never get calloused and that people would never become "just another patient" or "just another situation" that I was called to deal with. Entering into each of these moments with the awareness that this is someone's son or daughter—a young person who had dreams—is most certainly the harder way, but it is the richer way as well.

And Sharon is always the gateway to these situations. She is the bandleader handing out the sheet music before we are called to play. Each call brings a new, sad song. A sophomore has died in an accident while he was studying abroad. A junior has succumbed to the cancer that she so bravely battled for the last five years. A graduate student has passed away as a result of substance abuse. A young man has taken his own life.

I have a file in my office full of tear-stained memorial service programs from gatherings that I have officiated here on campus over the years. Each one is sad in its own way. Each one is a devastating, life-altering tragedy in the lives of a family and in the lives of friends. In moments like these, our job in the university chaplaincy is to be present, to cry and grieve alongside others who are crying and grieving, to hug, to hold up in prayer, to love, to journey with, to help gather, to dare to look upwards, to dare to sing blue notes and lamentations.

MAKING THE CALL

I remember one rainy afternoon on campus. The phone's caller ID once again revealed that it was Sharon calling, summoning us back to the stage. Blues tonight.

A young man, a senior, captain of our football team, was in critical condition at the hospital. "Chaz, here's the number. Will you call his parents?" Sharon asked me.

Making these calls has changed for me over the years. When you become a parent yourself, having to tell another father or mother that their greatest fear has been realized pulls a distinct kind of understanding tears from your eyes. There is no good way to break the news of tragedy to anyone. We have come to find that if it can be avoided, it is best not to share the worst over the phone, but rather to wait until they arrive on campus or at the hospital. This is often not feasible when the student is from out of state or out of the country. We then try to have someone go to their home to speak with the parents in person.

And yet, parents can often sense that something bad has happened the second they hear the voice on the other end of the phone. It is important for a university to think about who is best suited to make this phone call. This decision should not necessarily be made on the basis of title, but rather by considering who can hold it together while being present for the family, who can be a "non-anxious presence" (to use a term most ministers will be familiar with), and who will be the main contact person for the family. We tend to not have our campus police make this call, not because they can't, but because having a law officer call connotes criminal activity and can scare people. We prefer to not have our upper administrators (president, provost) call, as they are usually not involved in the direct response to a situation, and they won't be the ongoing main contact person. Some believe that having the chaplain call automatically signals the worst to a family—which might be the case. I remember that when I was working at the hospital, I would knock on a patient's door and introduce myself as a chaplain, and occasionally patients would burst into tears, thinking that their family had asked me to come and administer last rites. "Nope, just came to check in," I'd say with a smile. Sometimes they'd believe me.

I think that a chaplain is usually the best person to call, not only because we are often trained to engage others during these most difficult moments in life, but because of what we symbolize. Symbols are important. What a religious official symbolizes is different to everyone. But for most individuals, the chaplain symbolizes the presence of a higher power, of hope, of peace. Being reminded of these things can sometimes help to keep us grounded during those moments in life when the winds of chaos and grief threaten to carry us away.

After the captain of the football team was brought to our hospital, and after I had called his father and mother, the student intervention services band of Sharon, our campus police chief, the doctor, and I gathered in the hospital waiting room. Then, as his family drove the prayer-filled hour from their home to the hospital, we got the news. Their son had died.

The waiting room where I now stood, preparing myself to deliver terrible news, was the same place I often stood when I worked as a young trauma-bay chaplain at this same hospital. The sterilized hospital air filled a room that was for me full of ghosts and echoes. I could still very clearly see wailing families who had just found out about their brother, son, father, friend dying from a gunshot wound. I remembered an angry young person who punched a hole in the wall out of anger as he vowed to get revenge on the person who'd taken his friend's life. I could recall the screams of a daughter in a state of biblical grief, tearing her sweater while she wept on her knees. Some I held as they cried on my shoulders; some ran out, unable to bear the news.

These ghosts vanished as the football captain's parents walked in. I was left alone with the doctor to tell his mother and father the worst news that a parent can ever hear.

They asked to see him. Maybe because they didn't believe it. Maybe to say good-bye. One of the nurses and I escorted them back to see their son—this tall, strong young man whose diapers they used to change. The boy they used to give piggyback rides to and who they swung up on their shoulders. The sweet guy they used to cheer for at high school football games. Their son, of whom they were so proud—and who they had planned to see graduate in just one more year.

I couldn't help but cry with them.

After the parents left, our song did not end. The football team had heard that something had happened to their captain but they did not know any of the details. They were all waiting down near the field in a campus auditorium.

Sharon and I, along with our counseling office staff, walked together to the auditorium, where more than seventy large young men sat waiting in silence. They were the reigning league champions, who had been through so much together already, a very tight-knit group of physically and emotionally strong young men, a few of whom went on to play professional football.

Coach led us in, and I was asked to break the news.

I will never forget seeing an entire roomful of men cry in the way that they did. The counseling staff, the student intervention team, and the coaches stayed for a while to speak with them individually.

It was a long day, full of heartbreaking refrains, but eventually my set was over and I went home for the night. I cried for the entire subway ride.

LAMENTATIONS AND BLUES

I have had to "break the news" to many over the years. What an odd phrase "break the news" is, as it is more accurate to say that it is the news that breaks us. Or almost breaks us. The threat of brokenness looms over campus during these crisis times, and the moves that administrators and staff make over the days following a tragedy should be made very carefully. I have shared sad news like this with our school band, the senior class of our nursing school, various fraternities, different religious student groups, the residents of close-knit dorms, and other large groups. But our job is to be more than just messengers, more than just bearers of bad news. We must also be bearers of good news as well. We can't only sing the blues under the dim lights; we must also sing songs of hope under the brightness of the sun.

We have found over the years that in the aftermath of tragedy, it is crucial to have some type of gathering opportunity for our students and for our entire community. The director of our counseling office, Bill, and I have spoken several times over the years about the great importance of having either a memorial service or a time for friends to come together and share stories informally, not only for closure purposes (sometimes situations like this don't close so much as much as become bearable and held in a place other than grief), but also as a healthy and safe opportunity for our students to express their feelings and be together.

It should go without saying that each situation is unique. Each response should also be unique and appropriate to the discrete circumstances surrounding the situation, dictated in large part by the wishes of the family and closest friends and, we think, reflective of the person we are remembering. Once we had to say good-bye to a young man who played tuba in the band and was the co-captain of a team of students who designed and constructed an all-electric motor scooter. Thus his service featured not only remarks by classmates, faculty, and friends, but a display of the scooter that he worked on (renamed to honor him) and of course a performance by the band. The director of the band cautiously told me that "the band doesn't do sad music very well." They didn't. They ended up playing some of the same celebratory loud songs that they play at football games, and it was a tremendously appropriate way to honor a guy who lived life to the fullest.

These services are never easy. Tears and laughter often dance within the same moment. Families hear stories that open a window into an aspect of their loved one's life that they often only knew peripherally.

Sometimes, however, it's just too hard. We have had large candlelight vigils where there was no laughter. And at those very sad gatherings—for example, after a student has taken her or his own life—there is a different intensity of pain that we all hold; a sadness seldom voiced but certainly felt and understood. The best way these moments are addressed is not by any words said from the podium, but rather through friends holding each other and crying together.

I would be remiss if I didn't share a story about a campus memorial service that my predecessor shared with me. Occasionally those of us who are planning a service can try to do too much. The chaplain's office was called by a group of recent graduates whose friend had passed away. They wanted to return to campus and have a small memorial gathering in front of their old dorm as a way to remember their friend. The chaplain of course agreed to officiate the service and make the necessary arrangements for the day that they all agreed on.

One of the friends had an idea. The young man who had passed away loved butterflies. "What if, at the end of the service, we released live butterflies into the sky?" A lovely idea.

The butterflies were ordered from a monarch butterfly farm, which ships these beautiful little insects overnight in a cooled case that blocks out the light, placing them in a hibernation-like state, ensuring their safe arrival. Once the box is opened, the natural light and warmth of the day gently awakens them and they fly out. The plan was that at the end of the service, the chaplain would offer a closing prayer ending with something to the effect of "May you rest in peace and may you fly back to heaven from whence you came," at which point the butterflies would be released.

Well, the service went well enough, and the moment for the final prayer arrived. Upon uttering the words, "Fly back to heaven from whence you came!" the chaplain opened the box. One brave little monarch fluttered up about two feet and then fell to the ground. A few more thawed and also succumbed to the same crash landing. Not exactly how the chaplain and the friends planned it. It could have been taken as a bad sign, but I think everyone present laughed at the technical difficulty. Improvisation in a minor key.

"I DON'T KNOW HOW YOU DO IT"

Every chaplain at some point in their career has been told that "they have the hardest job on campus" or that "I don't know how you do it." I'm not sure that I agree that we have the hardest job on campus, as I most certainly think being a college or university president is far more difficult, as is being provost or dean, with the various aspects of the university that they must serve and articulate a vision for. Each job on campus brings its own challenges, whether in the classroom, staff positions in support of our students and facilities, or administrative work. Yet chaplaincy does indeed bring its own unique set of difficulties—particularly on those days when crisis and tragedy visit our campuses. On a regular day, a chaplain's work might include facilitating the journey from a multifaith to an interfaith community; advising and mentoring a tremendously diverse group of students; creating and executing programming that educates, affirms, and deepens; presiding over weddings; presenting invocations, benedictions, and sermons; writing and preaching sermons; planning liturgy; sitting on what is almost an endless number of committees; and being present daily with a community of students, faculty, and staff, who bring the full range of life moments to the couches in our offices. When you add to that the normal budgeting and staff supervision work that the job demands, it can make for many long days, weeks, and semesters. And yet, when the phone call comes letting us know that a member of our flock has fallen, everything changes.

In recent years, some of the challenges in responding to the death of a student have changed, making these most painful of all student-life situations even more difficult. There seems to be an increased caution by many universities around possible lawsuits. There are times, perhaps, when universities may be legally culpable. Yet even when they are not, as is most often the case, I have seen and heard of occasions where families in their grief threaten legal action against a university or one of its parts. Grief is complex, and it affects our actions in very complex ways. Sadly, this fear of legal action by families tints the way that some members of a university staff may reach out to grieving family members. Many become very guarded, putting their own legal protection above the care of the family. I understand this impulse, I get it, but it is tragic nonetheless. When the staff members of some universities need to correspond with the deceased student's family members, they run their e-mails by their school's general counsel in advance of sending them. Some staff members are coached to never "admit fault" in a situation, as it may incriminate the university in a future lawsuit. In their defense, I have heard of families who recorded phone conversations with university officials in an effort to catch them saying something that might be helpful in a possible suit against the school. All of this can potentially impede the care offered by a response team. Fear is one of the great impediments to a truly loving, care-filled response.

Along with anxiety around legal issues, the speed with which information is disseminated has greatly increased—bringing other unique challenges. Students share news via their portable devices—by phone, by text, and by social media—extremely quickly. News like the passing of a classmate is, I firmly believe, best learned when people can be together with friends or family members who can support them. I can understand the argument that it is better to hear from a friend rather than an administrator with whom a student has no relationship, yet finding out that one of your fraternity brothers has died while reading a text message in class is not at all ideal. This puts an interesting pressure on student support teams to plan gatherings quickly—not necessarily so that we can share the sad news first, but rather so that we can be there as soon as possible after students find out.

And yet the greatest challenge for chaplains when responding to tragedy on campus is something far more subtle. It is the self.

This is a holy tension that all ministers—all humans really—must wrestle with: finding the balance between a loving selflessness and lack of self-concern with a sincere focus on self-care. Let's consider the former first.

Prior to being appointed university chaplain, I was asked to serve as interim chaplain while the university carried out its search to fill the position left vacant by my predecessor. Being asked to serve as an interim while also feeling called to apply to that position can be both a blessing and a burden, for in many ways it is an audition for the permanent job—an audition that could go very well or very poorly.

For me, while this was a great opportunity, it was also a great trap spiritually. I recall with some shame and sadness the days leading up to our university's graduation ceremony that year. On our campus, the chaplain is asked to offer an invocation, which should not last more than two or three minutes, as well as a benediction, which should be under two. To produce these five minutes of prayer, I must have labored six hours, spread out over several days. I never spend that long preparing to offer a prayer, a sermon, or remarks anywhere. But that was not the worst of it. I remember that my motivating force in working so hard on the prayer was that I wanted to impress our university president, our provost, and the search committee. Thus I endeavored to make my little prayer sound as eloquent and as impressive as I could. I consulted the thesaurus to find better, more intelligent-sounding words. I rehearsed my reading of the prayer so that I could get the inflections in my voice just right.

On the big day, after I said "Amen," as I walked back to my seat, I glanced at the president and provost and delighted in their approving smiles. I glowed at being told later how much people "loved my prayer" and how they "loved the sound of my voice." I was supposed to be praying to the God of the universe, giving thanks for all that the graduates had accomplished, interceding for their future work, but my ultimate concern was not that my prayers were heard above, but how I was coming off while giving them. How sad.

This greater concern for self-image than for the care of others or for our service to the One who calls us is not only spiritually dangerous, but it also can potentially hinder us from offering our best pastoral care, especially when we are most needed. I am thankful that in my case, the temptation toward pride and the hindrance of insecurity have been tempered somewhat through experience and caring mentors (though like many of us, I imagine, I will always struggle with it). And yet worrying about "how we are doing as chaplain" can get in the way of actually doing "chaplainy" things, or rather, serving in the best way possible. The best chaplains are those who are fearless—those who are not afraid of what others may think. This is not to be confused with a lack of self-awareness. Rather, I'm talking about someone who is driven not by the opinions of others, but instead by their faith, by the One they believe in, and by those they are serving.

I recall a time when this overconcern for self-image crept into my attempts to care for a circle of grieving family and friends after the loss of a young woman on our campus. I remember that it was a particularly stressful time for me (an important detail, as stress can sometimes negatively impact our decision-making abilities), and I was preparing to fly out of town to preach at another university's chapel service that weekend. That Friday, hours before my flight, I received a call from Sharon informing me that a student had died. I, along with the rest of our team, was soon in her dorm, where her family, who lived locally, was already waiting for us. In between reaching out to the students on her hall and others in the building, I spoke with her family. Through tears and shock, they asked about the possibility of holding a memorial service on campus three days from then, on Monday.

I brought their request to the rest of our response team, and we all had reservations about holding a memorial service so soon. Yet, one of our upper administrators thought that we should follow the lead of the family. She asked me if I could pull together the service by then. My pride got the best of me and I answered yes.

I should pause to say that there is probably no perfect time to have a memorial service or funeral (however, it should be noted that certain religious traditions do have time requirements around when individuals should be buried and when services should happen), but there are indeed bad times. As has already been mentioned, each situation is unique. I do think that sometimes a gathering such as a candlelight vigil in the immediate aftermath of a tragedy, be it local or global, can be a powerful, deeply moving, and very helpful/hopeful response. Yet, after the death of a student, the "best" services that I have been a part of are those that have some time (around a week or more) cushioning the grief after a community first hears word of the loss. This time allows for better planning so that their friend can be remembered and honored properly. Likewise, it helps to make the memorial gathering into a positive experience as opposed to an added stress during an already trying time. In the end, regarding the situation mentioned above, we pulled together a beautiful service, yet afterward the response team was nearly burnt out. Each of us, to a person, wished that we had waited longer to have the service, but my pride in wanting to please one of the administrators whom I report to got in the way of wisdom and experience. With many so competing voices, it's especially important to make sure the rhythm doesn't get lost.

RESTS

Along with this loving selflessness and lack of self-concern, chaplains and truly all who serve in caring ministries should constantly dedicate a significant amount of time and energy to self-care. There are several books written on this matter, and they are not only very helpful, but they will convey this message with far greater clarity and far more convincingly than I ever could. And yet, I will share just a little of my experience and how I learned that all beautiful music changes tempo now and then—and always contains rests.

I find myself often giving thanks for the great opportunities afforded me by this ministry to which I have been called. When I am presiding at the wedding of a former student, when I get to meet and engage with the various world figures who are receiving honorary degrees at graduation, when I get to challenge and affirm the many wonderful students I meet each year, it is wonderful. Even in the more challenging times, I find myself giving thanks for the gift of being able to love others during and through their times of trial.

Still, this work can be exhausting—and not only physically. There is a daily demand to multitask. At any given moment we could be working on liturgy for an upcoming service, drafting sermon notes, preparing an invocation and benediction to be offered at an event, grading papers and working on lesson plans, running to meetings about funding for the upcoming year, mediating between two student groups, finalizing the power-point presentation of a religious diversity training, or counseling a student who has realized that she doesn't want to be a doctor any longer, or a staff member who doesn't like his boss, or a faculty member who is feeling anxious about tenure, or an administrator who has found a lump. This does not even include finding time to work on one's own writing projects and spend time with family (never mind exercise or just hang out!). Thus when a day of "normal" chaplaincy is extended by the advent of a crisis, the possibility of hitting a breaking point is very real. And a broken chaplain is of no good to anyone.

Stress demands a response. For some it is breakdown or burnout. I have encountered many colleagues in the ministry who have walked through painful seasons where their bodies (and minds and spirits) simply refuse to go on. I had an old mentor who used to say that "the body keeps score." He was referring to how many of us carry stress in our shoulders or back and anxiety in our stomach. The body indeed does keep score, and sometimes it calls time-out. That in the end is meant to be a gift. Our bodies are our friends, and this oldest of friends is trying to tell us what our mind may not be grasping. Yet if we do not heed this bodily warning, great danger may be looming.

For some the response isn't burnout, but instead it is lash-out. Their behavior changes, and they become short-tempered and impatient, as resentment at the current stressful life situation seeps out into the treatment of others.

For still others, the response is to self-medicate the stress, sometimes through prescriptions or, too often, with unprescribed, unhealthy behaviors. I've known many clergy over the years who deal with the stress of ministry by drinking or through other means of escape.

The temptation is to want to always be "on" for everyone, to always be ready to respond to every single request for help, every single hurt on our campuses. This of course is not a bad temptation, as it is an impulse toward doing good. Yet, it is dangerous—what had the potential to be a forty-year career can turn into a four-year career, after the strain of the work quickly deteriorates our effectiveness and endurance in ministry.

One of the great gifts of working in higher-education chaplaincy is the fact that we work on an academic calendar with built-in rests and vacation days. Use them! In fact, tell others that you are using them! During my first year or so, I remember wrestling with the question of whether I should leave an "away message" on my e-mail account. With smartphones, we can constantly be plugged in and always respond to e-mails, making it seem as if we are always in the office, working hard and staying busy. Sadly, being busy can often be a source of pride on our campuses. But at some point, I became convinced of the fact that the chaplain or the dean or director of religious life should probably be one of the main people modeling how to rest and who should demonstrate self-care on a campus.

I have to qualify this, however. As I mentioned above, whenever Sharon calls, I answer. This is true even when I am on vacation. And I have indeed been called back to campus from vacations when an emergency has arisen. The thing that I have learned over the years, however, is that I should work hard to get that time back. When I receive a call late into the evening that requires me to come to campus and not return home again for hours, if possible I will spend the morning at home resting and come into work later. If I end up spending part of the weekend on campus, I try to make sure that I can take a day off at some point the following week.

But rest and self-care are about more than just staying at home and taking days off from work. I find that I need to exercise, eat right, and most importantly have someone in my life with whom I can speak and process things. I firmly believe that everyone in ministry should be in some type of a counseling relationship. With the unfortunate stigma around being in counseling and therapy, many shy away from taking time to do this because they do not want to appear as if anything is wrong or as if they have a problem. But I've found I have benefited greatly from having someone in my life to "dump on" after having a few weeks of everyone on campus "dump on" me. After being the shoulder for everyone to cry on, it's nice to have someone who can listen to me cry.

There is so much more to the art and call of chaplaincy than responding to crises, yet being available to serve in these most vulnerable, most painful moments in life is an important part of our work.

During my college years, I sang with an a capella group called The Inspiration. I miss those days, even the three-times-a-week

practices. I will always remember the faces of individuals in the audience and the way that they would light up whenever we would sing
"their song" and get the harmonies just right. When we could work
together, each of us singing our respective parts, we made beautiful music—even when singing sad songs. When we kept the tempo,
going not too fast and not too slow, we could always move those listening to us. And after a long week of practices, I knew that I needed
to take care of my voice with tea, honey, and cough drops so that I
might be ready to sing a few days later.

Chaplaincy is music, and I pray that our song, with all of its varied notes, might move and bless people for as long as we are able to
sing and play.

CARING
AT THE
CROSSROADS

BETWIXT AND BETWEEN
Interstitial Dialogue, Identity, and Mending on a College Campus

Rev. Dr. Linda J. Morgan-Clement
College of Wooster, Wooster, Ohio

Barely tall enough to peer into the full-length mirror at the end of the hall, I stretched out a tentative finger to touch the unfamiliar face that stared back at me from the shiny surface. I traced the broad face whose eyelids disappeared behind dark, surprised, almond-shaped eyes. I followed the line of high cheekbones and a wide, almost bridgeless nose, leaving a streak on the mirror's surface. And I wondered at the way the stubbornly straight, almost black hair danced in response to my startled movements. Who was this small girl-child who did not look like anyone in my family or city?

From the time I came to "know" that the face in the mirror was my own, awareness of otherness has shaped me and, as a result, my ministry. I feel fully a part of the white, Midwestern family that adopted me, but I don't look anything like them. I am ethnically Chinese, but

Rev. Dr. Linda J. Morgan-Clement is chaplain and director of interfaith campus ministry at the College of Wooster in Wooster, Ohio. Her work has appeared in *We Ask Your Blessing: 100 Prayers for Campus Occasions* (ed. Donald Shockley). She finds it deeply satisfying as a campus chaplain to assist people—be it students, her own family and friends, or faculty and staff—to discover genuine connections with others. She welcomes opportunities to deepen ordinary human activities into encounters with self, others, and the holy in ways that encourage courageous and connective living.

I am confused and mute when I encounter cultural and linguistic Chinese people. As a chaplain, I am a woman in a traditionally male role. And on a secular campus with its sound-bite, media-fueled suspicion of religion, I identify as a progressive Christian.

There is no category into which I fit perfectly. But my dissonant identities are not in conflict with one another. In fact, the perspective my perpetual "otherness" has granted me is essential to my work as a chaplain. A vantage point from the margin allows me to help the people I work with discover elements of themselves they have been afraid to confront, and to guide people from different worlds toward a deeper understanding of each other.

I have come to think of my chaplaincy work as a spiritual practice of interstitial living: *enlivening the spaces between.* It is the experience of being "in" but not "of" the basic categories and of thriving in the interstitial where "all/and" allows for new life to emerge. In biological terms, the interstitial is what lies between the essential tissues of bone, organ, and artery. In part, it's the webbing that holds the body together, but it's not simply webbing, it's the spaces between—the openness required for the parts to perform their own essential functions. Without it, people and other living things would literally fall apart.

On the campus too, it is often easier to define a chaplain by what she is not. I am not faculty, not student-life professional, not support staff, not alumnae, not pastor, not custodian—yet I incorporate pieces of each and relate to all. In both my personal and professional life, I am constantly creating a whole from multiple parts. It's this peripheral perspective that allows me to create and hold interstitial space on my campus and to make those spaces large enough that people can meet others there and recognize each other's humanity, especially persons who may be marginalized elsewhere.

My experience as someone who has often not exactly fit any category has helped me understand and embrace the vital role of interstitial space. Both physical and metaphorical, it is essential to the social and spiritual health of any community. As Martin Buber, Thich Nhat Hanh, and many other spiritual visionaries acknowledge, we will not understand ourselves or meet the Holy One until we see ourselves in the other and the other in ourselves. As chaplain at the College of Wooster, I work to create and to invite others into interstitial spaces where our gaze turns toward the communal spiritual practices of translating, connecting, and holding.

CREATING INTERSTITIAL SPACE

When I came to the college in 1996 to build an interfaith ministry, the office was located on the garden level of the student center, not in the chapel. This meant that the chaplaincy was then located in the very center of the campus. The student center was a hub of activity that included a number of "essential communal services." In addition to the chaplaincy, it housed the main dining hall, the snack bar, the post office, and the bookstore.

By 2005 the basement area of the student center, with its chipped cinderblock walls, had become home for me and the many students, staff, and faculty who made up the campus ministry community. Memories filled the space, students sprawled on the worn carpet, books, crayons, art supplies, souvenir tee shirts, remnants of open house displays, and an Earth Day plant project crowded one another on the long open shelving that served as our storage area. But the administration decided to refurbish the space for a new advising center, and we were to be "given" an old building on the north edge of the campus. "This is such an ugly space," the president said of our beloved basement center, as he informed me of our impending move. "There is so much potential at Overholt, think what you can do with it!"

For almost ten years we had been building a ministry of hospitality at the center of the campus in this "ugly, windowless" space. It had become a casual, worn, and welcoming home for generations of students. Much of the character of the ministry was shaped around the location to which we had been assigned. Staff time, student accessibility, making all of campus our shared space, and the visible proximity of our tiny offices made collaboration and informal engagement core practices.

As a leader, I had to overcome my first upset response. My natural inclination to make the best—something I learned from my Depression-era mother—came to the rescue. Gather the community, dream together, ask for what we need to lean into the old house on the edge of campus. Old wisdom, gained the hard way, allowed me and the rest of the interfaith community to see a way forward. In part, we would now embody yet another location between, this time between the campus and the community.

With the move to the edge of campus, we would have lots of space and light, yet the change in location required essential changes in the ministry and in the ways in which we could now be a physical reminder of the presence of the sacred. Hospitality in liminal geography offered different challenges. We would lose the ease of access, accidental walk-ins, and the advantage of "being in the center." Working from the edge of campus, we now needed to intentionally open our space, create a safe and inviting place where unexpected connections could be discovered and nurtured, and provide reasons for people to make the trip north. With the move from the center of campus, the core practices of the ministry shifted toward valuing and connecting in a space that was neither/nor—the space between gown and town.

A group of students and staff members wanted to make this work. They were an interstitial community, diverse yet connected, who shared a deep sense of connection and interdependence that had grown over the years. With creativity, imagination, and lots of elbow grease, we packed and unpacked. We scrubbed walls, borrowed old furniture, painted woodwork, and started plants that friends gave to us (we had windows now). An office was turned back into a living room, and a basement bedroom was filled with huge yellow, red, blue, and green beanbags.

In the years since the move, many students and staff have worked to transform the building into a low-tech, on-campus retreat. Overholt has become a welcoming, casual place where students and staff come to breathe—to sit on the porch and think (or not) or to flop in the beanbag room and talk with strangers until they become friends.

The kitchen has become a place where challah rises on Thursday and candles flare at sunset on Friday; where early-morning Ramadan breakfasts fill the predawn air with the spicy smells of biryani, and Sunday evenings mean hymns on the old piano and Communion by candlelight. One of our seniors remarked, "When I first came to Wooster I was worried and disappointed that we did not have our own Hillel building and kitchen. But now, I am so glad we did not! Sharing Overholt with all the other groups made me ask and answer questions and share experiences that have made me a much better Jew, and none of that would have happened if we'd had a place of our own."

In working together, we had to articulate more clearly and carefully the commitments that we shared as well as our growing edges. In the midst of being pushed to the edges, we made a choice—the choice to engage in interstitial living, to offer places for all who find themselves pushed to the edge. It took the goodwill, the vision, and the hard work of many students and our staff to take on the challenge to create an interstitial ministry. Overholt now has a reputation as a good place to practice pondering important questions and a safe place to have big conversations. It has been a wonderful place in which to learn how to talk about our lives with each other until we discover a new narrative that we can share.

TRANSLATING

Not all interstitial space is physical. Part of my role is to facilitate times and occasions when people can reach outside of their own categories and open themselves up to another's experience. One of the most important examples of this is the multifaith baccalaureate tradition we've developed at the College of Wooster.

A multifaith group of seniors met in October to begin planning the ceremony that will accompany their graduation. I start by asking them simple questions, seeking to avoid religious language that is loaded or located too much in a single tradition: *Tell me stories about places and times you received something from someone else. What about a time when you were humbled because someone saw you more clearly and compassionately than you saw yourself?* Having shared the college experience and elements of their own development, similarities quickly emerge. As the stories pile up, we begin to bring in language from specific religious traditions: *When you told those stories, it reminded me of Paul's phrase at the end of the Corinthians love poem, "Now I know in part, then I shall know fully, even as I am fully known." Does that fit for you?* The process of working from personal stories toward existing practices, traditions, and terms allows us to discover commonalities in what might otherwise feel like contrasting religions. This process helps students simultaneously embrace the tradition in which they were raised and recognize the ways other traditions speak to many shared human experiences and concerns.

Each participant brings to the service a part of themselves and a piece of their religious and spiritual tradition. Together they tackle the daunting task of weaving together their diverse spiritual and religious lives with the goal of creating a worship experience that will be shared by other seniors, faculty, staff, parents, and family members. As chaplain, I experience the process and the creative product as deeply sacred. This interfaith translation is made possible by focusing on the interstices rather than comparing or contrasting traditions in their confining boxes.

What happens in this creative, sacred, interstice allows us to invite others outside the conversation to join us. The baccalaureate service emerges as a gift to the senior class and their families from the process of sharing deeply about the (often taboo) subject of spiritual experience.

At eight thirty on a Sunday morning a few years ago, twenty sleepy seniors straggled into the large stone-block chapel that serves as a constant reminder of the religious upheaval of the late sixties. Pushing back stray hair, barefoot with sling-backed sandals in hand, adjusting a tie or a sari; the cool cavernous space warmed to the rising energy of anticipation and excitement. This was the day that our group had worked toward for months: meeting, talking, planning, and creating an interfaith service of worship that would attempt to capture the spiritual meaning of the past four years.

Before we could complete the final setup, parents and families began arriving, eager to claim good seats for the service. Finally, the organist hit the opening chords of the processional. The faculty entered in their colorful academic regalia, and everyone stood to watch as they were followed by the senior class in black gowns and mortarboards. The president and the platform party processed forward, followed by the five students who would lead the opening call to prayer. The last note from the organ faded. The congregation sat, rustling into stillness. The first student raised the microphone to her mouth and began the invitation to prayer. One after another the seniors spoke, each using the language most familiar to his or her own religious tradition. In English, Hindi, Hebrew, and a dialect from Bhutan, we invited the gathered worshipers to acknowledge the sacredness of life.

Ali was the last to speak. He took the microphone and held it to his mouth. His left hand cupped his ear and his head bowed in concentration. Taking a breath, he raised his head and sang, *"Allahu Akbar, Ash-hadu an-la ilaha illallah...."* ("I bear witness that there is none worthy of worship except God. I bear witness that Muhammad is the Messenger of God. Come to prayer...."). He completed the recitation and slowly lowered the microphone. My lungs contracted sharply as I let out the breath I had not known I was holding. After a moment of silence, the organist began the introductory phrases to the congregational hymn, and the five students filed slowly off the platform and up the aisle to their reserved seats as the congregation rose to sing.

Following the service a tall middle-aged man stopped me. "Chaplain, thank you for all of your work with the students on the service. It was beautiful! But tell me, what religion was represented by the last student's singing? It was simply stunning."

I smiled and thanked him for his response. "That was Ali; he recited the Muslim Call to Prayer."

His eyes widened. "I thought it sounded familiar, but all the other times I have heard it have been on TV where it is the background to scenes of violence." His words trailed off. I felt my heart drop. "I had no idea what it meant," he said. He paused and started again, "I mean, in this context it was beautiful."

Touching his arm lightly, I responded, "For Ali, I think it is always beautiful, and every time I hear it, I can feel its power."

His hand reached out to shake mine, "Thank you for the service," He paused, still grasping my hand, before he finished his thought. "It was beautiful." As he moved off into the crowd, I stood still, awed, saddened, and hopeful.

I have never forgotten how moved the gentleman was to suddenly hear the Muslim Call to Prayer as beautiful instead of ominous. For me, this confirmed all the hard work the students had put into designing the ceremony and into connecting with each other across traditions. It was a reminder to me that when we are able to establish interstitial spaces, we make it possible for people entering those spaces to make their own, deeply powerful translations. It's those translations that help us live together more generously and peacefully.

CONNECTING

While every encounter is really an encounter of both difference and similarity, some are more obvious given the way we divide the world into categories. Because we deeply want to feel the same, our fear that we may not have a community can create barriers or say to someone who seems too different, "You're not a human being," or "You're a bad human being." Another response is to look over those walls of difference in a spirit of conversion and say, "Just come be like me and then we can be friends." Or we may respond by giving so much away to be like another that we become anything but ourselves. These are three common responses to a fear of being "othered." But interstitial space offers a fourth way.

In embracing the ambiguous and ubiquitous existence of interstitial space as a location for chaplaincy, I have come to see it as a creative space, a location from which the yet unimagined is given the room to emerge. What happens there is not a method but a dance with steps to be discovered along the way, invented by two or more persons who commit to being present with one another.

For four years, I met with a group of women who came together with the intention of engaging in an interfaith dialogue. Unusually diverse in terms of religious backgrounds (Jewish, Presbyterian, Quaker, Pagan, Baha'i, Hindu, Muslim), we shared many similarities including our political orientation and familiarity with the consistent pressure of our campus culture. When we first agreed to meet, I offered only one rule for our time together—that we would not "do" anything other than talk. In this I was honoring an awareness, painfully gained, about the difficulty of engaging in deep and committed dialogue. Running off to create a program, offer a panel, or engage in a political project could too easily serve as a distraction, mask felt but unarticulated tensions, or embody an undeserved sense of pride in our "tolerance for persons of different faith backgrounds." On our small campus, there was no need for us to create common experiences. The space between dining hall and classroom, co-curricular clubs and community service was an interstice for sustained and committed exploration of one another's religious life and the ways in which our faith and religious identities (and those of others) shape us and our actions.

While we all had a sense of the difficulty that might be ahead, I don't think that any of us really "believed" that we were going to run into problems. We all wanted to go deep, and for that we knew that we had to be able to listen deeply. The slow and difficult process of listening and clarifying became a norm as we practiced by hearing one another's faith narratives. Each woman took the floor for a full eighty minutes to tell her story and respond to the questions that arose in the group. We focused on the experiences, the people, and the encounter with mystery rather than structure, belief, or even practice. At the end of the first round of narrative sharing, we almost started again, because our own narratives and memories had been significantly reshaped and informed by the narratives that we had heard from one another. But instead, we decided to shift gears and begin to address some common topics. Taking turns, the members of the group started bringing in news articles or personal experiences from the week that we would discuss through the lens of our religious and spiritual traditions. For the entire first year, our shared experience was one of increasing comfort and acknowledged points of commonality.

As facilitator, participant, and interpreter, I drew upon multiple worldviews to understand what was happening. I drew upon my personal history and education, including Christian theology, therapeutic encounters, mothering mixed-race daughters, navigating multiethnic communities, and simply living. For all of us, being "in the group but not of the group" was a familiar experience. It takes time to practice the kind of vulnerability and self-awareness that grounds us enough to be open to others. This way of living is countercultural in our fast-paced society and campus environment. Too often students' experience is that their human value is measured by output, and busyness has become a form of competition. Interstitial connections require a more deliberate pace that involves risk taking, silence, self-awareness, compassion, and careful listening that is willing to set aside assumptions for clarity.

HOLDING

As the friendships among the college women deepened and the level of sharing continued to intensify, I found myself more and more in the role of observer as they facilitated their own conversations. Then one evening I was sharply pulled back into the role of facilitator and space maker, as conflict threatened to shatter our carefully nurtured dialogue.

The light was starting to fade from the sky as we gathered in the familiar circle for our weekly dialogue. Carol was curled up in her chosen corner of the couch, and Lydia and Sarah shared the couch with her, while Amelia chose a spot on the floor, sitting cross-legged under her long skirt, leaning back against my chair. Ashita and Megan sprawled on the other couch, feet resting on the coffee table. Nancy hurried in, dropped into an armchair, and flipped on the light. Fatima arrived last, settling calmly, almost regally, into the remaining chair.

When Fatima had settled in, Carol leaned forward and launched in. Waving a clipping from the newspaper, she spoke: "So this is from this morning's paper, and they are about to execute another prisoner in Columbus. I know we promised not to 'do anything,' but this seems like something we ought to speak about. I mean, it would be great for us to write in protest as a multifaith group of women." It was clear that this cause was important to Carol. Sarah, Amelia, and Nancy nodded in agreement. "This might be something we really should do," Lydia spoke softly.

Carol's feet hit the floor with a thud. "It's really wrong to execute people! There's tons of research that shows how racist and classist the criminal justice system is. The statistics on execution do not reflect the general population or even the prison population. And the demographics of the prison population are so messed up anyway. I really don't think that you can be a person of faith and support this kind of gross injustice! I really don't get it. Even the Catholics don't support the death penalty." For a few moments others in the group joined her passionate condemnation of the death penalty. I found myself wondering whether Carol might not be right. Perhaps this was the time to break our rule and take some action other than talking. We had been learning to listen and share, building a community for more than a year—maybe this should be our next step. I knew that they wouldn't move unless I gave permission—even with their growing skill in interfaith dialogue they still deferred to me, giving me the final say. Pulling back, I listened and watched, trying not to go with the moment, trying to value their wisdom and intuition.

"I really don't agree." Fatima spoke in a low voice. In the sudden silence, all attention shifted to Fatima's tense face. As if the quiet, almost diffident words had been a gunshot, faces that had been animated now registered surprise and confusion.

"What did you say, Fatima?" I felt myself pull back even further, curious and cautious, as startled as the others.

"I really don't agree with you." Fatima was sitting very still, tightly composed. "I believe that Allah has given us a structure and laws to shape our lives together. The death penalty must be carefully administered, but at times it is the right thing to do." I held my breath. Our cherished multifaith community that had been a source of growth, intimate connection, and pride for all of us suddenly felt incredibly fragile. Carol inhaled audibly, winding herself back up into her corner of the couch. Amelia leaned into my chair, her arms now hugging her raised knees. Megan crossed and uncrossed her legs, while Ashita became absorbed in the fringes of her scarf.

"I just assumed that since we agree on so much, we would all agree on this issue as well," Carol broke the silence. "I don't see how it works, you know, executing people who might be innocent. That can't be God's desire."

"No, I don't think that it is," Fatima continued. "There is so much that we do that is not God's will. But if the executed person is innocent or a victim of the structure, then it is God's to judge and to forgive, not ours. And if we condemn another unjustly, then the punishment may also rest in God's hands." As Fatima spoke, her measured and thoughtful words became more assured. For the rest of the hour, we struggled to listen, to clarify, and to understand as best we could while she shared her deep faith in God's justice and human limitations, articulating her belief in the necessity of law that, at times, might feel harsh to us. I was awed by her faith and ability to articulate her theological position. Her clear faith and courage challenged all of us in the room. This was a moment of interfaith dialogue that cut through to the core of an essential difference. What surfaced were very different ideas about the nature of God and the relationship between human society and law and an afterlife.

Conflict is scary for many of us. My throat and gut were tight with the anxiety that surrounded the very real differences that suddenly stood before us. All of the theory about moving beyond tolerance and the wise sayings about learning our most important lessons from failure raced through my head. As I recall those tense moments, I am deeply grateful that I was able to hold back from trying to "smooth it all over," to mend the rift that threatened to tear us apart. The interstitial community hovered on the edge of never becoming. The silence on my part came from the trust that had been nurtured, and it allowed us to move forward into a deep communal experience. Silence, conflict, anxiety, and even fear were held gently and firmly in the interstice because each of us could remain who we were. The spaces between us bonded us even more closely.

"Same time next week." I spoke the words that had become our parting ritual. By now the sky was dark. Uncharacteristically quiet, the group dispersed. I paused to turn off the lamps and push the chairs back into their places, wondering what next week would bring. Questions about next steps and how to trust and encourage the group spun in my head. Who needed care, who needed challenge, what were they capable of without my intervention? I had been lulled into inattention and worried that I had made a critical error.

"So did I ruin it all?" Fatima stood next to me in the dark. Tears glistened in her dark eyes. "I don't think I should come back next week. They won't want me to be part of the group anymore."

"No, no!" The fierceness of my words startled me, loud in the dark room. "What you did took so much courage, and you were wonderfully clear. Fatima, you must come back, we need you, your faith, and your courage to help us see our differences clearly so that we can celebrate our common bonds." I touched her hand, seeking to reinforce my respect for her courage and my care for this tall, beautiful Pakistani woman who had given us the gift of allowing us to travel on what was, for all of us, a difficult spiritual journey.

"I don't know, I just don't know. We'll have to see, but thank you for wanting me to be here." While a moment before I had worried, her question suddenly left me very clear. There was nothing more to be said; all of us would have to wait and see. Fatima and I stood silently, watching the stars come out over the football field.

"Good night, rest well," I said when we parted. I left hopeful that this was not an ending but the real beginning that none of us could have anticipated when we first agreed to listen, to learn, and to share our faith with one another.

Part of my role as facilitator of the interstitial space we'd all created together was simply to hold it, to continue to ask that we not turn away from one another, now that the conflict we'd all feared had emerged. In the context of interstitial living, "holding" can mean holding accountable, holding as an act of comforting, holding in mind, holding a place, holding the center. In this group, I felt that my job was to simply hold the space so that it would anchor each separate member in the storm that threatened to wash us away.

It had taken us a year and a half to get to the place where we could hold onto the trust we'd created, and even then it was so fragile. To this day, I don't know how close Fatima was to walking away or how close I came to letting her go or how near the rest of the women were to saying, "Get out." As it turned out, the shared narrative that emerged during the process of sharing individual stories brought us back together and held us together through several more years. That shining, tension-filled encounter illuminated the contours of the interstitial spirituality that we shared while reminding us that it was actually the space between our lives and our traditions that had given us all so much life and faith.

I know from my own life that when someone with multiple identities, racial or otherwise, experiences repudiation of parts of herself, the result can be brokenness and bitterness. Integrity and identity can only be redeemed through honoring her non-dualistic complexity. In the same way, the religious and spiritual brokenness and bitterness that individuals and communities feel can also be redeemed in honoring the complexity of our individual and collective religious and spiritual landscapes. As more and more persons become aware of their own multiple identities and the fractures that inhibit our ability to see other people in close proximity, we increase our need to develop the capacities to dwell interstitially.

In interstitial space we cannot focus on a single spiritual or personal narrative. When many share a space and each is honored, a shared narrative may arise so that the intuitive awareness of our connection is nurtured into bloom. The intimacy of sharing our personal narratives with each other allowed us to see the co-dependence of our lives, illuminating the connective web of similarities and differences that make us human.

I have found that when one nurtures the interstices, it's not a matter of "hoping" that connections will happen—they *do* happen.

In doing this, we open space to work through emotionally intense conflict peacefully and with goodwill or to hear a call to prayer for the first time as a prayer and not a call to war. These in-between relationships teach us much about what it is to be human, complex, and beautiful in ways that transcend material limits. The spiritual practices of translating, connecting, and holding that we learn here may allow us to move forward into the complexities of the future, from a place of mutual understanding.

PASSPORTS
The Chaplain Moving
across Boundaries

Rev. Dr. Richard E. Spalding
Williams College, Williamstown, Massachusetts

I arrived at Williams to take up my new job as chaplain to the college during the dog days of summer. The campus was almost deserted, and I'd been warned that most of the people I'd find most helpful to my acclimation wouldn't appear until late in the pre-September adrenaline rush. *Well, there'll be time for people soon enough,* I thought, and decided to start out by introducing myself to buildings. So sometime that first morning I walked from my office in the student center over to the chapel to survey some of the landscape I was now responsible for.

The Gothic revival chapel building is an architectural icon on our campus—in spite of the fact that regular Sunday services there were discontinued in the early 1990s, when the last remnant of a congregation had all but evaporated. During my interview several months before, there had been a few appreciative

Rev. Dr. Richard E. Spalding is chaplain to the college at Williams College in Williamstown, Massachusetts. He oversees religious and spiritual life at Williams, especially for students affiliated with underrepresented traditions and students who are exploring spirituality generally. He is an ordained pastor in the Presbyterian Church, (U.S.A.). One of his great joys at Williams is leading a Winter Study course in Nicaragua called Explorations in Solidarity. If you stop at his office on campus, you'll probably also meet his dog, Monty.

murmurs around the search committee table when I wondered out loud about multifaith services and late-night, candlelit meditations. But my revival reveries came to an abrupt halt at the heavy Gothic door. Not only did the key I had just been issued not turn in the lock, but the door sported a sign that said, "DO NOT ENTER."

By the time a week or so later that Aisha invited me to her house for supper and what she described as a chance to meet a few good people she was sure I'd find it helpful to know, I felt about as hungry for introductions as I've ever been for food. Aisha had been a member of the search committee that chose me and she was also director of an administrative office on campus. Indeed, in the absence of still-vacationing faculty and administrators, she seemed to be the only one on campus to have noticed my arrival. Things I'd heard about her hospitality and sumptuous cooking burnished the eagerness with which I looked forward to that evening. "It'll be very informal," she said. At last, I thought: a few key people, and an open door.

When I pulled up in front of her house, both sides of the quiet street were solidly packed with parked cars, and the house was ablaze with sound and light. The front door was indeed open— mostly because the crowd had outgrown the living room and spilled onto the porch. Evidently her dinner party was the annual harbinger of the end of the summer diaspora. Inside, I recognized only one or two of the few people I'd already met in the course of meandering around campus. Finally I spotted Aisha on the far side of several dense knots of conversation. It took a minute or two to thread our ways to a greeting in the midst of the crowd—but she lived up to her reputation for warmth, scooping me up and maneuvering me to a sofa. "Just sit," she said. "I'll bring you a plate." And then, just before she disappeared, with her hand on the shoulder of the distinguished-looking bearded man beside whom I was now sitting, "You need to meet Bert. He's one of our very best people," she said, her eyes sparkling. "Bert, this is our new chaplain. I'll be right back."

Channeling as much as I could of Aisha's bright energy, I reached for the low-hanging conversational fruit: "So what keeps you busy at Williams?"

"I teach statistics," Bert said.

The pause that followed lasted just long enough for a bit of desperation to set in under the murmuring roar of the roomful of people. "Statistics," I finally said, astutely.

"That's right," Bert said, looking down at his plate. Another pause. Then he made eye contact again and said pleasantly, and as deliberately as seemed possible, "I ... hate ... organized religion."

Every now and then I get a new idea of a reply I might have made in that moment: "I ... hate ... numbers," maybe—or, "Thank you for moving our relationship so quickly to this level of intimacy by sharing this important piece of your spiritual journey"—or, "So, you're a Unitarian?"

There are always those who are determined to try to pin you down with pointed assumptions that reduce faith to dogma, or to contain you in the very small box that is all the space they need to embalm a very withered understanding of "organized religion." But despite these experiences of closedness in my first days as a chaplain, over the subsequent years I've come to discover and to practice in my chaplaincy a subversive and delicious litheness of movement.

Far from being stuck, I have an extraordinary privilege of movement across boundaries in realms that are often marked "closed" or that are off the map altogether: areas of people's lives that are off-limits to standard academic processes but of the essence of education; realms of towering questions that don't fit on syllabi; vantage points from which one might even glimpse, fleetingly, a sense of some whole that might possibly encompass all the parts. Chaplaincy can slip through permeable membranes to get to these places and gain swift passage between opposite poles—inside and outside, depth and surface, here and there, now and then. I've found the work to be filled with lessons about a grace of movement that I now see as inherent to this calling: grace, that is, not in the sense of artfulness—the beauty of a dancer, say, or the poise of a diplomat—but grace in the sense of intrinsic blessing, inherent freedom.

None of this, of course, is easy to explain to the people I work for.

Notwithstanding the fact that it was the institution that posted our positions and hired us to fill them, I know I'm not the only member of this guild to have been charged to write my own job description not long after beginning work, because no one else knew how to do it. The days when catastrophe strikes campus—a death, a security threat, a hate crime—remind our colleagues in senior administration why we're here. But on many other days the institutional doors to the spaces in which we're supposed to do our work are hung with mixed messages—or mined with ambivalence, if not with Bert's overt antipathy. And still, every one of the dozens of times in any school year that someone asks, "So, what exactly do you do?" I feel a certain edge to the question—whether it's there or not.

What I do is *keep moving*.

It took a while, of course, to figure out how to apply for the passport that confers this kind of mobility—or, rather, to realize that I'd been carrying it all along in the alloy of conscience, critical reflection, compulsive hopefulness, and a love of stories that are intrinsic to this vocation.

At first I thought that getting unstuck, unpinned, finding an open door must mean getting out, getting away. I watched the almost offhanded way many of the students around me seemed able to cross boundaries back and forth between risk and stability, between the unfamiliar and the familiar, between entrenched pragmatism and flagrant idealism. Sometimes it seems that the mainspring of young adulthood is wound by the paradox of change and resistance to change. That's the same continuum, of course, that our institutions navigate—though at their own lumbering pace, and generally risking far less than students do in the process. I noticed that students are, in general, more agile in transit between continuity and discontinuity, comfort and discomfort, balance and dislocation.

So, I thought: let the chaplaincy follow them.

I decided that one place I could trust to start teaching me chaplaincy was ... Nicaragua.

It was made clear to me when I first arrived at Williams that my appointment to a position in "student services," rather than in an academic department, meant that I should not expect to teach. But it turned out that that locked door swung open annually during our January "Winter Study" period, a midyear punctuation mark between semesters, when a staff member or alumnus can slip across the bright line between "faculty" and "others" with a proposal for a month-long course off-campus. In my pre-Williams life as pastor of a progressive urban parish church, I had had my own boundaries and values rearranged by several visits to a sister parish community in rural Nicaragua. All right then, I thought—there'll be time enough to figure out religious life on campus. Let me begin by introducing students to some of the *campesinos* I've met: the daily rhythms of their lives, their stories and songs, their take on our history and their revolution, their practice of liberation theology, their passionate politics and poetry. Not accidentally, the purpose of the Winter Study course I proposed, a year or so into my job, was just to do what I had mostly been doing anyway as the new chaplain: to listen. When the students started listening to our Nicaraguan hosts, I somehow knew I'd start hearing things I needed to know about accompanying them.

I was not wrong.

A few days after arriving in Nicaragua, with the process of orientation still very much under way among us, we made our way through the chaos of Managua morning traffic to a quiet side street and pulled up in front of a house that leaps out of the block: the wall surrounding the front door was swathed in brightly painted murals. There were vines, flowers, a sunrise, birds, and, in one corner, a grasshopper—a symbol, I'd learned, of blessing and good fortune.

So the entrance was already steeped in irony—because this was the Casa Benjamin Linder, named for a young engineer fresh out of university in the United States who had been inspired to come to revolutionary Nicaragua, like so many others in the 1980s, to offer whatever help he could. In April 1987, he and two young Nicara-guans were killed at the site of a hydroelectric project they were building in a remote village near the Honduran border by a band of counterrevolutionary guerillas who'd been armed and trained by the CIA. Linder and his companions were unarmed and did not resist; they were killed execution-style. The village that (eventually) benefited from the project they were working on had never before had reliable access to electricity.

Ironic, then, in that the grasshopper arrived too late in Ben Linder's life; whatever blessing and peace it might confer came post-humously. The courtyard in this house named in his honor over-flowed with bright murals that showed communities working and living in joyful harmony. There was a grasshopper perched in some corner of nearly every one.

We strolled into this house of peace where, each week, a ragtag col-lection of North Americans still living in Nicaragua offered whatever help they could to what was left of the revolutionary wave, gathering to share news and stories and to hear presentations of different kinds. That week the speaker turned out to be a Honduran man, an activist in exile from his country in the immediate aftermath of a coup d'état the previous year that unseated the democratically elected president. The activist described the political situation: international calls for the reinstatement of the president, turmoil in the lives of ordinary people as their government reeled, and the urgent fear that the United States would intervene militarily or economically before the people of Hon-duras could resolve the struggle for themselves.

When the speaker asked what we from the United States thought about the situation in his country, one student in our group responded. "At Williams," she said, "we have the privilege of educa-tion—but we are so wrapped up in it, so busy with everything we're doing, activities and classes, preparing for our careers, planning to make money, that we don't know what's going on in the world. I'll admit it: I didn't even know about the coup in Honduras."

The activist replied, in a voice both calm and urgent, "And in whose interest do you think it is that you are so occupied in your own life that you don't know what's going on in the small places in the world? Who benefits from a large, apathetic, and uninformed population in the United States?"

After the talk, I made my way over to the student to see how she'd weathered his question. She just repeated his words, and they seemed to land in a deeper place in her each time: In whose interest is it that we're too busy to know what's going on in the world?

As we spoke, in one corner of my field of vision, on the wall behind her, I could see one of the grasshoppers.

LEARNING TO NOTICE WHAT YOU DON'T SEE

A friend in our math department is fond of saying that education comes down to this: learning to notice what you don't see.

As is true on many campuses, most of our students are effectively blinded by the comfortable and familiar bounty of their own college experience. Days are so full of commitments, appointments, errands, and the commerce of friendship that the idea of stopping to look at the stream you're stepping into, contemplating the big picture, seems naive. Time is the drug of choice among our students: it's the stuff you can't get enough of, the compulsion you swear you could get under control if you had to, the craving that can blind you even to the beauty around you that seems to cry out to be noticed. The appetite for time is insatiable, and the habits that emerge from ways of using and abusing it turn out, on occasion, to present a real threat to health and well-being. Recently I heard a student say, "If I keep achieving at this rate, how will I ever have time to think?"

On the face of it, the project of learning to notice what you don't see would seem as absurd as learning to listen to what you can't hear, or remembering the touch of something that you can't reach. But the long view, overlooking a small New England college from the Casa Ben Linder or from the two-room house of a subsistence farmer, is breathtaking. And vulnerability to the unfamiliar is the thing that knocks you off-balance enough to be able to take it in—to get you paying attention.

The first part of the path to that vantage point is well-enough traveled. In recent years, many colleges and universities have been zealously introspective about finally noticing what they were unable or unwilling to see through so much of their history: that not all have been equally welcome at the table of higher education. These days colleges are making significant efforts to correct for the inequities of previously unnoticed privilege—resources, experience, status—that the academy has replicated from its surrounding culture and that students (as well as faculty and staff) bring onto campus with them like a virus.

But a bit farther along, the trail of critical distance gets more challenging. We still resist noticing the privilege conferred upon all of us, regardless of our origins, by virtue of citizenship in an elite private college—privilege that we all carry with us (consciously or unconsciously) wherever we travel beyond its boundaries once we leave, regardless of how much or how little we brought in with us when we came. It's easy to get too occupied with the self-important errands of education to notice what's going on in the small places in the world.

And the path to that wider, riskier view can be further confused by the overgrowth of affection in which colleges like Williams are held by a great many of their alumni. The breadth and depth of the gratitude that many students feel for their college is palpable even on the shortest visit to campus. I'm told it's one of the first and most obvious things prospective students have their antennae up for when they take the campus tour. How can the work of learning to notice what we don't see be advanced in an environment that is already so self-conscious on the one hand and so self-satisfied on the other? How shall we learn to listen to something that is so hard for us to hear?

It turns out that, of all things, this is a religious problem—in a sense of that word that doesn't have anything to do with neo-Gothic doors, locked or unlocked. The intentional cultivation of humility in the encounter with a whole that is greater than the sum of known parts is, in itself, a spiritual discipline. The decision to embark toward a wider truth that integrates even as it unsettles matches the paradigms of both young adulthood and pilgrimage. The companionship of a guide for whom the way of the journey is both familiar and also profoundly mysterious is intrinsic to pastoral and prophetic ministry. And the effort to remember the experience of the touch of that which we cannot reach is the essence of mysticism.

It may not be that every undergraduate needs to leave campus to climb up to some literal vista overlooking the limitations that are inherent even in the bounty of education—or that every chaplain needs to dust off his or her actual passport in order to start crossing boundaries in search of a vantage point from which to point out things we seldom see. But there is no substitute for the most literal journey to stand outside the nurture of the institution. The issues and struggles that await beyond familiar academic routines may have made an appearance back in the classroom, just long enough to be discussed. But stepping out into them in ways that call the nature of education into question is uncomfortable, sometimes counterintuitive. Paying attention—after all, one of the dearest forms of contemporary currency we have—is a form of travel for which a passport may be required.

And, of course, it's a journey I need to take myself, even as I accompany others. In whose interest is it that I spend my days caring for the spiritual well-being of some of the world's most privileged young adults?

THE RADICAL POWER OF ENCOUNTER

Over the course of that first year, as I slowly unpacked my books and sorted them onto the shelves of my new office, a bumper sticker surfaced in one of the boxes—an artifact from a faith-based community organizing campaign in which the urban church I'd previously served had been involved. It said:

> The most radical thing we can do is to introduce people
> to each other.

I tossed it aside as a relic of a closed vocational chapter.

But then, as those first months passed, that little vessel of words began to seem more portable and more refreshing. And when I got back from Nicaragua, it burst into song; I gave it a place of honor on the coffee table where everyone who comes into the office can see it.

Stuck as I had been in those first weeks, it had been a relief to find a role for myself as chaplain in inviting students to move with me across boundaries. In my excitement, I had taken this literally at first. But now, as I settled into the job, I came to realize that I didn't need to leave campus in order to stop running into walls or feeling pinned down; I just had to keep crossing boundaries. As I started to think about the walls and divides between people, even within our comfortable liberal arts context, more possibilities for my role opened up.

Now I recognize the words on the bumper sticker as an indelible mark in the passport of my chaplaincy. It helped me realize the radical power of helping people move out of their own social groups into encounter with others. It helped me see that part of my job is to gently pull circles apart to open them up, to recombine them. Every year brings many opportunities to wield that bumper-sticker line as an instrument of my work: a prod for nudging students to take risks, a lens for noticing connections, a template for thinking about the difference relationships make.

And actually, I find the words oddly comforting. They've been a kind of visa for passage from the relative clarity of pastoral ministry in a parish into the relative ambiguity of chaplaincy on a pluralistic, secular campus—authorizing movement between realms. When I urge students to expect to feel most awake to the unfolding meaning of their own lives as they extend themselves to greet the unfamiliar, the words remind me that I, too, should expect the perennial clumsiness of introductions, re-beginnings, rediscovery of the nature of this work.

The essential meaning of "radical," of course, is "of the root"—and with the help of this bumper-sticker mantra and ten years of relationships with students and faculty, I'm learning that what I'm about is awakening or uncovering an elusive but palpable sense of things going on in the depths. It's about access to what's going on below the radar, down at the place where our overlapping experiences of humanity and, perhaps, divinity are less about maps and more about intimations, less about evidence and more about faith. As a Christian whose chosen ministry, now, is to celebrate the nobility of all of the world's religious families, even while standing firmly rooted in my own, I'm publicly committed to the proposition that encounters with the stranger whose roots tap a different creed or sensibility are always potentially sacramental.

Though I work at an institution whose cost, resources, reputation, and clout help put the "high" in higher education, it turns out that the task here is deeper education. One of the most faithful acts of chaplaincy I can perform is to open the way to encounters that draw on roots far below the surface on which we pass so much of our lives. At college, there are always people to introduce to each other.

But we live, as President Barack Obama has observed, in a time when, for whatever reasons, we human beings seem to be suffering from "a diminished capacity to see ourselves in one another." So many of the debates that presently swirl so angrily around us are fueled by that diminishment. Every human life, of course, is brimming with narratives of things that have happened—fears, journeys, images, sorrows, symbols. The infinite importance and value of those narratives would seem obvious. But, in a world greatly diminished by our inability to recognize ourselves in each other, no one can take for granted that anyone else will understand the things that have happened to her, to him.

T. H. White's wonderful novel about the young King Arthur, *The Once and Future King*, includes a memorable bit of wisdom with which Merlin the magician tries to buck up the young Arthur, who is locked in the depths of a kind of dark night of the soul. Merlin says:

> The best thing for being sad is to learn something. That is the only thing that never fails. You may grow old and trembling in your anatomies. You may lie awake at night listening to the disorder of your veins. You may miss your only love. You may see the world around you

devastated by evil lunatics or know your honor trampled in the sewers of baser minds. There is only one thing for it, then: to learn. Learn why the world wags and what wags it. That is the only thing which the mind can never exhaust, never alienate, never be tortured by, never fear or distrust, and never dream of regretting. Learning is the thing for you.[1]

If we were to take such counsel to heart in the midst of this storm of civic anger and the despair or detachment it can incite in us—what might such a project of learning look like? How would this world be different if we asked each other, across every line we've ever thought to draw between ourselves and another, to tell about the things that have happened?

Several years ago a handful of students came into the chaplains' office with an idea. It was not long after one of those hateful, probably alcohol-soaked episodes of graffiti appearing nocturnally on somebody's bathroom wall. It occurred to them, the students said, that the stories that all of us are carrying around with us have the power to redirect our efforts to be a community, if only there could be an opportunity for those stories to break the surface of our life together. So they invented what we now call StoryTime.

Every Sunday night at nine o'clock, people gather by the fireplace upstairs in the student center to hear someone simply tell a half-hour-long handful of their story—with as much honesty as they can, going as deep as they care to, and without any fear of judgment or embarrassed self-consciousness. With some gentle coaching during the preceding week from one of the student organizers, the story someone finds to tell is usually a scrap of the narrative of their lives that they haven't often or ever told before: not necessarily a deep-dark secret, just an episode or a narrative strand that comes from a different place—often a more vulnerable place—than most of the incoming calls that crowd the air of our social cohabitation. The first Sunday night there were about a dozen people there; a week or two later there were a hundred; by now we've lost count. The transformation that the hearing of these stories enables, of course, happens too slowly to be visible to the naked eye; the effect is less like a wave of Merlin's magic wand and more like the splashing of waves on a solid rock at the edge of a great sea. But it's one of the single most powerful instruments of education to find its way into our hands in a long time.

And, interestingly, along the way it has unlocked a door into an unlabeled but unmistakable sanctuary. In the mounting anticipation as we gather each Sunday night, I sometimes think about the "secret passage" in the board game "Clue" that enables a player to jump the longest diagonal distance on the board from the kitchen to the conservatory in just one move. Suddenly, just because collectively we want to, in the twinkling of an eye we cross the boundary between ordinary time and holy ground. Rituals apply: the steering group who selected and coached that week's storyteller passes around a bowl of his or her favorite cookies, then rings a singing bowl to set the time apart and usher in the silence from which the story will emerge. While the story is being told, a thank-you card circulates among the listeners—draped all over the lounge furniture and each other—to gather whatever gratitude all that authenticity might provoke.

As chaplain, I participate week by week and year by year in a number of events that would seem to have a better claim to the label "religious" than StoryTime: weekly vespers, text studies, events that need invocations and benedictions, encounters of interfaith dialogue. But, all sectarianism aside, few if any of them feel as close to the marrow of my vocation in the secular academy as StoryTime. Week by week, the study of the sacred texts of students' lives at StoryTime scatters at least as many clues to the great mystery as most Bible studies I've ever facilitated.

The word "religion," of course, stands as a name for much of what so many students want to protect themselves from. Many of them, like Bert the statistics professor, think that once it gets "organized," it serves only to compromise or manipulate their spiritual explorations—as though the imposition of any cogent framework or common history would limit their movement or constrain their freedom to meet what is waiting at the outer edge of the familiar. They notice the barbs and toughness that religion grows in a climate of moralizing, dogmatism, and breaches of trust, and they steer clear.

But the roots of the word, well below the surface of this arid condition, are full of a different kind of life. *Religare* signifies reconnection: the tying back together of things that have come apart—the intimation of a whole that is greater than the fragmentary pieces of experience, the splintered community, the partial insight. To notice what we don't see about religion would be to allow ourselves to be led out into relationship to the great mystery on whose threshold students are fascinated to encamp.

Those Sunday nights are tying us back together, one story at a time. They've become almost a template for other constructive ideas and events: these days, about all we have to say to each other is "it might do for us the kind of thing that StoryTime does ..." and another journey across another frontier is in the offing.

AN OPEN DOOR

It's been true since my first days at Williams that at night in the bustling student center, it only takes turning the office light on and leaving the door ajar to bring some compelling story or other to roost in my office. There was an autumn night during my second year, though, that almost cured me of the habit forever.

Often those conversations begin with a disclaimer of sorts from the student visitor: "Can I talk to you even if it's not about religion?" But this time, the topic was overtly sectarian. She introduced herself, sat down in the conversational chair, and fired her question at point-blank range: What does the Bible have to say about homosexuality? At that point, of course, the conversation could have taken any of several trajectories; to find out where this one would be headed, I asked what was making her wonder about that. She let me know that she was actually well acquainted with the Bible's teachings on the subject—she had verses and an interpretive précis to prove it—and that what she was wondering about, in fact, was how I could profess to be a Christian minister and to serve as chaplain of this college despite my being gay.

It wasn't the first time, or the last, that I'd fielded that question or had it land on such a sharp edge. But some combination of factors—the time of year, probably, and the invisible presence of family, certainly—turned this query into a disputation. None of my deft evocations of the wide interpretive spectrum available to any serious reader of the Bible succeeded in broadening the focus or softening the urgency: she was angry, and her desire that I account for myself began to burn.

Pushed, I pushed back: Did she see any role for interpretation when engaging with scripture? Did she feel called by her education to find a way to exercise both faithfulness and intellectual responsibility in relationship to these texts? Did she consider all the things we've learned about ourselves and the world in the centuries since the texts were written? The temperature in the room rose. Before long, she left. It might be appropriate to say that she stormed out, except that she left the storm behind: I went home to a mostly sleepless night, wishing I hadn't pushed so hard, hadn't let her tone color mine—and wondering how indeed a gay man can serve as a chaplain to a community that includes some who see his sense of ministry as an offensive oxymoron.

It was one of those conversations that one doesn't forget. In fact, the memory of it helped me achieve a more satisfying alloy of both gentleness and conviction in similar conversations I had with other students over the next several years—even while it contributed to my heart-heaviness about how steep and high the mountain is that has to be climbed before we who disagree about these things will ever find our way to reconnection.

And then one evening, a couple of years later, there she was again at the open door. In the intervening years I'd barely glimpsed her, but now here she was, seeking me out. But even before she spoke, I could see that something was different. She apologized for having been so hostile years before. She said she'd been thinking about that conversation a lot. And she told me that she was gay.

Generally speaking, the word that names what happens in the college classroom is "discussion." But there's trouble brewing in the root of the word. The Latin *discutere* means to dash or shake to pieces, agitate, disperse, dispel; it suggests some kind of productive collision.

That, I suppose, is what happened with this student that first night in my office—it was a mode of interaction for which we were both academically conditioned.

We could wish it had been a bit less concussive and a bit more reflective, from *reflectere*, to (re-)bend, (re-)direct. To reflect is to return to text or evidence or experience, to retell a story in order to reconsider its meanings. The stories of which we're custodians, like the journeys we accompany and the often unnoticed things we struggle to see, are subject to both discussion and reflection. I hope that the chaplaincy is helping students, as it is helping me, to discover more freedom of movement between those two modes of exploration than we had imagined.

PROFESSIONAL AMATEUR

In the context of the academy, the word "amateur" is freighted with unfortunate comparative overtones—as though it denoted the opposite of expertise, the absence of serious purpose, the equivalent of dilettantism. Actually it's a word that has a great deal to contribute to an understanding of the liberal arts—where disciplines are meant to be tried on, not only because they may harbor intimations of vocation, but also because the disciplines in themselves are intellectual enticements and because energetic encounters with them are playful in the best sense of the word. If the liberal arts have done their work, the history major who eventually goes on to law school and becomes a practicing attorney will always be something of an amateur historian—one who, at a key formative moment, came to love the rigors and habits, the tools and lenses of the field.

As students come to love the disciplines and to develop some preliminary grace in wielding them, their principal models are thoroughly credentialed experts. The guidance that these experts offer, the knowledge to which they enable access, the skills they demonstrate, are essential to learning and growth.

But I have come to understand that there is a role in that developmental trajectory, too, for the companionship of the amateur. The conventional view of the adult companion as supervisor, chaperone, or safeguard is only a shadow of the real power and educative value of the role of co-witness. By choosing to return to a vantage point that explodes a familiar worldview, to an experience that overwhelms the mind or breaks the heart, the one who accompanies exercises a particularly vital form of the ministry of presence.

When I served as a parish pastor, choosing to be with someone who was reeling in the fresh spiritual trauma of grief or tragedy often felt like a way of encamping with them, keeping watch at the unfathomable synapse between life and death. Now, as a chaplain, I recognize the analogue experience: at the moments when experience humbles, when long-estranged truths are reconnected, when the mist lifts briefly to open a vista on the whole, I hope my presence bespeaks a willingness to return to the threshold of the great mystery, to join in the vigil of pondering meaning that is always in progress there.

Using my passport to return again and again to that liminal place between worldviews, sharing fully in the experience and weathering all of its demands out of something like love, I've come to see the chaplain as a kind of professional amateur—one who models the habits and disciplines of listening and reflection on the near side of expertise. In the role of companion, the chaplain models ways of giving and receiving hospitality, observing respectfully, taking to heart the struggles and the suffering of others, and even contemplating the possibility of being complicit in them. The chaplain becomes an outward and visible sign that the experience of having one's perspective upended, one's mind overwhelmed, and one's heart broken, is survivable—and, even more, that in the long view of learning, it is desirable and even fruitful to re-experience vulnerability.

Passport at the ready, the chaplain can pass with impunity between tenacity of mind and tenderness of heart—between the realm of whatever professional wisdom or skill he or she may have accumulated and the role of amateur human being, permanent student of the mysteries. Even where expertise falls short and knowledge is not yet sufficient, there is value in simply abiding at the place of deepest vulnerability, to model being moved by suffering and the shared desire to do something to ease or to end it once and for all—even when all the experts in the world have so far failed to demonstrate what that something is.

Whether the companionship provided to these journeys by chaplaincy qualifies as "organized" may depend on the eye of the beholder. Most of the best work I do transpires below the sectarian or dogmatic radar, down at the root place where intimations of common humanity are interwoven among the taproots of insistent questions—questions that may not be fully encompassed by the curriculum but that are essential to the growing that's in progress up above the surface.

But, "organized" or not, I venture to hope that the companionship can qualify as religious—which is to say, that it is outwardly and visibly about remaking connections, revisiting revelations, re-noticing things the seeing of which widens the view of both the college and the world, reintroducing people to each other at the outer edge of the familiar. The ability to pass back and forth across boundaries and among realms of experience is the most essential credential of this work. And, even in the absence of some simple declarative sentence that pins the job down or that parries Bert-the-statistician's antipathy, I hope it is about exploiting as flagrantly as possible the freedom of movement that the role confers—between inside and outside, between depth and surface, between here and there, between full and empty, between sacred and secular.

I hope all that movement has left some tracks across the institution. I know it has left its marks on me.

The summer that I came to Williams—the same summer of the locked chapel door, my encounter with Bert the statistics professor, and the bumper sticker in the packing box—a friend gave me a scrap of poetry as a gift to see me across the threshold. It promises a visit of angels, not to those who plead for their company, but to those who know themselves to be novices, amateurs, beginners. Every summer since, I've included this little vessel of words in the letter I send to each incoming first-year student, hoping that it might help them name and embrace the work that lies just ahead of them: to be a "beginner" in the most flagrant, exhaustive, playful senses of that word. I walk out on faith, a bit, to promise them that they're very likely to be met along the way by many angels incognito (remembering that in Hebrew and Greek the root meaning of the word for angel is, simply, "messenger"), bearing messages of challenge, possibility, solidarity. I'm thinking, of course, of the Honduran activist, the storyteller on any particular Sunday night ... and also of their professors (including Bert), and perhaps their first true loves, and certainly the friends with whom they'll burn countless hours of midnight oil keeping vigil at the synapse between the known and the unknown—anyone they'll meet who'll profess the integration of conviction and action. Many of them will find that their keys don't fit, either, in the ponderous doors of our chapel or other outcroppings of organized religion. But almost every one of them will be seeking sanctuary of some kind, at some point. And there is no reason why they should have to seek it alone.

So each summer now, in the pre-September adrenaline rush, I get ready to re-begin my own journey with them: to re-cross the boundaries between here and the beginning—to re-notice the blessing and the blindness that their years of sojourning in this rarefied place will confer on them—to re-love the sheer audacity of the project of holding learning and believing together. I recognize myself as one who, knowing how essential freedom of movement among the realms is to the spiritual journey of deep learning, tries to be in the right place at the right time to just stand there, at the boundary, and help them cross. I brace myself for the awkwardness of being reintroduced to strangers I have somehow always known yet never known— rejoining a conversation that has been in progress since the world began. And I remember again the sublime touch of that which I, too, cannot reach.

RELIGIOUS HYBRIDS
A New Interpretation

Rev. K. P. Hong
Macalester College, Saint Paul, MN

*Z*en master Wuzu once asked a monk, "Ch'ien and her soul are separated. *Which one is the true Ch'ien?" Which is the true person, what is our true self?*

Wuzu raises an old Chinese folk story to make his case. Once, in a provincial town on a great river, there was a father who loved his daughter Ch'ien dearly. He told her how beautiful she was and that her beauty was very like that of her distant cousin, a boy named Chou. Ch'ien and Chou played together throughout their childhood and fell deeply in love. But to their dismay, Ch'ien's father told his daughter when she became old enough to marry that he had already chosen a husband for her.

On the night before the wedding was to take place, unable to stay and see his beloved be married off to someone else, Chou stepped into a boat to leave forever. He began making his way up the river when he noticed someone running along the shore, calling after him. It was Ch'ien, tear stained and unwavering in her love. Together they traveled to a distant province where they married and happily started a family.

But Ch'ien could not forget her father. As a mother herself, now knowing what it was to love a child, she imagined his anguish. She said to Chou, "I

Rev. K. P. Hong has served as a chaplain for religious and spiritual life at Macalester College, Saint Paul, Minnesota. He has also held pastorates in Asian-American and multiethnic congregations in the United Methodist Church. Rooted also in Buddhist practice, he is especially interested in interreligious work in the increasingly relational context of world religions.

long to go back to my village and see my father and beg his forgiveness." He
replied, "I also feel that way. Let us go." They got into a boat again and went
back down the river. When they reached the village at night, Ch'ien stayed in
the boat while Chou went first to her father. Chou bowed low and begged for-
giveness for having run off with Ch'ien. But the old man listened with incre-
dulity on his face. "What? Who are you talking about? Ch'ien is lying in bed.
She's been sick all these years, and we haven't known what's wrong. She's
been lying there like a shadow of herself. She hasn't spoken since you left."

"But she followed me that night," Chou said, "and we've been married,
and have two children. She's returned now to ask for your forgiveness." Chou
rushed to the boat to bring Ch'ien to the house, even as the father went to tell
his sick daughter of all this. Still not speaking, she got up out of bed and
walked out of the house. Ch'ien rushed from the boat, and Ch'ien walked
from the house. Two lives, two stories, came together and at last embraced.
"I never realized that I was at home all this time," said Ch'ien. "I saw Chou
leaving and I dreamt that I ran after his boat. But which one was I? The one
who went away or the one who stayed at home? And who am I now?"[1]

My perceptions about chaplaincy reverberate with Chi'en's story:
the themes of leaving home, transgression, displacement, and living
between stories. At the edges where plots soften and blur, characters
dissolve into larger fluid themes and imagination expands in search
of greater mythologies. And at the edges, in between stories, anomalous strands wait in the shadows. Try as we might to fit them into
available stories, they will not be interwoven and may even threaten
to unravel entire canonical narratives.

Some of us would like to organize words and stories into single-
stranded, bright, linear forms, with each word and thought marching
according to prescribed, orderly sequences. No collisions, no blur-
ring of boundaries, no shadows and ghosts. But without shadows,
there is no fecundity, growth, or life. Only with shades of light and
dark can meaning be sculpted and depth given to two-dimensional
realities. Only with darkness can there be any sense of illumina-
tion—revealing who we are even as it concedes to the mystery of love
that separates us in one way and unites us in another way.

When my father cautioned us as children that we were "honoring" our Korean ancestors strictly according to Christian memorial, and never to mention at church "worshipping" our ancestors, he gave voice to the shadows of idolatry, syncretism, and heresy in the unavoidable comingling of his Protestant Christian faith with his Korean Buddhist, shamanistic, and Confucian ancestry. In my remembered or imagined past, I hold a memory of my family gathered around old family photographs, bowing to our ancestors and listening to stories that illumined with their dark intensity the shape of things to come. It is a memory of something that belongs to many worlds and differing stories, a memory that blurs and questions the boundaries we keep and the anomalous strands that bide their time in the shadowy folds of a richly interwoven religious journey.

Looking back on his own spiritual journey, Father Raimundo Panikkar once famously wrote: "I left Europe [for India] as a Christian, I discovered I was a Hindu and returned as a Buddhist without ever having ceased to be Christian."[2] Needless to say, his multiple belonging and the consequent irresolvable tension he maintained throughout his life speak to both an enormous existential risk and the depth of his intellectual work, without which such multiple belonging runs the risk of being a shallow, fashionable pastiche. If such religious hybridity is to be credible, without violating the unique identities of religions by syncretism and indistinct synthesis, it must reach for a symbiosis of "cross-fertilization and mutual fecundation"[3] through which new forms of religiousness can emerge creatively and dynamically, offering coherent worldviews, however provisional they may be.

Similarly, for theologian Paul Knitter, the only way to be religious is to be interreligiously religious. He asks at the conclusion of his spiritual retrospective on being a Christian who takes seriously the Buddhist path—*Without Buddha I Could Not Be a Christian*—"Is what I've been trying to do in this book a kind of religious promiscuity?"[4]

Is multiple religious identity or belonging about hybridity or promiscuity? Is it a form of cheating that dilutes and corrupts religious commitments, or is it an acknowledgment of an intrinsic plurality to religious identity, providing fecundity and growth? Knitter writes, "So if we take the etymological meaning of 'promiscuity'—the inclination to 'mix it up,' from the Latin *miscere*—we can say, with a dangerous stretch of words, that not only are we all promiscuous; we *have to be!*"[5] For Knitter, Buddhist practice is not auxiliary to his Christian spirituality nor merely a hermeneutical resource for Christian theology. He is Christian only by also being Buddhist.

OUR SHIFTING IDENTITIES

However clichéd it may be to speak of living in a world of flux—where mobility, experimentation, and transgression beyond given structures have turned into core motifs of postmodern lifestyles—religious identity is inevitably a promiscuous, selective reconstruction from an array of possibilities that work to provide meaning and purpose. Appreciation for such promiscuity anchors the broad range of perspectives through which I can understand my own hybrid religious-spiritual experience of being Christian and Buddhist, and moreover within a Korean-American context. Those perspectives—ranging from the personal, remembered, and imagined to critical theories about cultural exchange, colonialism, and interreligious dialogue—each activate their own multitude of distinct frames of reference and clusters of ideas and emotions.

But has not religious practice always been hybrid and religious identity increasingly plural, nomadic, and ambivalent in the postmodern world? Do religions have consistently shared centers of understanding, or rest on unchanging foundations? Is there an exact or exclusive criterion by which Buddhists or Confucianists can be identified? Are not the criteria themselves constantly in flux and undergoing transformation? Do not the sectarian divisions among Buddhists and Christians, and the contradictions and polarizations that bespeak differing visions and paths *within* each religion, let alone without, raise the question of who has the right to question the status of belonging?

Religious identity seems inevitably a *selective* reconstruction from the array of possibilities that work to provide meaning and purpose.

Calling oneself a Christian, or a Buddhist, means that one has selectively appropriated aspects of a vast array of practices and beliefs that have been identified by those who came before as "Christian" or "Buddhist."

Outside of religious identity, we also must take into account the profound challenges to a conception of self that historically formed the horizon of our thought: the self as coherent, bounded, individualized, author of its own actions, beneficiary of a unique biography. We have considered our life meaningful to the extent we could discover our self, be our self, express our self, and step into a larger sociality that honored this regulative ideal of self. But now, far from being a rarefied academic exercise or simple shift in cultural fashion, postmodernism has forever altered the terms by which authority, knowledge, selfhood, and reality are conceived. With more young adults growing up in interfaith households, and many of them likely to change their religious affiliations, being alert to the ways our students are experimenting with dual or multiple religious belonging on an unprecedented scale remains a lively question and challenge for college chaplaincy.

Rather than focusing on the validity of multiple religious belonging, or mapping models of interreligious dialogue, I will seek to register the value of hybrid identities encountered in college chaplaincy. This chapter is thematic, analytic, and illustrative rather than comprehensive, primarily inquiring into the virtue of exploring religious hybridity as critical for our diagnostic understanding of the spiritual and religious challenges of our times. But given the contemporary situation of religious pluralism and the hybridized character of religious and spiritual identities ever more familiar on our campuses, the need to make multiple religious belonging spiritually fruitful is more urgent than ever before.

RETHINKING HYBRIDITY

We all recognize students like "Sarah" (a composite portrait drawn from the cultural mosaic of modern life), who practices Zen meditation intermittently, watches public television on yoga and nutrition, and through her academic work in translating Arabic texts has become increasingly interested in Sufism. At home, she is mostly vegetarian, and on Sunday mornings she attends the local Episcopal church. Sarah's family tree reveals generations of notable Presbyterian elders, with intriguing connections to philanthropic work in Jerusalem. She has never joined a Buddhist sangha but plans to visit Dharamsala while studying abroad in India. Doubtless, she has certain nodes of identity like name, gender, age, hometown, and significant relationships to anchor herself in an ever-unfolding process of making meaning. These are the elements of stories that she lives in, as fish live in water. But given an ever-multiplying array of global resources from which to enact hybridity, and aggravated by the postmodern suspicion of historical precedents that can authoritatively address her, is she free to explore and choose new narratives unhindered by self-limiting stories—or is she abandoned to the task of inventing herself without possessing the actual means to do so? However much the idea is discounted by those skeptical of the vagaries of spiritual consumerism, religious hybridity may serve as strategic repertoire and practice of symbolic resources, available to be mobilized in response to sociopolitical challenges, cultural dislocation, and existential uncertainty.

Postmodernity's penchant for difference, multiplicity, and suspicion of metanarratives and other totalizing absolutes is patently clear today. Hybridity has become fashionable, especially in cultural and postcolonial studies, moving beyond the duality of hyphenated identities to capture the more dynamic multiplicities of culture, ethnicity, gender, class, and more, especially for diasporic populations. "Hybridity," however, remains an elastic and disputed term, with its analytic value routinely questioned and its many tonalities registering the complex human response to sociocultural change. To what extent does hybridity point to the impurity of mixings occasioned by the dissolution of political, cultural, geographic, gender, religious, and aesthetic boundaries? Is it simply a celebration of naive multiplicity rooted in excessive individualism, unbridled consumerism (spiritual or otherwise), and loss of the collective memory that characterized modernity, with little regard to their truth values and mutual compatibilities? Is it a prevalent form of "believing without belonging" as public religion is privatized into countless forms of personalized spiritualities?

Students like Sarah are confronting a new condition of subjectivity, exposed to the full force of a requirement to authentically "be oneself" without recourse to a "credible collective enunciator."[6] If this is the case, then it becomes clear that such students would be easy targets for powerful mechanisms like the consumer market that offer options to satisfy immediate needs whatever their truth value or coherent meaning. Such students, uprooted and abandoned in the postmodern shift, would be open to recruitment by diverse and contradictory causes and social movements. And in particular, when the interconnectedness of the world, with the rise of cloud services and social networks, continues to reorganize and reconstitute everyday lived experience, the import-export and displacement of larger cultural narratives, values, and practices itself has become a new cultural value. Technology, particularly information technology, no longer remains merely an aspect of culture but has itself become a culture that registers not only *that* we are interdependent but structures *how* we are interdependent—and at profound levels of complexity and pace—without careful reflection upon the secondary effects of ambivalence and unease.

But what if religious hybridity is not simply a matter of technology, modern consumer choice, and the conceptual untidiness of syncretism, but of complex identities within boundaries that have always been inherently slippery? The combining of beliefs and practices from multiple religious traditions—crossings between "isms"—can be seen in the impact of Shinto on Japanese Buddhism, of shamanistic and Confucian practices upon Korean Christianity, of Santeria on Cuban Catholicism, or of keeping kosher while on a *sesshin* meditation retreat. There is hybridity all the way down. From "night-stand Buddhists" with their copies of *Tricycle: The Buddhist Review* to environmentally conscious students dancing with pagan druids, self-identity (religious or otherwise) has always been a plural and shifting hybridity of worldviews. In its most generative usage, "hybridity" emphasizes identity not simply as the fusion or collection of disparate pieces but a dynamic field of differing forces that re-invent, re-imagine, retell, and reframe in an ongoing reiteration of identity.

Proponents of religious hybridity point to multiple-religious cultures like China, where Confucianism, Buddhism, and Taoism have lived side by side for thousands of years without being considered mutually exclusive, but each having specialized functions responding to different needs and circumstances in a person's life—a sort of division of labor: you don't look to Buddhism for reflection on political and social structures, and you don't look to Confucianism for an understanding of rebirth. Rather, you might see Confucianism dressing mourners at a funeral, Buddhist chants helping the departed reach the Western Paradise, shamans exorcising evil spirits who might harm the departed on their journey, and Taoist geomancers supervising the digging of the grave. Within my own Korean immigrant community, there is a saying that one is "Christian in the head, Shamanist in the belly, Buddhist in the heart." Each tradition offers something different and valuable to the greater mutuality. And double religious belonging seemed a common form of life of the earliest Christians as is evidenced in the Book of Acts. They maintained both their profound newfound faith in the risen Christ and their inherited Jewish beliefs and practices: "They went to the temple area together every day, while in their homes they broke bread" (Acts 2:46).

Such hybridized religious identities have served as catalysts for questioning orthodoxy and launching reforms throughout the history of religions. And in the rapidly changing landscape of American religious life, of plurality heightened by postmodernity and globalization, hybridized identities are progressively common among students today. To ignore those who identify with hybrid traditions would be to ignore an increasing population of students actively interested in and engaged with religious and spiritual life on campus. They are expressing their dissatisfaction with existing religious models. They may know just enough about Buddhism or Quakerism to know that it does not have the congenital defects of their own religious traditions, although they do not know enough to see that these other traditions have their own defects. Embracing a hybridized religious identity becomes a way for students to express and project their hopes for a better global religion for the twenty-first century.

Hybridity may hold the very possibility for collaboration, re-imagination, and healing from across religious traditions that is necessary for our time. Admittedly, the practice of religious hybridity reflects a measure of spiritual consumerism—often quite savvy consumerism—amidst an unprecedented availability of spiritual options and a postmodern penchant for self-stylization and self-celebration. In the popular culture where "enlightenment" rolls off our lips as easily as *café latte* and we run from weekend retreats to popular guru to the next esoteric spiritual experience, spirituality is a commodity, bought and sold, an elective identity, a club to belong to, and in high demand.

Such consumerism itself may be symptomatic of the postmodern existential insecurity of attempting to live meaningfully in a Western, capitalist, and psychologically wounded culture. Hybridity may be a register not only of the sociocultural shifts taking place but, more deeply, a register of the existential challenges facing the uncertain epistemological status of the self and our cognitive grasp of the world. From what may appear at first as a loose and precarious assemblage of odds and ends, dissimilar forms and practices, careful stitching and darning (particularly applied to worn spots) come together to reveal a patched identity that offers stabilizing meaning and function. Far from some clear and unimpeded alignment of disparate traditions, there is intrinsic tension between hybridity's challenge to fixed categories and its simultaneous reliance upon those stable classifications, a creative tension that serves to assimilate as well as to disrupt the logic of the larger context, through strategic alignments with and against religious belongings. This tension proves strategic and indispensable for survival and continuity, offering hybrids a wider horizon of maneuverability and agency, which is needed within their social environments.

Rather than either offering glosses about hybridity as a slippery slide into untenable identities or valorizing a generalized hybrid condition, college chaplains and religious professionals can recognize that not all hybrids are equal and so focus diagnostically on the particular appropriation of religious identities by students. What accounts for students who are Jewish-Buddhist or Pagan-Hindu? What accounts for the heightened interest in meditation and Eastern spiritualities? Constructions of religious-spiritual identity for students may reveal insights into how and to what ends cultural-religious discourses are being strategically used to destabilize particular identities that constrain them, while reshaping other identities that offer greater agency, self-authorship, and authenticity grounded in sacred, transcendent narratives. Such diagnostic proficiency seems only increasingly *de rigueur* for modern chaplaincy in order to help students be more clear and articulate about maneuvering among multiple religious identities.

Such maneuverability in college students—traversing identities, orientations, traditions, and other boundaries—carries echoes of and may be illuminated by a nomadic trope. Like nomadic cultures, for whom movement is not about romantic excursions but is a necessity for survival, hybridity requires the capacity to be ecologically attuned to changing terrain and available resources, recognizing unique spaces and/or creating new spaces. Far from wandering aimlessly or traveling with a fixed destination in mind, nomads and hybrids exist on thresholds between existing orders. Mobility, adaptability, the ability to interpret signs, and the capacity to recreate home in new places, remain vital skills and resources that continually redraft nomadic cartographies. For nomadism is not fluidity without borders but an awareness of the non-fixity of the borders themselves.

Even as nomadic peoples depend upon larger, sedentary cultures, so too do sedentary cultures rely upon marginal cultures to give shape to fluid identities, revivify practices, and offer redrafted cartographies for emerging truths. Hybridity offers a liminality in which learning from the other and allowing our own convictions to be made fruitful through the insights of the other can provide vital transformation. Our identities, both in their origins and in their ongoing life, take shape and flourish only through mixing them up with others. For Knitter, "hybrids are stronger, live longer, and have more fun than purebreds."[7]

But perhaps this is overstating the case of college students and the presumption of their strategic use of hybridity. However much hybridity may intend to democratize the spiritual playing field or disavow privileged religions (namely Christian), an uncritical valorizing, even romanticizing, of nomadic lifestyles remains much in vogue in Western literature and consciousness. If anything, in the postmodern collapse of enduring truths and stable identities, religious hybridity may be less a strategy than an indiscriminate reach for anything to substantiate the self in the face of its gnawing sense of lack and disorientation. Whether following *A Course in Miracles* or buying into the participation mystique of guru worship—readily available in the contemporary pick-and-mix spiritual marketplace—the prevalence of a "self-spirituality" cannot be disputed. Even more seriously, hybridity may serve as a cover for the nihilistic argument that social categories of difference do not ultimately matter at all. There is only the postmodern "economy of differences"—an endlessly fleeting play of differences, with only traces of traces of difference that finally are of immaterial consequence—from which any identity or truth claim remains a limited, particular construct, continually vulnerable to erasure and deconstruction. Whatever the intended effect, hybrid identities draw our attention to a wider postmodern malaise, diagnostically indicating collective suffering in our compulsive attempts to ground ourselves and to make ourselves feel more real in the world.

THE POSTMODERN SELF: FROM IDENTITY TO SUBJECTIVITY

During a spring break retreat on Whidbey Island, on the northern boundary of Puget Sound, thirteen college seniors wrestled for a deeper integration and understanding of their undergraduate experience. They refused to accept an increasingly compartmentalized world where they often resolved the cognitive dissonance among multiple worldviews and commitments by ignoring them and were especially frustrated with academia, where the continuous expansion of knowledge discourages attempts for deeper, wider comprehension. In one activity near the end of the week, students were surprised with and invited to re-examine their college application essays, written when they were seniors in high school.

After bursts of laughter and embarrassed comments, a palpable and vulnerable silence settled over the circle of students caught by the innocence of what they had written. And in that silence, one could hear the quiverings of remembered hopes and dreams, of a younger, more innocent, and reverent reach for knowledge, love, and commitment worthy of the person they dreamed of becoming. Hopes and dreams that still breathed with wonder without getting drowned by an impressive repertoire of sociocultural insight, feminist critique, deconstructive strategies, and proficiency at dismantling ideologies of oppression, injustice, and neocolonialism. Hopes and dreams that spoke of Paul Ricoeur's second naiveté, that "beyond the desert of criticism, we wish to be called again."[8]

One of the students, visibly affected by what she had written, found words for her tears:

> I wrote so beautifully, so honestly, better than I know how to write now. And it's amazing how clearly I remember that moment, looking out the classroom window to Detroit and realizing how much I loved my city ... and wanting to work to make my city a better place for all. It's amazing ... I knew what I wanted to do with my life back then, and however much college may have challenged my dreams and ideals, I'm still that person!

Here, on an island at the northern boundary of Puget Sound, she had rediscovered an integration of her experience that revealed how nothing is an island. She had heard the call again from a deeper place of being—not just of values but the very source of her values—that named her various commitments not as separate affairs but different expressions of a fundamental way she belonged to the world. In that place of integration, she reclaimed a vital source and dream which had not been erased from her. A source from which she would dare do something innocent and dangerous.

Postmodern identities operate under erasure that leaves only deteriorated and deconstructed forms with which to think and speak our lives into being. Such is the endless play of postmodern difference, with identities sutured episodically from momentary construction to momentary construction. The postmodern identity becomes a trace of a trace of differences, an echo of an echo, bereft of any transcendent, sacred narrative or worldview. We are finally left with only the subjective realm of identity—preferences, opinions, and tastes— that is our main foothold in reality. What was epistemically true versus false, fact versus fiction, is now supplanted by optionality among endless preferences. And trying to ground our constructed identities in an ever-changing world where everything, including ourselves, is constantly being reconstructed only exacerbates an existential anxiety about our cognitive grasp and our very place in a meaningful cosmos.

Whatever the liberatory prospects of unfettering individuals from absolutes into the wider freedom and play of shifting contexts, such optimism is conspicuously at odds with the paralyzing anxiety increasingly seen in student populations. In the absence of any historical or generational antecedent that can still legitimately address the young, any credible cosmology wherein they have both a home and purpose, we no longer know in what or in whose name to address them. The situation of the postmodern subject is characterized by the lack of any credible collective enunciator, and she is summoned to invent herself without possessing the means to do so. Lacking coherent basis for shared exteriority and interiority, the individual subject remains unable to confidently deploy herself in the world, always uncertain about self-appraisal and left only with indeterminacy and myriad subjectivities that do not necessarily cohere into an identity.

What is ultimately "true" and valuable will be decided by power in a world where each of these terms have been rendered suspect: *knowledge, truth, revelation, authority, scripture, tradition, evidence, verifiability, falsification, correspondence, coherence.* When epistemology and the reliability of enduring knowledge have been defeated by extensive skepticism, power—the ability to impose one's stories—offers the best promise of determining reality. Consequently, relations with others become complicated by power, the survival of personal agency, and a hermeneutic of suspicion. For theologian David Krieger, this is not an affirmation of the idiomatic freedom of "to each his/her own" but the pervasive anxiety of "to each his/her own power."[9]

Cultural critics have described this postmodern self as an embodiment of the absence of community, tradition, and shared meaning; an absence and its consequence experienced as a lack of personal conviction and worth; an absence, loneliness, and disappointment experienced as a chronic, undifferentiated emotional hunger. Such hunger is psychologically and spiritually evident in colleges and universities, with students exposed to the full brunt of existential scarcity trying to compensate for what has been taken away and desperately trying to be filled up. It is hardly surprising that contemporary cultural discourse, academic or otherwise, increasingly reflects controversies that refuse resolution, and that any encompassing moral vision for our culture is progressively characterized by confusion and exhaustion.

Despite cultural theorists now pointing to newly emerging paradigms of authority and knowledge succeeding postmodernism—with little consensus as yet among proposed designations—the essential postmodern challenge to authority, knowledge, selfhood, and reality remains indelibly inscribed in contemporary life. If anything, theorists predict a further slide into existential uncertainty and impairment to human sociality. In place of the neurosis of modernism and the narcissism of postmodernism, an impaired sociality of autism increasingly defines contemporary life. This is a generation of students experiencing a new condition of subjectivity in which nobody—certainly not those responsible for their education—is regarded as definitively and authoritatively holding the answer.

To this condition of subjectivity we have seen a number of responses in student life that are in fact, among other determinations, attempts to compensate for the subject's felt sense of lack and attempts to realize (or make real) the self. One such response is the reach for instant community facilitated by a growing number of online communities, blogging websites, and social networking sites like Facebook and Twitter. One cannot bear the weight of autonomy and self-definition alone, without others who wear our tags or logos to mark our shared identities, however virtual or trivial or unquestioned in their fundamentalism. Technology provides a way of revealing beings to one another, however fleeting. But its overwhelming mediating presence tends to eliminate other human modes of sociality, leaving us more isolated from one another and dependent on surrogate forms of intimacy.

Another response readily available is substance abuse, codependency, or addiction of whatever kind, a form of substituting and relocating the anxious subject in the realm of *need* rather than conscious *choice* or *decision.* Addiction concedes to lack and removes the burden of choice by pointing to the obvious procuring of what is needed. Yet another response goes further—with terrifying and terrorizing consequences, which we have seen across college campuses, as in the Virginia Tech massacre—when the subject endows himself with omnipotent agency, assuming power of life and death over peers, and grounding the sense of self in violence and existential nihilism.

Hybridity reflects yet another attempt to substantiate and ground the self, however compulsively amidst the proliferation of "sources of self" available. Pushed by the postmodern critique to concede every identity as an "elective identity," what remains essentially is agency—agency for the individual subject to actively construct self-identity; to avoid being named, sorted, collectivized, and defined according to larger categories that attempt to confine individuals within politically determined identities. So with the poststructuralist recognition that people are not simply *socialized* into the world but undergo a process of *subjectification*—to/by forces of economics, cultural conventions, legal codes, historical circumstances, and the material world in general—a shift occurs away from any particular *identity* to the individual *subject(ivity)* enacting multiple selves into existence and participating in an ongoing construction of identities.

This very sense of oneself as a subject who can transgress beyond any given religious identity, unfettered by any sense of truth or undisputed authority, and forge something new and even hybrid through a combination of previously unrelated discourses, captures the shift in consciousness of our college students today. Identity and subjectivity—*Who am I?* and *Am I free?*—two very different but related frameworks for orienting the self, focus the issue properly on the postmodern subject who cannot be present in the world in an innocent and disinterested manner. While identity employs stable categories of race, gender, religion, class and other forms of acknowledged social relations in order to categorize people, subjectivity attends to an individual's self-authorship, both accommodating and resisting settled meanings that would seek to confine meaning within a singular or particular identity. Subjectivity remains committed to categories that structure our lives through stable identities but simultaneously questions any identity that would categorize people with little regard for their aesthetic and existential horizons of value. Subjectivity is that *interior* movement among *external* identities as individuals shift and renegotiate alternative ways of being in relation to various structures of value, meaning, and power at work in their lives.

But even as emphasis on subjectivity brings greater attention to agency, agency (as means) liberated from a grounded and transcendent sense of purpose (as ends) becomes anxiously self-preoccupied. Without agency rooted in some historical location, without a sense of tested and confident belonging, such individuals have little to stave off chronic revisionism and radical reappraisals from short-lived relationships. This is indeed a self made precarious and disoriented, exposed to an unprecedented uncertainty about its status and exposed to the full brunt of existential turmoil.

It should not come as a surprise then, that the burden of interiority, reflexivity, and self-scrutiny has given shape to an irony all too familiar in cultural discourse today. What is authentic and what is constructed lose their difference; what meaning anything holds is reduced to its function. Nothing means what it says but merely serves an intended effect. There is only the play of individuals caught in their own parody, irony, and the suspected taint of hypocrisy not far off. Irony is the self, trapped in an endless and compulsive self-interrogation, having to expose all possible conspiracies that would conceal the "authentic" self. Irony is the banality of Bart Simpson or yet another episode of *Family Guy*, a refusal to take anything seriously, a way of putting "air quotes" around speech or action, a habit of a mind weary of depths, sincerities, and the truth of anything—especially of anything earnest. Such irony too easily becomes a substitute for genuine action and engaged thought, a form of subjectivity without substance or commitment. And while the postmodern penchant for ironic diagnosis reveals and debunks, human subjects cannot live on social commentary alone but by words that come from the mouth of the Sacred and Transcendent—or at least larger narratives and meaning that can confer a more reliable world. But what transcendent horizons or authoritative truths are available to ground reality and anchor students from being existentially adrift? What will provide a stronger account of human subjects who actually believe in something and have the courage to lay claim to it?

As college chaplains, our attention to subjectivity divested of sacred, transcendent narratives remains an urgent challenge for our time. Academicians and student affairs professionals bring important focus to the challenge of pluralism and an epistemology that can critically manage difference; but for chaplains accompanying students through the exile of postmodern displacement, however significant an epistemology of *difference* may be, an epistemology that *heals separation* and existentially grounds students in original relationship must bear the greater weight. For how we *know* has always shaped and been shaped by how we *relate*, and any construal of a knowing subject separated from an ethical intersubjective relationship remains deeply flawed. Epistemology has historically been bound up with the course of ethical and religious life—"to know as we are known"[10]—and finds its proper functioning within an ethics that grounds knowledge in relationship. If Paul Ricoeur's second naiveté resonates diagnostically in any way—that "beyond the desert of criticism, we wish to be called again"—then chaplains must offer a voice that speaks to students' need to substantiate and ground their selves in more sacred, transcendent relationships. The challenge of returning a prodigal epistemology, hungry and abandoned in a far-off place, properly back home to an embracing ethics remains a pivotal opportunity for chaplains and religious professionals.

HYBRIDITY AND THE RETURN OF ETHICS

The look on her face holds frustration and excitement. "Abby" has just returned from an afternoon at the Occupy Saint Paul rally, part of a sweeping movement bringing attention to the problems of corporate greed, laws favoring the "1 percent," a national debt from wars being balanced on the backs of the poor and the most vulnerable, a politics of unsustainable fuel supplies, the degradation of human rights and freedoms, and an overall brimming discontent with the world as it is. As I listen, Abby gives voice to her passion and encompassing life-purpose of living more sustainably and reverently before the urgent needs of a complex ecology of both human and environmental relationships.

She recalls a conversation shared with her housemates in the EcoHouse, where environmental advocacy converges with a nascent sense of democracy attuned to a new, emerging consciousness. And as I listen, fragments from the author and explorer Jay Griffiths come to mind:

> Accepting that there are different ways of knowing, different ways of speaking, is the beginning of democracy, and forests are a model of wild, tatterdemalion democracy, of seedpod, riverbank, wind and caiman. As if pollen mattered and the beetle had a vote, an ultimate parliament, a *parlement* (literally, "speaking") where all voices can be heard. For democracy is not only a matter of voting, but of talking and discussion … extending democratic ideas into ecocratic wisdom.… The Lakota referred to the creeping people and the flying people and the swimming people, all of whom must be heard in human councils.[11]

"We need a more generous way of listening and knowing," asserts Abby with the fervor of an evangelist. Our lives, our very being, are inextricably bound together with the songlines of the earth in an ethical ecology. How do we move past an arrogant and impoverished sense of self that stands apart from life's interdependence, and begin to hear the wind and breath that speak in many tongues?

To claim that hybridity somehow encapsulates the postmodern condition would be to overstate and trivialize the case, but the prevalence of religious hybridity seen in college students today may warrant a modest proposal: that maneuvering among multiple religious identities suggests a creative search for new foundations, worldviews, and more robust epistemologies to ground the anxious self.

Carrying the burden of parody, irony, indeterminacy, and hyper-self-consciousness that accompanies the postmodern self, students are less effective at allaying anxiety, and more extreme measures may be needed in defense of their identities and commitments. Theirs is a precarious, intersubjective self that stands exposed to an unprecedented epistemic doubt about its status, anxious about its existential grasp on life and frantic for agency. The self becomes the site for one frantic achievement after another, rather than life experienced as sacred, entrusted gift. And it should not surprise us if students today are turning to religion and spirituality, even if guardedly, as traditional forms of consolation, to reassure them that their lack will be filled and their groundlessness grounded in God or some transcendent Ground of Being. This epistemologically unfettered self—both abandoned and free—may suggest seminal ways of actually shifting away from epistemology's dominance in modern thought, moving toward a more expansive moral-ethical understanding of intersubjectivity, which is urgently needed for the contemporary world. Indeed, an ethics of intersubjectivity that attends to an original and originary sociality of all life may elevate ethics to the position philosopher Emmanuel Levinas called "first philosophy."[12] For what is unveiled at the heart of being itself is *be*-ing that verbalizes our ethical relation to the other as preceding and exceeding any sense of an autonomous self.

If ethics is prior to and serves as the basis and frame for epistemology, then the postmodern takeover of epistemology, and the ensuing politics of suspicion-agency-power (suspicion of master narratives, agency to construct self-identity, and above all power to determine what is true), is not the only sequence available for accounting the modern self. Rather, a pre-existing ethics of responsibility makes available a differing epistemology altogether—an epistemic regard for the self that begins with involvement, communion, mutuality, and accountability, offering possibilities for healing the distortions of an alienated epistemic status of the self. Subjectivity, then, is not only the effect of power and subjection but liberation into our primary and constitutive intersubjectivity with others. Agency and freedom become acts of renegotiating connectedness, a practice of mutuality and interdependence.

Even more, such knowing-as-relating strongly advocates for a different category of knowing altogether, a different form of intelligibility beyond formal relations of rationality. Academic communities and educational research continue to show increasing interest in rehabilitating a more generous approach to knowledge, reconsidering defeated forms of knowledge, and exploring more holistic means of educating the whole student within living ecologies—both human and environmental—that are made increasingly fragile by the conceit of narrow epistemologies. Such emerging epistemologies have already opened new frameworks for serious consideration, particularly redressing the constructed self with its literal embodiment, as embodiment has yet to be taken seriously enough in Western thought, which still largely denigrates all that is corporeal. There is no purely poststructuralist person for whom all meaning is entirely relative and historically contingent, unconstrained by the body. Neither is there a purely linguistic person for whom language is primary and all other forms of meaning parasitic upon linguistic meaning. Nor is the mind the only site of linguistic rendering between the self and the world. Contrary to such forms of intellectual segregation and dominance, not all human experiences and perceptions are semiotic or linguistic. Whereas the postmodern emphasis on multiplicity pointed to an eclipse of the essential self and a lack of enduring presence or self-identity, alternative epistemologies that draw on embodied practices have argued that postmodernist modes of abstracted thinking superimpose psychological categories and reify it into something that eludes immediate experience.

Postmodern theories of the self, for all their perceptiveness, seem ultimately incomplete. Concerned with the self as constructed idea, such epistemic constructs slip too quickly and easily past the self as embodied experience. They leave the impression that apprehending and addressing the problems of the self is ultimately a matter of acquiring the correct intellectual perspective. But to package and dispense with the self in this manner assures its perpetual anxiety and its inevitable search for new foundations, including the practice of postmodern hybridity.

Hybridity as a contemporary expression of existential hunger and attempt to search out different, more adequate epistemologies, seems diagnostically evident in religious and spiritual life. Religious identity—perhaps the most fundamental of all identities—offers the consolations of an identity embedded in sacred, transcendent life-worlds that are ultimately intractable to the power of rationality alone. Perhaps for this reason, chaplains and religious professionals are seeing students more likely engaged by the practice of spiritualities than by the intellectual contents of religious dogma, more interested in a mode of experience than a systematic theology or metaphysics already held suspect.

Of course, there is no such thing as experience pure and simple, but through spiritual practices, hybridity may open a reconsidering of faith traditions not confined to the politics of words, ideas, and beliefs alone, to the mutual benefit of traditions and those seeking. Hybrid spiritual practices may confer a deeper appreciation and renewal for the place of memory, narrative, emotion, symbols, intersubjective relations, and embodiment in the formation of religious identities. And beyond the confines of *interreligious* engagement, hybrid spiritual practice may signal a growing need for *interspiritual* engagement in chaplaincy, wherein religious professionals are called to be responsive to the great diversity of human experience itself, religious or otherwise, without losing the normative force of their spiritual compass.

The central issue is not that we have failed to notice the complexity of religious identity, but that we have not fully applied the best insights about the hybrid character of religious and spiritual identities. Some still draw on essentialist-normative definition of religious identity, meeting certain standards of orthodoxy and orthopraxis. But our master stories have been disrupted, and we each hold only some of the threads and emerging patterns of a more encompassing sacred fabric. How do we attend to those individuals, and to a wider emerging cultural pattern of those who are claiming their religious identities with very little trace of orthodoxy or orthopraxis? Hybridity remains both precarious and precious, and a bid for inclusion in the modern project must respond to some of the inescapable and axiomatic realities of contemporary life, including hybrid religious identities.

THE
CHAPLAIN
AND THE
SECULAR

STEWARDS
OF THE NEW SECULAR

Rev. Dr. Samuel H. Speers
Vassar College, Poughkeepsie, New York

Early on in my now fourteen years at Vassar College, I organized and moderated a faculty panel on Mel Gibson's controversial film *The Passion of the Christ* (2004). The film served as a bellwether for aspects of the culture wars at the time—uncovering old wounds over Christian portrayals of Jewish responsibility for Jesus's crucifixion and revealing fault lines between evangelical and liberal Christians. I thought I was organizing the panel to provide an educational forum for students, helping them to understand the anxiety and misunderstanding surrounding the film. What I did not expect is how much a student's criticism of how I had organized the panel would educate me.

Gina was a leader of the campus chapter of InterVarsity Christian Fellowship, an evangelical Christian student group. As moderator of the panel, I noticed that Gina raised her hand and then withdrew it during the question-and-answer session with the

Rev. Dr. Samuel H. Speers is director of the Office of Religious and Spiritual Life and assistant dean for campus life and diversity at Vassar College in Poughkeepsie, New York. He is project coordinator of "Secularity and the Liberal Arts," a Teagle Foundation multi-institutional working group. He is author of "The Secular Thesis Revisited" in the *Journal of College and Character.* He is easily confused (as his loved ones remind him) and finds the experiences of poetry, being outside, and being with family harder and harder to tell apart.

panelists. I waited for her question, but it never came. In the post-discussion conversations, Gina did come over to speak with me. "I was disappointed," she said, "that there was not someone [on the panel] who embraced the film, who said they liked it. I see there was considerable diversity, but still there was not someone on the panel who agreed with the movie, who saw how it agrees with scripture, who saw the movie as generally positive." She described the diversity I had included, making clear she did not experience her evangelical perspectives as part of it.

I wish I had had a better response for Gina. I explained that I had deliberately not asked people to offer their opinions about the film, for fear of turning the panel into a debate and further polarizing our community. I had instead invited people from a range of scholarly disciplines and religious commitments (or lack thereof), in the hope that our panelists would help us understand what was making the movie so polarizing.

In the years since, I have come to think that Gina was essentially right. In the name of open discussion, I should have invited an evangelical perspective onto the panel, rather than panelists who said they could speak to evangelical concerns. Since my encounter with Gina, I have worked to incorporate evangelical perspectives into our interreligious initiatives—often precisely for the ways evangelicals unsettle my campus's and my own liberal assumptions. I have come to see that evangelical Gina was essentially outing me as a liberal Protestant, and I am grateful for that.

While I thought I was taking a secular approach with the panel I had organized, her comments made me realize how difficult it is to be fully secular in the generous and capacious sense of this often misunderstood term. We call ourselves secular at places like Vassar, and encountering our secularity is a defining aspect of the college experience for many students; yet we are not sure what we mean by the term, nor how it defines the liberal arts education we seek to provide.

Even more, Gina helped reveal an often unremarked trace between the secular ideals of the college and its founding in an era of high Protestantism. The unifying ethos for the college in its early decades was Protestant. For good reasons, the college's leaders have worked to distance Vassar from this earlier Protestant predominance, and now people generally think of the college as a secular institution. Yet, as I hope to show, Gina showed me how a kind of hidden liberal Protestantism can stand in for the secular in our context. Paula Cooey, who teaches the history of Christian traditions, Christianity and culture, and theory of religion at Macalester College, calls this the "faded Protestantism" behind our secular assumptions.[1] Gina's challenge to me brought out the importance of distinguishing these lingering Protestant assumptions from our campus's secular ideals.

Gina also helped me to see the vital role chaplains have to play in helping their campuses come closer to achieving their secular ideals, or what my Vassar colleague Jonathon Kahn calls "the new secular." It may seem strange for a chaplain to understand her or his work as stewarding their campus's *secular* ideals and practices. Most of the time we think of religious life, not secular life, as the purview of chaplains. I hope to show through this chapter that being stewards of the new secular is a creative means for chaplains to serve the changing dynamics of campus religious life.[2] Critically, playing this role provides a way for chaplains and religious life administrators in former chaplaincies (like myself) to reclaim our partnership in the learning enterprise of our institutions.

VASSAR'S ERSTWHILE CHAPLAINCY: A BRIEF HISTORY

Vassar College, like a number of its peer institutions, is historically Protestant. The college was founded in 1861 to provide women with a college education equal to that being provided for men. People here take pride in Vassar's ecumenical vision: the college's founder, Matthew Vassar, a brewer and a Baptist, wanted the college to be free of denominational ties. In the context of his day, this meant the college would not be affiliated with any single Protestant denomination. The first four presidents of the college were all Protestant clergymen. Daily chapel was a mandatory part of life at Vassar as elsewhere, and those services were, of course, Protestant. In short, Vassar's ecumenism was *Protestant* ecumenism—the college was and wanted to be part of the Protestant establishment of its day.

The conventional way of narrating what has shifted between now and then is to say that the college has become more secular. In many ways, of course, it has. Students applying to the college are no longer expected to provide a letter of recommendation from their minister, as they were in the early decades of the college. The days of the clergyman-president are long past, as are the days of mandatory daily chapel; Franklin Delano Roosevelt, then governor of New York, chaired the committee in 1926 that recommended this change as the college sought to recognize increasing numbers of Roman Catholic and Jewish students. If the Protestant triumvirate of faith, learning, and service was once the glue of a liberal arts education, now faith and learning are seen as strange bedfellows, and service is understood as one of many extracurricular activities among which students may choose.

All of these developments reveal the fractures being felt in Protestantism's sway as a unifying force in U.S. culture in the early part of the twentieth century. It was at the beginning of the twentieth century, after all, that William James was presciently identifying the crisis of belief and unbelief in modernity;[3] however, the changes to campus religious life that are probably most felt now resulted from the cultural and political upheavals of the 1960s and '70s and their aftermath. In many ways, Vassar's Protestant history mirrors the developments historian David Hollinger has recently traced: its decline is its triumph.

My liberal Protestant predecessors used their pulpit to critique the privileges of church, society, and college. In the self-critique of their own power, chaplains of the day—the majority of whom were white and male—sought to undermine their own cultural privilege and make room for communities that had been historically excluded. For many today, a more traditional and conservative Christianity is the public face of religion; yet the multicultural education many campuses now embrace is in no small part the legacy of liberal Protestantism's self-critique during the movements for civil rights and women's rights and against the Vietnam War (as Rev. Ian Oliver's chapter in this book insightfully outlines).[4]

In ways that current students cannot fully comprehend now, the chaplaincy at Vassar was embroiled in these controversies and often at odds with the college's administration. To describe a colorful chapter in the office's history in a rather distilled fashion, the chaplaincy became a lightning rod that the college then decided it could do without. College officers tried but could not eliminate the office entirely, yet they did dramatically reduce its scope. The chaplain's position, which had included faculty responsibilities, became one of full-time administration, and the chaplaincy model was replaced by a managerial one. The chaplain became a "director" and the chaplaincy became the "Office of Religious Activities and Chaplaincy Services." As one alumnus described the office's renaming to me, the president at the time "was an old bureaucrat who knew how to kill something with bureaucracy."

As fascinating a story as these controversies provide, what is most important for my purposes here is their outcome: Vassar created a new model for religious life on campus. By replacing the chaplain who taught in the religion department with a non-faculty director, the college's leaders were offering a model commensurate with their understanding of the shifting terrain of religious and spiritual life at the college. It is tempting to personalize this new administrative model for religious life at the college as a story of righteous chaplains versus their secularizing administration, yet the personality struggles can obscure the way these shifts were also part of larger forces at work across many historically Protestant institutions of higher education.

Clay Steinman, humanities, media and cultural studies professor at Macalester College has insightfully described some of the cultural and religious changes happening at that time:

> In the last mid-century, the question of religious diversity at liberal arts colleges, whether explicitly elite Protestant or culturally so, might have been framed as: *How*

*open are these religiously grounded institutions to religious dif-
ference and indifference in their students?*[5]

Steinman's analysis is apt for Vassar. Already in the 1950s, the "Vassar
Community Church" that was run by students with the assistance of
the chaplain had been renamed the "Community Religious Association" to signal the college's opening to ongoing increases in Roman
Catholic and Jewish presence. Along with the public acknowledgment of the college's increasing religious diversity, the numbers of
religiously indifferent students—and faculty—were also increasing
at Vassar and elsewhere.

In response to these cultural changes, the college's leaders
were not only trying to quiet their prophetic chaplains in ways that
reflected an ambivalence one still feels about the public expression
of religious commitments; the college's leaders were also trying
to distance the college from its founding norms, when its liberal
Protestantism was understood as the unifying ethos of the college's mission. Part of the solution this new administrative model
offered—akin to the way many interpret the so-called separation of
church and state in U.S. politics—was to privatize religion. Turning
the chaplaincy from a faculty position into an administrative one
worked to separate students' intellectual life from their religious
life. Students' spiritual lives became understood as part of their life
beyond the classroom. It is this model, one that seems to assume
religious life is fine on the secular liberal arts campus as long as
it is kept private, that is now under pressure. As Gina's criticism
makes clear, there are students at the college now—and it is not
only religiously conservative evangelicals—who are uneasy with the
constraints they feel are placed on public expression of personally
felt spiritual commitments.

This new administrative model for the increasing religious difference and indifference on the secular liberal arts campus received
its intellectual support from the so-called secularization thesis. This
thesis is the notion, born in the heyday of early-twentieth-century
optimism in human economic, scientific, and technological progress, that as societies become more modern, they necessarily

become less religious. The corollary assumption to this line of reasoning is that the more religious a society is, the less modern it must be. The problem with the thesis, of course, is that it is not what has happened; at the beginning of the twenty-first century, religion in its many and changing varieties has not gone away. It has declined in some societies, emerged in new forms in others, and generally refused any single or simple story. In short, it has become clear that the secularization thesis itself relies on a set of untenable assumptions: about advance or progress, about the role of religions in societies, and about the secular itself. In an era marked by increasing religious and secular diversity, how are campuses that used this thesis as a pillar for designing chaplaincies—and liberal arts education—to respond?

THE DEFINING EXPERIENCE OF CAMPUS SECULARITY

I will describe below a project I initiated to address this question, but before I turn to administrative and faculty responses to these pressures on the secularization thesis, I want to consider another student, Tiffany, whom I met while doing a qualitative research project for my doctor of ministry (DMin) studies. I turn to Tiffany in part because I have come to appreciate students as lucid interpreters of the changing religious and spiritual landscape of our campuses. A good number of students I have worked with understand their encounter with the background secular assumptions of campus life as a defining experience. Even more, Tiffany has helped me to see the unusual position in which chaplains find themselves working on today's secular liberal arts campus.

My DMin research included a focus-group project on two historically Protestant campuses with similarities to Vassar College. Tiffany was actively involved in and curious about a number of the different Christian communities on her campus—including both progressive Protestant and evangelical groups. My research questions were designed to get a feel for what it is like for students to navigate the religious and secular terrain of campus life: what kinds of support and obstacles do religiously engaged or curious students encounter?

Tiffany talked about the surprise she herself experiences when she encounters peers who are also religiously involved:

> I would say that, at least in the Christian communities and student groups on campus, I think a lot of it [being religious] tends to be discreet. Within each group there will be a handful of individuals who end up representing the whole they're part of; they get tagged as being a religious person. But, as an example, when I attend Christian Fellowship, or when I first attended this year (I went all last year), I myself was surprised by some of the people who came, because I didn't know they were religious, and I was kind of surprised. Likewise, when I go to church and see people who aren't members of the Christian Fellowship, I think, "Oh, they're religious?" *I think that here, you're assumed nonreligious unless you prove otherwise. You have to prove you're religious instead of proving you're unreligious* [italics mine].

In these few sentences, Tiffany incisively describes a number of social dynamics she inhabits on the secular liberal arts campus. In the taxonomy of the diversity our campuses seek to foster, she points out the ways religious commitments are enlisted within the discourse of "identity." Students actively engaged within their communities find themselves getting "tagged as being a *religious* person." In the social milieu of campus life, their behavior seems to need an explanation; it is experienced as unexpected by religious and nonreligious students alike. Tiffany realized her own learned sense of religious practices as anomalous when she found herself surprised at her own surprise: "Oh, they're religious?" she asks herself on seeing someone in church whom she did not expect to see there. It has become a surprise in her context, including to her, that people behave in this way that is labeled "religious." The organizing force of this set of operative assumptions is that religiously engaged students seem to feel put on the defensive—having an identity that needs "proving." When Tiffany described her context as one where "you're assumed nonreligious unless you prove otherwise," her peers in the focus group nodded appreciatively at her framing of default assumptions they also experience.

I do not believe Tiffany and her peers in that focus group had kept abreast of current scholarly debates on secularity and Western secular assumptions, but her observations lucidly confirm the unsettled terrain these debates describe. Influential philosopher Charles Taylor argues that Western modernity has "changed from a condition in which belief was the default option, not just for the naïve but also for those who knew, considered, talked about atheism; to a condition in which for more and more people unbelieving construals seem at first blush the only plausible ones."[6] In her descriptions of life on her campus, Tiffany seems to have this sense of lived belief as unlikely, implausible, outside of the norm. Taylor knows this condition is not a universal. There are many contexts and communities around the world where other conditions are operative, including those where religious observance is not a matter of personal and private choice and is instead, as in many Islamic societies, for instance, and throughout much of India, inextricably linked with cultural and community practices. "But," Taylor notes, "the presumption of unbelief has become dominant in more and more ... [modern] milieux; and has achieved hegemony in certain crucial ones, in the academic and intellectual life, for instance."[7]

Tiffany's insights and Taylor's analysis point us, in short, to see higher education as a peculiar context, one in which students encounter a particular understanding of religious belief as one among many possible worldview options—and "frequently not the easiest to embrace."[8]

These presumptions put college chaplains in the odd position of being hired to tend to a dimension of human experience that is widely understood within our hiring institutions as implausible. Rather than see this dilemma as untenable, I have worked to make it an occasion for what learning institutions seek to bring to human dilemmas: critical reflection and creative engagement. It is not surprising that those who come to me from otherwise disparate backgrounds—say, agnostic Jewish, evangelical Christian, and mindful Buddhist students—all report finding our campus a difficult place to be religious. In response, I find ways to ask gently whether students want or expect my colleagues and me somehow to make it easier for them. Rather than pretend we can take away the challenges of integrating religious and spiritual questions into student learning, we try to help students see that their felt dilemmas are not simply personal to them or our campus, but part of historical forces they will be encountering throughout their lifetimes.

THE "SECULARITY AND THE LIBERAL ARTS" PROJECT

Secularity has become part of the background assumptions on our campus, but finding language to explain these secular presumptions is often challenging. A professor on my office's advisory committee talks about how "secular" seems to be a placeholder, a marker that conveys a kind of studied vagueness. Part of "getting it" seems to be not needing to explain whatever "it" is. Part of getting it also seems to be understanding that there are some things we are not supposed to talk about. With Clay Steinman, I wonder what kinds of religious expression the secular campus actually does support and encourage—in the residence halls, the classroom, the dining hall, the chapel, the theater? Many people think that secular is the opposite of religious, and this meaning seems to have become the commonsense use of the term. However, the history of the term tells another story and provides other, more generous ways to think about the religious and secular—not as opposites but as changing and contextually specific terms to distinguish carefully and see as interrelated.

Building on the doctoral research that led me to Tiffany, I initiated a project that has taken up this question: What do we mean on the liberal arts campus when we call ourselves secular? I reached out to chaplain colleagues on historically Protestant campuses whom I knew were dealing creatively with similar issues, and together we put together a proposal to the Teagle Foundation (a higher education philanthropy dedicated to enlivening student learning).[9] Our proposal brought together a working group of faculty and chaplains across four different campuses. The initial organizing question for our project was whether and how secular assumptions structure students' engagement with their "big questions"—their questions of meaning, value, ethics, and purpose. Our multi-institutional working group and its representatives on each campus implemented an array of activities: a qualitative research project across all four campuses, faculty-administrator seminars, campus forums, a collection of papers, and a concluding public conference featuring leading educators and scholars, including religious ethicist Jeffrey Stout, Swarthmore president Rebecca Chopp, and Harvard Divinity School professor Stephanie Paulsell. At the conclusion of our initial grant project, our working group put together the "Reconceiving the Secular Liberal Arts" workshop to widen the circle of campuses engaging the questions of our project. As I write this chapter, these workshops are continuing.

This is not the place to describe in detail our whole Teagle project; our work is well-summarized elsewhere.[10] I do want to emphasize here, however, how difficult we found it to bring the workings of our secular assumptions into view. Toward the end of the first full day of our discussions in our opening working-group meeting, Jonathan VanAntwerpen, a consultant to the project, observed how often we kept talking about religion, even though we said we were trying to talk about secularity. VanAntwerpen reminded us of social scientist Pierre Bourdieu's analytically useful notion of *doxa*, which are those fundamental unthought beliefs we hold to be self-evident.[11] As studies of race and ethnicity have worked to bring the construction of whiteness into view, now a range of disciplinary fields are working to bring secular assumptions and constructions into view. I expect readers of this chapter will also experience similar struggles with secularity's slipperiness.

"SECULAR, NOT SECULARIST"

The critical distinction that has helped the term feel less slippery to me is Jeffrey Stout's distinction between "secular" and "secularist."[12] Using Stout's normative distinction, the faculty and chaplains in our group have proposed a substantive working definition of our secular ideals for campus discussion. The most important accomplishment of our secularity project has been the conversations about the purposes and practices of a liberal arts education that Stout's distinction sparks.

A secularist, for Stout, is someone who "says that striving to minimize the influence of religion on politics is essential to the defense of democracy."[13] It is this secularist position that atheist Stout wants to unsettle. He understands that secularists are motivated by warranted concerns about the rise of theocratic movements, where theocrats are inherently antidemocratic: they seek to make their religion the governing force for all people, of any or no religion. "But," Stout pointedly argues, "not all religious people are theocrats. Why, then, should we take religion as such to pose a threat to democracy?"[14] Secular—not secularist—talk is Stout's proposal for making room for non-theocratic religious speech in open, democratic discussion.

Stout calls the kind of open speech democratic practice requires "secularized discourse." In an often-cited passage, this is how he describes the freeing goal of such speech:

> What makes a form of discourse secularized, according to my account, is not the tendency of the people participating in it to relinquish their religious beliefs or to refrain from employing them as reasons. The mark of secularization, as I use the term, is rather the fact that participants in a given discursive practice are not in a position to take for granted that their interlocutors are making the same religious assumptions they are.[15]

What Stout makes clear here is that secular speech is a set of practices for different people to talk across their differences. Contrary to secular*ist* talk, secular talk welcomes religious beliefs and reasons into public discussion—on the condition that everyone involved understands they cannot expect their conversation partners to share their own presuppositions. To my earlier discussion of secular campuses as places where religious perspectives seem at first to be implausible, Stout challenges those of us who are religious not to marginalize ourselves but to bring our religious reasons into public discussion.

Jonathon Kahn lucidly develops Stout's critical distinction for democratic practice in ways that have compelling implications for learning communities:

> The secular becomes a discussion between religious and non-religious citizens who are acutely aware that the demands of secularized democratic life require an extraordinary balance between prizing and cherishing one's own convictions and the awareness that these same prized and cherished convictions are contestable, and may at times act as a bludgeon against other democratic citizens. A further type of knowledge emerges in this secular: a self-critical consideration of how one's own commitments might be heard by citizens with differing ones, a knowledge required for acting compassionately, civilly, and democratically.[16]

Stout's insights point at the critical role college campuses have to play in giving a new generation of leaders skills, understanding, and experience in secular discourse as a practice of creating and nurturing democratic community. Stout thus reimagines and, in Kahn's term, revalues secularity. Stout's secular is an ethic of hospitality, a way of speaking and relating that allows democratic community to form and sustain itself.

This hospitable secular is what Kahn calls "the new secular." This new secular invites the evangelical perspective Gina wanted in the panel as much as it invites an atheist or Jewish or Roman Catholic perspective. All voices are welcome as long as they recognize that their "cherished convictions are contestable."

To my earlier reflections on campus life as a difficult place to be religious, Stout thus offers a compelling challenge. He makes clear that the sympathy I harbor for students who find it difficult to be religious is somewhat nostalgic or, more precisely, misplaced. Students find it difficult to inhabit religious commitments because bearing witness in our time *is* difficult. It is difficult *and* needed in a world where religion's ambivalent force—toward both misunderstanding and reconciliation—is so much a part of current national and global conflicts. This difficulty is not new, of course, but the reasons for it are particular. Liberal arts education has a role to play in giving students skills in navigating this historical moment. How might our campuses become learning environments for religiously different and indifferent students to experience and learn from their differing perspectives on our common public life?

THE NEW SECULAR AND FADED PROTESTANTISM

This vision of college campuses as ecologies for the new secular calls me to reconsider what I have learned from Gina and her critique of the ways I organized that campus forum on Mel Gibson's film *The Passion of the Christ*. How does Stout's "secular, not secularist" distinction help me evaluate my framing of that faculty panel? How well did I do at creating a forum that acknowledged the contestable character of what matters most to us (and to me)? In my reflections on my exchange with Gina, I initially thought the tensions between us had to do with our differing perspectives on Jewish-Christian relations and scriptural interpretation. Liberal Protestant that I am, I hoped part of what the panel might accomplish would be to introduce members of our campus community to the difficulties and challenges for Christians of being faithful to the Christian scriptural accounts of Jesus's passion without continuing the history of the church's anti-Semitism.

Without apologizing for my commitments to criticize anti-Jewish interpretations of Christian scripture, I have come to learn that the more important tension between Gina and me was between my theologically liberal presuppositions and her evangelical ones. If the new secular means letting the different voices of our community have their say, then the panel I organized fell short. As I indicated from the outset in my introduction, I think Gina was right that the program would have been stronger if I had included an evangelical panelist.

When I say that the panel "fell short," I do not want my self-critique to be overstated. My focus here on Gina's critique afterward probably skews the perspective that most people there had of the program itself. In many ways the panel accomplished my goals of providing a public forum for engaging polarizing religious questions in a context that tends to keep religion private. At that time in my work at Vassar, I was still feeling the lingering effects of the controversies surrounding my office's tumultuous history; making space for such discussion even without an evangelical voice felt somewhat risky.

My interest in Gina's critique comes from how it unsettled me. Her question spurred me to consider my own presuppositions in all the uncomfortable ways Stout's new secular requires. It is these hidden assumptions that I want to explore more fully here. In order not to use my position as director of the office to authorize my own views on the film, I thought it best that I organize and moderate the panel, but not serve on it. I knew that an evangelical voice was missing from the panel, but a number of the panelists I had confirmed conveyed insightful sympathy for how evangelical Christians on campus were experiencing the controversy. I told myself at the time that I did not know of a faculty member at Vassar or one of our nearby campuses who was both an evangelical and trained in a discipline that would help shed light on the film.

There is not room here to repeat the whole conversation I had with Gina after the program, but even the opening framing comments we each spoke reveal our very different starting places. After some pleasantries between us, Gina shared the heart of her concerns: "I'm disappointed there was not someone who embraced the film, who said they liked it. I see there was considerable diversity, but still there wasn't anyone on the panel who agreed with the movie, who saw how it agrees with scripture, who saw the movie as generally positive." I replied, "Well, I understand what you're saying, but I didn't ask people for their opinion about the movie in inviting them to participate. I sought people who could bring the perspective of their training in a particular field." Our conversation continued for several minutes, but these opening comments already show our contrasting presuppositions.

Gina's comments reveal that she is well aware of the personal commitments that motivate her. Her primary concern is that I did not include anyone on the panel who not only agreed with the film but who spoke to how it "agrees with scripture." She experienced the panel as challenging her notions of scriptural authority. Crucially for her, the conviction that the authority of scripture is paramount is a defining trait for Gina and most evangelical Christians.[17] This commitment of hers is critical for me to understand as director of the office that thinks of itself as helping students integrate their commitments into their learning experience.

My comments reveal the more administrative approach I thought I was taking by removing myself from the panel. My comment about seeking "people who could bring the perspective of their training in a particular field" sounds academically innocuous enough. I am confident Gina understood I was referencing the different fields that were represented on the panel—Jewish studies, film, Roman Catholic studies, and early Christian literature. Yet on closer examination, my "innocuous" framing reveals a set of liberal presuppositions about the norms for interpreting religious tradition. For when I identify sources outside the church as adequate for interpreting *The Passion of the Christ*, I am embracing a theological turn that Gina does not share. The liberal Protestant assumptions of the panel—and the ethos of the college—are the elephant in the room Gina's question helped me to see.

This theological turn is the innovation—initiated by the liberal Protestant church in which I was raised—to widen the sources for theological reflection. As theologian B. A. Gerrish observes, for the emerging liberal Protestantism of the nineteenth century, the theological dilemma was the "credibility gap [that] had opened between the dogmas of the church and the outlook of the Enlightenment" thought of the day.[18] The new task for Friedrich Schleiermacher and other founders of liberal theology was to work at bridging this gap. Gerrish summarizes concisely this change in theological method:

> The problem, for the liberal, is no longer "Scripture
> and tradition" but "tradition (including Scripture) and
> modernity." And its characteristic expression is the rec-
> ognition that Scripture can no longer serve alone as
> the exclusive critical norm for the language which the
> believing community is to hand on.[19]

This opening to norms outside of Christian tradition is a critical
aspect of liberal thought and method. It is also precisely the turn
that theological liberalism's critics have found problematic, finding
it too accommodating of norms outside of Christianity, in ways that
too readily compromise the church's distinct claims.

I sketch in broad strokes the background debates to my encounter with Gina not to apologize for my liberal Protestantism, but to
acknowledge it as the critical hidden tension between us. While I
thought I was admirably removing myself from the panel, in fact
I was structuring the whole discussion in accordance with my own
theological presuppositions. It is no small wonder that Gina felt
excluded from the panel. I had used my presuppositions to structure hers out of it.

The impact of my unthought presuppositions on Gina's experience of the program also has a larger force. For while I might have
wanted to think I was using my authority lightly, it just so happens
that my theological presuppositions align with the founding ethos
of the college. The liberal opening to modernity is a critical premise
that guided the Protestant founders of Vassar College, who saw no
conflict between piety and learning—their liberal theology helped
mediate between the claims of modernity and the claims of faith.

As I note in my introduction, Paula Cooey speaks of one version
of the secular on some of our campuses today as a kind of "faded Protestantism." I now see that my uncritical use of my own assumptions to
organize the panel was a version of what Cooey describes. I thought I
was creating a public forum for religion that would fit my secular campus; yet I did not understand that my "secular" default drew primarily
on lingering Protestant presuppositions that have faded from view but
are still part of the cultural formation of campus life.

By not including a space for personal, deeply held evangelical faith on the panel, I was asking Gina to conform to the unstated norms of faded liberal Protestantism that often stand in for the secular on my historically Protestant campus: keep your religion private; check your enthusiasm; avoid getting too emotional; be wary of singular truth claims. I have come to see as well a host of other particularly Protestant assumptions that pass as general ones: the definition of religion primarily in terms of interiority, belief, and the individual in relationship to God.[20]

There are historical reasons, of course, that liberal Protestantism has developed in the ways that it has in the United States. This is not the place to review this rich history and its intertwined relationship with U.S. higher education. But it is the place to say how much I have come to appreciate the rich resources of liberal Protestantism's opening to modernity—its bold insight into culture as an arena for God's free and freeing activity in the world. The language we now use in the liberal arts to talk about the importance of "educating the whole person" has significant roots in this liberal theological tradition. Coming to a better understanding of my community's insights into the compatibility of spirituality and all human experience is one of several ways I feel grateful for—and freed by—Gina's question.

Gina's challenge and what I have learned from it reveals another aspect of the power of Stout's secular, not secularist distinction: it creates a space for listening respectfully to the viewpoints of others while clarifying one's own. The problem with my framing of the panel is not liberal Protestantism per se, but its hiddenness. The problem, to paraphrase Barnard women's studies professor Janet Jakobsen, is not my norms, but my presumption that they were an adequate frame for the liberal-evangelical conflict between Gina me, rather than a party to it.[21] Here, too, Gina helped me to see how and why critiques of secular norms as expressions of power call for chaplains' diligent attention. Public forums for religious engagement require a level playing field for all participants in the discussion in order for all voices to have their say.

I am not sure what Gina took away from our exchange. I continue to feel in debt to her. My encounter with her, when combined with the central insights I take away from the secularity project, has given me new ways of understanding that continue to guide my work. Instead of thinking of religion in higher education through the lens of decline, I have learned to be clear that what has changed at our historically Protestant institutions is that Protestantism is not—or can no longer be—the enabling tacit frame of reference. What one scholar has called the "educational Christendom" on U.S. campuses is coming to an end.[22] Rather than see this significant shift as a cultural turn to lament, I have learned to see it as an opening, an accomplishment—and honestly, a relief. I have learned to see campus religious life as shifting, complex, contested—and crucially, all the more vibrant for being so.

STEWARDS OF THE NEW SECULAR

I have come to think of the calling of chaplains, given that we work in contexts of deep and growing cosmopolitanism, as a call to be stewards of a renewed secular.[23] The language of stewardship makes secularity a spatial term. Such stewardship becomes a practice of holding open a space between—between different and sometimes incompatible modes of being and being religious, between competing claims and incompatible convictions. If we call this space between different claims "the secular," as Stout seems to, then one crucial role for chaplaincies is the work of holding open such spaces, of cultivating an expertise and nurturing practices that make such room.

In my work, I have developed some approaches to stewarding the secular that others may be able to adapt in their own contexts. One way to hold open a space for students to consider their own presuppositions is to turn Tiffany's insight about her context into a question for student discussion. At Vassar and a dozen other campuses, we have organized student panels to engage the question, "Are you presumed nonreligious until proven otherwise?" Faculty and chaplain facilitators meet ahead of time with our panelists—anywhere from five to ten of them—to give these students some experience in considering their own presuppositions and commitments. Following Jonathon Kahn's insights into Stout's "secular, not secularist" distinction, we also ask students to consider what passions and commitments they check at the door—in the classroom, the residence hall, and campus forums. In all cases, having faculty and chaplains facilitate this student discussion makes for one of those campus conversations that is difficult to bring to a close.

Turning Tiffany's insight into a question opens up a host of questions at the fault lines of our campuses' secular borders: How are our campuses' secular presumptions experienced by the different people who reside and learn here? Should religion be thought of as a private aspect of individuals, without public or collective frames of reference? Do our secular assumptions have parochial understandings of religion embedded in them? Are religious convictions at odds with critical thought? As this last question already suggests, these discussions reveal a series of anxieties that are not at all limited to questions of the religious, but also include the goal of the liberal arts, the place of students' questions of meaning and purpose and ethics, and the relationship of wonder to learning.[24] At one workshop, a student with evident analytical abilities spoke of feeling the need to check his enthusiasm in the classroom, noting the vulnerability such enthusiasm entails. Is this what the secular classroom requires? Chaplains need not and should not pretend to have resolved these questions, but they can and should be part of campus deliberations to better understand where and how all of our students learn.

Being stewards of the new secular can also apply to apparently mundane administrative practices. One of the ways many chaplaincy offices attempt to map our changing religious landscape is through the annual ritual on today's secular campus that we call the "religious preference card." I inherited this practice from one of my predecessors, who initiated it during the early 1980s. During the summer each year, I send a letter asking incoming freshmen to respond to two questions. I ask them to share their religious affiliations, if any, so that we might better understand the student demographic we are serving. I also ask them to share what current groups on campus they would like to learn about—so that I can share their names with the community or communities in which they indicate an interest. I also make clear I will only share their "religious preference" information with those groups they indicate on the form.

Having learned what I have through the secularity project, I administer this card with some unease. The card helps us track some sense of the college's changing religious and spiritual demographics, however statistically imprecise. This is important and needed information for the office's work to understand the community we are to serve; yet the name of the card and the way we administer it already asks students to accept a set of assumptions that the secularity project has taught me to question. It presupposes religious life as a matter of "preference," of private choice and individual conscience. There are hidden Protestant notions implied as well about religion as a matter of personal decision; however, this is not how a good number of students coming to the college understand their religious affiliations.

Any number of students come to Vassar from contexts where religious and cultural life are not separated and compartmentalized as unexamined secular norms seem to require—including students who have attended religious schools, international students where religion is not merely one among many cultural attributes, and some first-generation college students. It is thus strange and even alienating for some students to feel their religious affiliations being reduced to a check mark in a box, an "identity" that marks them as distinct and unusual in a context they experience as strangely nonreligious. As Tiffany came to see, such uncritical secular assumptions can make some students feel as if the ways they have long inhabited the world are now unexpectedly implausible—parts of themselves seem not to belong. I thus oversee the process uncomfortably aware that I am presenting a particular view of religion—as a matter of private and personal preference—as if it were a universal norm, and certainly the norm for our campus.

I do not imagine I can avoid this dilemma in administering the religious preference card; yet examining my presuppositions—often with the needed help of my interreligious colleagues—can also begin to transform our use of the card into a useful measure and mirror of our context. Each year we reevaluate the card, seeking to convey my office's attentiveness to the changing religious and secular terrain our students are navigating. By opening up the categories of affiliation on the form, we seek to better reflect the range of ways students are putting together their religious and secular identities.

To communicate that we understand the changing relationship people have to their traditions over time, my rabbinic colleague Rena Blumenthal suggested we allow students to indicate both current religious identification and religious background. This way students who might otherwise indicate no religious identity because of their current disaffiliation can tell us about the religious communities in which they grew up. With this little change, the form thus indicates to students our interest in their religious narrative, whatever direction it takes.

Rabbi Blumenthal also recently initiated a new option for affiliation in the form's section of Jewish identifications. Working against hidden Protestant assumptions that religious identity is a matter of personal belief, we have now added cultural or secular Judaism as one of the "religious" preferences students may indicate, along with Reform, Conservative, Reconstructionist, and Orthodox Judaism. The notion that cultural Judaism is a category of religious affiliation helpfully unsettles hidden Protestant assumptions that religious practice—to be religious—requires belief. A Jewish student in a class I taught once said, to the confusion of her classmates, that she thinks of herself as religious but not spiritual. As Rabbi Blumenthal has shown me, in Judaism, religious identity is more connected to communal and embodied practices than it is to belief. So if the religious preference card is to make room for the communities we serve, it needs to include secular Judaism as an option—an option that creatively points at religious and secular not as opposed terms but as interrelated ones.[25]

These examples reveal how the administrative work of chaplaincy provides continual opportunities to examine latent Protestant assumptions and uncritical notions of the secular as simply the absence of religion. Our hope in paying attention to such details is that our administrative practices over time will better convey my office's interest in, and stewardship of, the variety of ways students navigate their relationship to their current or past religious affiliations. The religious preference card thus becomes a means for communicating our interest in the hybrid combinations of religious, spiritual, and secular identities that students from more than just Jewish traditions are inhabiting and exploring.

Lest educational administrators imagine students are not paying attention to the presuppositions implicit in how we present their spiritual options, I want to mention briefly one last example of what we have learned from seemingly small changes in the language we use on the card. Several years ago I worked closely with the energetic student leader of our "Zen Meditation" group as he sought to expand the mission of the group. He proposed renaming the group "Buddhist Sangha" to reflect this increased openness to a range of Buddhist teachings and practices. When it came time to prepare a new religious preference card for the next year's incoming classes, I included this change in our form, deleting "Zen Meditation" and replacing it with "Buddhist Sangha."

What I probably should have seen coming is that this name change also resulted in a dramatic numerical change in student interest on the religious preference card. When we called the group "Zen Meditation," it had become the single most popular group among our listing of current student groups at Vassar—with four hundred or so students wanting to hear more about it. But apparently linking Zen practice to Buddhist traditions—itself a complex relationship—dampened student interest. Instead of four hundred students, the number decreased to around eighty students. Only the name of the group had changed, not its primary weekly activity of sitting meditation. While Eastern practices have a cultural allure, Zen meditation was appealing in a way that the more institutional sounding "Buddhist Sangha" was not.

There is not a tidy bit of wisdom I feel capable of drawing from this Zen experience. Would we still have four hundred students if we had changed the name from "Zen Meditation" to "Buddhist Meditation" instead of the unfamiliar term *sangha*? I do not know. I can only mark again, knowing that this is deeply Protestant of me, that language matters in how chaplains name the spiritual options we try to offer students.

These examples of our efforts to steward Stout's secular hospitality work generously in multiple directions. Holding open the space between different ways of being and being religious commends itself as much to Gina's evangelical Christian faith as it does to Tiffany's surprise at her secular assumptions, as it does to secular Jews who understand themselves as religious but not spiritual, as it does to meditation seekers unsure of the relation between Zen and Buddhism. Such is the space of possibility opened by Stout's demanding ethic of hospitality. This is an ethic of hospitality because it welcomes all perspectives. This is a demanding ethic because it does not privilege any perspective or protect it from critical questioning. The unfinished business to which Gina pointed me, perhaps unawares, is this lifelong work of holding open such a generous "space between."

THE ONE AND THE MANY
Old Language, New Engagement

Fr. Roc O'Connor, SJ
Creighton University, Omaha, Nebraska

I have been blessed to minister at two very fine and yet very different institutions of higher education. I recently completed my service as the rector of the Jesuit community of Creighton University in Omaha, Nebraska, one of twenty-eight Jesuit colleges and universities in the United States. Before coming to Creighton, I worked for six years with Rev. Lucy Forster-Smith as the Catholic chaplain at Macalester College. Macalester is a liberal arts institution, recently ranked tenth on a list of "least religious" U.S. colleges by the Princeton Review.

The invitation to address my rather divergent experiences at each school afforded me the opportunity to reflect on their differences, to be sure, but also their similarities. For example, each was founded by a particular religious denomination, and each lived out its distinctive religious history well into the middle of the twentieth century. However each handled the cultural shifts that affected U.S. colleges in the 1960s, notably the multiple concerns relating to diversity, by developing quite different responses. I

Fr. Roc O'Connor, SJ, recently completed his service as rector of the Jesuit Community at Creighton University in Omaha, Nebraska; associate pastor at St. John's Parish; and an instructor in the theology department at Creighton University. While on sabbatical, he plans to complete a manuscript on liturgical participation. He is deeply grateful to have served with Rev. Lucy Forster-Smith and Rabbi Bernie Raskas at Macalester College for six years.

began to wonder whether a study of these two fine institutions might yield useful insights to questions chaplains across the country deal with today.

It was in conversation with two of my colleagues in this project that an intuition began to take shape. Rev. Ian Oliver, senior associate chaplain for Protestant life at Yale, remarked, "Our times are different. The university in this postmodern era abounds with multiple ethnicities, diverse experiences, and a variety of voices each making claims about life and truth and meaning." Rev. Dr. Richard Spalding, chaplain to the college at Williams College, added, "There is no clear rallying point, no cause that calls people together as one. There is no special seat at the table for Christianity today in the university. *As a Christian, I am one voice among many.*"

His account immediately brought to mind Plato's theory (put forward in the *Parmenides*) called "the One and the Many," an idea that I have found to be useful in considering the following fundamental philosophical, theological, and spiritual question: *Does one best approach reality from an "either/or" perspective or from a "both/and" orientation?* For example, when answering big issues about health care, immigration, gun control, or the economy, does a group set two factors in opposition to each another, thereby establishing an irreconcilable difference between them? Or does a group hold two alternatives in some form of creative tension that keeps them alive and in relationship?

Spalding's observation, "As a Christian, I am one voice among many," clearly expresses what chaplains are dealing with today as each grapples with how best to situate religion and the role of the chaplain within secular educational institutions, no matter their current or historical religious affiliation. This institution prioritizes the one singular religious perspective of its founding tradition. Another emphasizes the plurality of the many divergent faiths or non-faiths represented on even today's most "traditional" college campuses. So, how does the chaplain navigate a balance between remaining true to her or his own religious affiliation while also finding common ground with the many other faith communities in the same institution? Spalding's reflection led me to a preliminary conclusion that colleges and universities today operate largely from an "either/ or" system when it comes to dealing with the presence of religious persons in their institution. Next, I wondered: *might the language of "the One" and "the Many" contribute something significant to the conversation around the role of religion in educational institutions today?*

NAVIGATING THE ONE AND THE MANY

Thinking of an institution's relationship with religious tradition as a starting place, I delved into ways that schools navigate the relationship between the One and the Many. Colleges that continue to identify with a particular religion, like St. Olaf (Lutheran), Bard (Episcopal), Ave Maria (Roman Catholic), Moravian (Moravian), and Baylor (Southern Baptist Convention), stress the One by virtue of their acknowledged affiliation. To a greater or lesser degree, an institution that affirms the One relationship has made some commitment to endorse its founding religious tradition as the primary voice that will be heeded within the institution. It will support, in the main, one consistent view of the world, teach that point of view to its students, and ensure that it influences campus policies.

By contrast, secular institutions that identify themselves as nonsectarian, like Boston University, Brandeis, Cornell, Howard, Northwestern, Quinnipiac, Rice, Syracuse, the University of Chicago, and Washington University, put the accent on the Many—some from the time of their founding, others more recently, after their institutional identity shifted explicitly toward the secular.

When any sectarian college or university promotes the One, a particular overarching religious tradition, it does so as part of its fundamental identity. For example, when Creighton University designates itself as Catholic and Jesuit, it makes an overt claim about its character in the world. And yet, it's ironic: while yet putting the accent on the One, many sectarian schools have a growing population of those who do not claim affiliation with the dominant religious tradition. At the same time, more explicitly secular campuses, like Macalester, stress the Many by supporting diversity, at least in theory, through welcoming a wide array of viewpoints to the table.

Most American universities today, it would seem, operate from the "either/or" schema, at least in their institutional relationship to religious organizations. That is, they handle the modern reality of diversity on their campuses by either orienting themselves fully toward that multiplicity *or* toward reasserting the centrality of their religious heritage. In both cases, choosing one focus over the other creates a tension—campuses that emphasize the Many sometimes find themselves in an awkward, even embarrassed, relationship with their own, singular founding religion; campuses that emphasize the One risk excluding other religious voices in their community from important conversations.

It's not hard to understand why institutions facing these tensions might choose to move more definitively toward one pole or the other. However, what if a college chose to dwell within the tension of the powerful contraries found in the One and the Many as a way to discover a more creative way of living in this complex, postmodern world? Might it be possible that, by learning to abide within the tension of the One and the Many, both religiously sanctioned colleges and secular universities would mature in ways not anticipated by the "either/or" approach? I am coming to see that both religiously affiliated institutes and secular institutions can navigate the challenging waters of diversity by incorporating the notion of the One and the Many into their corporate processes. In other words, sectarian colleges could benefit as much by dealing more explicitly with the Many as secular colleges might profit by dealing more overtly with the One. Both Creighton and Macalester could learn a lot from each other!

Throughout the rest of this chapter, I will recommend that the paradoxical relationship between the One and the Many points to a new and potentially creative direction for the work of chaplains and campus ministers at colleges today. By suggesting approaches drawn from my experience at Creighton and Macalester, I hope both to offer chaplains in secular institutions a new way to draw from tradition while deepening relationships across the campus community and to offer campus ministers in sectarian colleges a challenge to associate in new and resourceful ways to connect with students and colleagues of diverse backgrounds.

Quite a number of religious communities founded colleges in the United States beginning in the seventeenth century, to form clergy (seminaries), educate the laity, and equip members with skills to advocate their beliefs. Education came to be respected as a way to learn virtue, become an informed citizen, grow in moral uprightness, and instruct ministers. A number of these colleges maintain strong ties to their founding religious traditions. Today, in the early twenty-first century, 65 institutions of higher education belong to the Association of Presbyterian Colleges and Universities. More than 40 colleges maintain official ties with Lutheran bodies (mostly ELCA or Missouri Synod). There are 11 schools listed as Jewish, and 20 are Quaker by origin. More than 110 colleges and universities are affiliated with the United Methodist Church, and 244 claim affiliation with the Roman Catholic Church.

I don't think I overstate the situation by saying that before 1970, few colleges and universities demonstrated much of an inclination to attend to divergent voices among students or within the academy. For the most part, institutions of higher education maintained some form of support for the One voice, whether explicitly religious or that of the dominant culture. Diversity and multiculturalism had yet to appear on the scene as significant forces with which to contend. It is at this point that I want to examine how the history of two particular campuses, Macalester and Creighton, diverged in interesting ways.

HISTORICAL MACALESTER: EMBRACING THE MANY, DISAVOWING THE ONE

Many major U.S. colleges and universities owe their beginnings to particular religious bodies. The founding of Macalester College in 1885, however, came about from the rather complicated intermingling of the personal vision of Edward Duffield Neill, the practical needs of fund-raising, and the situation of the Presbyterian Church in Minnesota at the time. Neill promoted a vision of a "nonsectarian Protestant college steeped in latitudinarian thought"[1] (what we might call nondenominational today) in response to ongoing conflicts shown in interdenominational rivalries.

Yet, Neill's inability to raise sufficient financial support for his dream led his successor, Rev. Thomas Alexander McCurdy, to establish a more direct relationship with the Presbyterian Synod of Minnesota for funding and direction. As a result, the early years of the college were devoted not only to the development of students' moral character but also to a solid Bible-based Christian formation in what resembles pre-seminary training. Over the decades that followed, the tension between Neill's vision and that of McCurdy continued. Both viewpoints vied to become the the governing perspective for the institution.

Several other movements affected the college in the aftermath of World War I. Liberal Protestantism with its emphasis on the social gospel merged with the recently embraced theory of evolution and historical-critical method of biblical analysis to begin to undermine the authority of the Bible and promote an orientation toward service and science, separate from religious meaning and influence. This guided Macalester's shift toward secularism.

Further tension between science and religion grew. Controversy over new curriculum proposals in the early 1930s, for example, drew denunciations concerning the threat of "secularism" by former president James Wallace. The confirmation of Charles Joseph Turck as president in 1940 demonstrated the growing influence of liberal Protestantism within the Presbyterian Church at that time. It stressed service over missionary activity and advanced a heightened sense of civic engagement and internationalism. For example, the board of trustees confirmed this stance in a 1958 statement on Macalester's identity: "(1) it was a liberal arts college; (2) it had a mission to provide 'useful citizenship' and a responsibility to the world, nation and community; (3) its curriculum provided undergraduate preparation for graduate work ... and (4) it had a mission to develop Christian faith and character, though in a nonsectarian spirit."[2]

Other events signaled additionally significant changes at Macalester. First, following the establishment of the United Nations in

1948, President Turck committed the school to recruiting a more international student body, a very forward-looking move indeed. Macalester opened its doors to the likes of Kofi Anan (former secretary general of the United Nations, Macalester class of '61) and many other distinguished students from across the globe. They brought an ever-expanding world perspective to the campus. Today, Macalester can proudly boast welcoming students from more than eighty-five countries.

Secondly, while there was no simplistic or abrupt changeover to secularization at Macalester, a whole series of decisions gradually distanced the institution from its complex religious roots. Especially in the 1960s, administrators and faculty increasingly found common ground with the nondenominational vision of Edward Neill. The board of trustees, for example, removed the stipulation that two-thirds of the members of the board ought to belong to and practice in the Presbyterian Church.[3] A 1961 long-range planning document employed a decidedly imprecise set of descriptors to define the college's connection to the Presbyterian Synod: "Taking good will rooted in faith to be basic ... Christian in spirit and Presbyterian in background, but not sectarian in outlook...."[4] The curriculum ceased to require courses on religion in 1970. Yet, in the midst of it all, the Weyerhaeuser family funded a nondenominational Christian chapel.

The third "event" had to do with the consciousness-raising campaigns of civil rights marches and anti–Vietnam War protests in the 1960s and early 1970s. These movements exercised enormous influence on all of American society. In their wake, other so-called minority groups gained access to the public forum. African Americans, Hispanics, Asians, the LGBTQ community, and women found their voices and discovered ways to have them heard in and through academia.

While to the dominant culture it seemed as if diversity materialized out of nowhere, it had been a growing reality at places like Macalester since World War II. The concept that all voices needed to be heard and respected (at least, in theory) merely heralded the recognition by many in the dominant culture of realities in others' lives that had been roundly ignored. And in a relatively brief time, broad acknowledgment of the Many became an essential tenet by which much of the academy began to gauge itself. Diversity became axiomatic at Macalester, as at many other progressive, liberal institutions.

During the 1970s, students and faculty pressured the college administration to move toward a more "secular" environment, all but rejecting its religious affiliation. Over the course of the twentieth century, Macalester shifted from an institutional emphasis on the One to the promotion of the Many.

As a result, Macalester retreated from its previously strong and direct association with the Presbyterian Church, leaving the chaplain and the chaplaincy on the periphery of campus life. Some, like historian Jeanne Halgren Kilde, lamented the loss of an underlying source of inspiration, compass, and direction that the college relinquished when it forsook its Christian roots:

> If the church-related component of the college's identity were abandoned, what ... would replace it as the college's central unifying factor? Indeed, the *function* religion had previously served as informing the college's underlying purpose had never been fully addressed, much less replaced by a new central component, either intellectual or ethical. As the college worked to tighten admission and improve faculty credentials, the discussion of values shifted to a secular concern for achievement and national recognition for its own sake and for the sake of the financial well-being of the institution.[5]

When I arrived at Macalester in the fall of 1993, I encountered an interim chaplain who regularly grieved the passing of the significance of the chaplaincy, the influence of the church, and the advent of an era that no longer regarded his ministry as significant. This was the setting into which Rev. Lucy Forster-Smith walked in January 1994. It was part of her genius that she invited Rabbi Bernie Raskas and me to join her as colleagues in the effort to bring divergent religious groups to the table and raise the visibility of religion and spirituality on campus. She started "Why I Believe What I Believe" dinner discussions with faculty, staff, and students and formed the Inter-Faith Council. Together, our "God Squad" went anywhere and everywhere on campus to keep dialogue about religions and religious issues alive. It was important work toward fostering and nurturing the Many at Macalester.

CULTURAL SHIFTS AT CREIGHTON: FACING THE MANY, EMBRACING THE ONE

Two brothers, John and Edward Creighton, moved from Ohio to the Omaha Territory in the 1840s with their wives, Mary Lucretia and Sara Emily Wareham. Edward died young after amassing a small fortune in the banking and telegraph industries. He left instructions in his will to provide for the founding of a Catholic college. Mary Lucretia established an endowment in her husband's name and petitioned Bishop James O'Connor (no relation ... really) to help found and staff the school. The bishop in turn petitioned the Jesuit superior in St. Louis to provide personnel for what opened as the Creighton College in 1878, serving the Catholic immigrants of eastern Nebraska and western Iowa.

Sometime near the beginning of the twentieth century, Creighton College differentiated itself into a high school (Creighton Preparatory School) and a university. From its founding until about 1970, the student body at Creighton University remained approximately 95 percent Catholic.

As elsewhere, the civil rights movement and antiwar protests shook Catholic campuses. But two other historical events also shaped Catholic universities. The Second Vatican Council (1963–65) had introduced for Catholics a new sense of belonging in the world and instilled a desire to relate with Protestants and Jews. The ecumenical/interfaith age had begun. In addition, thanks largely to the stunning success of its educational efforts throughout the latter half of the twentieth century, Catholic families moved out of poverty into the middle and upper middle classes.

No longer confined to "Catholic ghettos" by economics or bias, generations of Catholics adopted behaviors and attitudes not all that different from their Protestant neighbors—moving to the suburbs, joining country clubs, and choosing colleges for sons and daughters based on factors other than religious affiliation, but rather answering the question "Which school will help my child get ahead in life?" For example, when I started to apply to colleges (1967), I had one choice, since I was Catholic and lived in Omaha—Creighton. Yet, today, students investigate upwards of a dozen universities, preferring any school that aligns with their standards for advancement. Religious affiliation has for the most part become one option in a long list of other requisites.

While Catholic students were enrolling at Stanford, Harvard, and Yale, ever-increasing numbers of Protestant, Jewish, Muslim, Baha'i, Buddhist, and Hindu students also registered at sectarian universities not affiliated with their own faith traditions. Quality of education and hope for advancement replaced religious affiliation as the primary motive for selecting a college. Thus, Creighton went from being 95 percent Catholic in 1968 to 64 percent Catholic in 2011. The Many had arrived.

It may seem rather improbable, then, that in this same period, Creighton and other Roman Catholic institutions of higher learning chose to reaffirm and reengage their religious origins, especially after 1968, when many decided to separately incorporate by establishing lay boards. This move legally (but not religiously) disengaged the institution from their founding religious communities. Even more surprisingly, colleges and universities founded by various Catholic religious communities (Benedictines, Franciscans, Dominicans, Mercy Sisters, RSCJ, Salesians, Jesuits, and others) responded by enriching their campuses with their recently recovered spiritual charisms.

Nevertheless, it was the charismatic leadership of Pope John Paul II (1978–2005) that promoted clear-cut distinctions from other Christian denominations, clarified theological doctrines, and sharpened the understanding of what it means to be Roman Catholic. In his encyclical *Ex Corde Ecclesiae* (1990), the pope set forth guidelines to foster unambiguous relationships between Roman Catholic institutions of higher education, local bishops, and Rome, thus ushering in an era of greater focus on Catholic identity. For example, *Ex Corde* required every Catholic university or college theology department to receive a *mandatum,* or mandate, from the local bishop for each professor teaching Catholic morality or theological doctrine. (Creighton is one of a handful of Catholic universities whose theological faculty has been granted the *mandatum.*)

John Paul II's influence prompted a new trend: a growing number of Catholic families began to put religious identity at or very near the top of their list of conditions affecting choice of college. Still, it seems curious that a clearer consciousness of its Jesuit *and* Catholic identity took hold at Creighton during the same period that its faculty, staff, and student body were becoming more and more diverse. As the Many emerged on campus, the university made a conscious decision to accentuate the One.

THE ONE AND THE MANY IN RELATIONSHIP

There are a number of expressions that have been used when of speaking of the relationship of opposites. For example, Carl Jung borrowed the term *conjunctio,* "conjunction," from alchemy and applied it to the psychological coming together of the conscious and the unconscious (individuation). The science of electricity understands *polarity* as "the quality of exhibiting opposite or contrasted properties or powers in opposite or contrasted directions; the state of having two opposite or contradictory tendencies, opinions, or aspects."[6] The Tao itself embodies the interaction between yin and yang and offers an ancient model for the dynamic relationship between opposites demonstrating the worth of maintaining actively energetic connections between them.

Permit me to use the term "paradox" here. Over the past few years, I have noticed that this term has been used in a similar manner to "the Tao," even though it seems to be related historically more to words like "contradiction," "incongruity," or even "absurdity." I will use this term to indicate the dynamic interaction of opposites, of contrarieties, even of absurdities held in creative tension.

Paradox abides deep in the heart of life. Over the ages, theology, philosophy, and other academic disciplines have faced the temptation of resolving the fundamental tension between the One and the Many by emphasizing one component over the other: unity *or* diversity, the universal *or* the particular, conformity *or* variety, univocal *or* multivocal, and so on. Setting one against the other offers precision that allows clarity in making judgments. It also characterizes the stage of development known as *adolescent.*

Perhaps children or adolescents don't notice paradox. There are always enough people willing to tell them how and what to choose. Yet as human beings journey into adulthood and are faced with more and more weighty choices, it is possible to discover how many of our "either/or" alternatives have become "both/and" opportunities. For example, young adults face significant choices like "career or calling," "making money or meaning," and the like. As people mature, I believe we realize how truly human tensions like "independence/dependence," "security/insecurity," and "sovereignty/surrender," or "individual/community," for example, are best resolved not by selecting one over the other but by abiding in the tension between them.

With this in mind, I've come to better appreciate the apparent conflict between the One and the Many on college campuses like Creighton and Macalester. Although these two institutions have both changed dramatically, I find an unconventional relationship between them. It seems to me that even though Creighton is more religiously diverse today, it is also more consciously Catholic and Jesuit than it was sixty years ago. At the same time, Macalester has become both more religiously diverse *and* secular than it was sixty years ago. As both institutions have grappled with the increased diversity of their student bodies since the 1970s, their relationship to their historical, founding tradition has moved in an opposite direction—Macalester toward secularity and Creighton toward reaffirming its Catholic identity. Perhaps enough time has passed now for us to recognize that simply prioritizing the One or the Many does not satisfyingly resolve the tension between them. Another, more mature, solution is needed.

What if each institution forged a new and creative synthesis by relating more intentionally with the opposite term of this paradoxical relationship? This means that students, faculty, staff, and administrators at Creighton (or other religiously affiliated colleges), which emphasize the One, would work out a more conscious relation to the Many. At the same time, Macalester (and other secular colleges or universities that emphasize the Many) would seek to dwell intentionally in tension with the One. In both cases, the chaplain or campus minster would assume an essential role of fostering creative dialogue with colleagues.

My basic thesis is that college and university chaplains or campus ministers have our work cut out for us in different yet oddly paradoxical ways that reveal variations on the theme of the One and the Many. At now-secular schools founded by religious groups, chaplains of the original religious traditions find themselves as one voice among many. At schools that maintain their association with their founding religious traditions, chaplains or campus ministers are invited to relate to a breadth of other traditions in the student body, staff, faculty, administrators, and alumni.

I recommend that dwelling creatively within the tensions of opposites, especially within the One and the Many, offers a way through the relatively monadic existences lived out on our campuses. The choice to abide in such tension *in relationship* calls us to recognize the limitations of the ideologically compatible groups to whom we now offer allegiance. The act of living within this tension offers a difficult route to maturity for institutions of higher education today for both types of college. At Macalester, I was able to see how a secular institution worked to include the Many; at Creighton, I'm aware of how our relationship with the One offers us a clear institutional and moral perspective. Drawing from both of these experiences, I would like to offer some frameworks by which secular and sectarian institutions might borrow from each other's strengths and work toward a more constructive relationship between the One and Many on their own campuses.

EXHILARATING DIALOGUE: THE ONE AMONG MANY

In many ways, Macalester's emphasis on the Many is an earnest response to the reality of religiously diverse campus life—a reality that's increasingly the case even at One-oriented institutions like Creighton. During my time at Macalester, I learned the value of honoring the Many religious and nonreligious voices on campus. It's a perspective I've taken with me into my work at Creighton.

As the Catholic chaplain at Macalester, I found it invigorating to engage with all kinds of students—Catholics as well as those practicing other religions or none. I loved learning about the life experiences of students who came from around the globe. I found that young people often had profound questions to which they had discovered tentative answers and were looking for someone to hear them. My job for six years was to go around and talk and listen—to students, faculty, staff, and administrators. I simply listened and asked questions about their experiences.

These conversations were often informal, but I also learned the importance of creating more formal spaces for free-ranging discussion. "Cigar Club" grew from the practice of two students (Mike and Dylan) who met on the bleachers of the football stadium in the evening. They would watch the sunset, smoke some cigars, and talk. Hearing about their experience, I suggested opening it up to more students who wished to speak about important things. It became a sort of philosophical and theological conversation society. Together, we learned how to converse with each other. In doing so, we also learned how to maintain respect for each person's individual experience and difference. By trying to listen and not just babble on, we also called each other into a sense of inquiry into the experience of others that was respectful and engaging.

This kind of conversation across differences is something that secular institutions like Macalester have been working hard to develop for the last forty years. But because increasing diversity is a reality even at sectarian institutions, dialogue, discovery, listening, and discussion between the One and the Many takes on greater importance at those colleges as well.

By constructing formal environments for dialogue, institutions can create a kind of holding tank for people to be in discussion and share about what they understand, believe, and do. In a way, the discussion space works likes a crucible in which different chemical elements retain their own integrity, even as they react and produce something new. The point of dialogue has nothing to do with one group *becoming* the other or subsuming the other. Rather, each maintains its particular distinctness in the *presence* of the other. Thus dialogue serves as the process by which creative tension between the One and the Many is fostered.

Dialogue like this achieves at least two ends. First, participants grow in self-identity. By meaningfully encountering the other, participants' commitment to and understanding of their own traditions grow and deepen, even as assumptions and expectations are challenged. At the same time, participants' openness to listen and engage the other in dialogue, action for the common good, and eventually theological exchange creates actual community by gradually relaxing barriers with those who at first seemed so distantly "other." For institutions like Creighton who have reaffirmed institutional commitments to a single religious identity, formalizing dialogue offers a way to dwell creatively in tension between the One and the Many.

In fact, such institutions may be able to look to their own traditions for invitation to dialogue. Instead of making it up out of whole cloth, they may find already existing paradigms for commitment to relationship between One and Many. In my own tradition, contemporary international Jesuit documents on interreligious dialogue have laid out a fourfold strategy including the dialogue of living as good neighbors, of action for the common good, of religious experience, and of theological exchange. The fact that these recommendations exist but are often ignored or overlooked speaks to me of the need for institutions oriented toward the One to consider the perspective and example offered by Many-focused institutions where fostering interreligious dialogue has been a priority for decades.

I would also like to offer an example of how one group of religiously affiliated institutions mined its own tradition for invitations to dialogue and fashioned a new relationship with the Many while remaining consistent to its own commitment to the One.

DRAWING FROM THE ONE TO ENGAGE THE MANY

Today Creighton University acknowledges up front that it is Catholic and Jesuit. This choice obviously orients the school more strongly toward the One and less toward the Many. And, like other Roman Catholic institutions, Creighton is involved in an ongoing realization of what it means to be connected to the One while incorporating a diverse population of students, faculty, staff, and administration.

For the past forty years Creighton, as well as the twenty-seven other Jesuit Catholic colleges and universities, has attempted this by articulating what we call the "Jesuit values" as a way of inviting commitment to a common mission from the broader population.

Having ruled out both proselytizing and requiring adherence to Roman Catholic practice from students, staff, faculty, and administrators, Jesuits and lay colleagues at all our institutions of higher learning have identified various articulations of "Jesuit values" or "Ignatian charisms." The following have become operative at Creighton:

Magis: This Latin term is best translated "the more" or "the better," indicating discernment of the next "better" step.

Women and Men for and with Others: The Creighton mission involves encouragement of sharing gifts, pursuing justice, and concern for the poor and marginalized.

Cura Personalis: This Latin phrase means "personal care" or "care for the whole person." It is rooted in respect for each person as a child of God and for all of God's creations.

Unity of Heart, Mind, and Soul: This not only points to personal integration within each individual, but the work for union among all.

Ad Majorem Dei Gloriam (AMDG): "For the Greater Glory of God" served as Ignatius's motto. It signifies an orientation toward the One who is Greater.

Forming and Educating Agents of Change. The Creighton mission means to teach students to reflect critically on the signs of the times and take responsible action on moral and ethical issues.

These expressions of the guiding principles of the university are rooted in the *Spiritual Exercises* of Saint Ignatius and were formulated with an eye to make a way for as many as possible on campus to connect with the mission of the university. Because they are highly distilled expressions that summarize key spiritual currents from Ignatius's *Spiritual Exercises*, they are embedded in the Jesuit Catholic tradition yet leave the door open for further and further exploration. Since proselytizing is not our practice, we have carefully distilled these statements of Ignatian values to permit deeper dialogue, collaboration, and even investigation. In other words, they offer a way of focusing the Jesuit Catholic mission of Creighton University to invite the Many who are not Catholic or Christian to participate authentically in the mission of the institution. The common experience on campus today is that people from many and varied religious traditions readily resonate with these "Jesuit values."

So here's the question for my colleagues on secular campuses: *Might this approach serve as a model for chaplains at colleges that have moved away from their founding religious tradition?* That is: What if a chaplain could articulate a spirituality intended to nurture conversation with his students faculty, staff, members of the board, and administrators in order to bring about a new level of relationship? What does the chaplain have to offer from her own tradition that could connect with those from many other points of view on campus? Might the chaplain serve as a unifying force for the college by engaging many different voices (the Many) with his or her voice (the One)?

Here is a brief sketch of my proposal:

1. A study of the university's mission statement yields values to connect with the religious tradition's founder.

2. A distillation of the spiritual writings of the religious founder generates potential value affirmations to relate to mission statement ideals.

3. The chaplain articulates five to six values from the religious tradition and demonstrates their connection to the university's mission statement.

4. The chaplain seeks broad support from students and colleagues through dialogue about these values and works toward ways to strengthen the university's mission.

A fuller explanation of the process: The head chaplain at a secular college or university articulates from his or her own religious tradition a coherent, distilled expression of the religious tradition's spirituality that speaks to the Many from the point of view of the One as related to the university's mission statement.

This religious tradition looks to the biography and writings of its foundational figure as a source from which to propose a coherent spirituality to students, faculty, staff, alumni, and administration to foster dialogue between the Many and the One. That would mean, for example, that Hindus could draw upon the life story and writings of Mahatma Gandhi; Buddhists on the life and writings of the Buddha and subsequent teachers; Muslims on Muhammad or Avicenna; Jews on Moses, Solomon, and the prophets; Lutherans on Martin Luther; Presbyterians on John Calvin; Methodists on John Wesley or the hymns of Charles Wesley; and so on.

This practice draws upon the fundamental wisdom contained in every religious tradition that is held and passed along in the writings and the life story of its foundational figure or figures. By studying the life and words of the foundational figure(s), colleagues gain insight into their own lives, catching a glimpse of the processes at work that led to their transformation.

Similarly, making the effort to offer a spirituality of the religious tradition's founder as it stands in relation to the university's mission statement reveals three things. First, it shows how the religious tradition is deeply connected to the life and mission of the college. That is, as the religion's ideals square with *these particular* values of the college, the chaplain can offer support from a surprising quarter. Second, the religious tradition can offer further insight, depth, and even collegial appraisal of the *practice* of the mission. It is not enough merely to support, but must enrich the mission of the school by offering a coherent foundation for reviewing its practices. Third, it leaves the door open for students and colleagues to delve further into the depths of the religious tradition if they decide to do so without the onus of coercion.

Such a statement of distilled founding principles would not only show the chaplaincy's support for the college, but also provide standards for helping the administration and faculty evaluate its progress. I believe that such an expression of the religious tradition can serve the college or university community and open new levels of dialogue within the institution.

So much has changed since the founding of these colleges. At that time, the One ruled; its sphere of influence was pervasive. Today, the One competes with the Many, to the point that the One is sometimes considered expendable. So does the future hold only estrangement and hostility between these contrary forces? In this multicultural, postmodern world where we live, with so many voices competing for ascendancy, can the chaplain became a force for union rather than uniformity, for relationship instead of homogeneity?

I propose that religious leaders live out the fundamental meaning of religion (*religare*, "to bind together") by bringing people together. I suggest that representatives of the One draw the Many into dialogue toward mutual and reciprocal communion, not conformity. At sectarian colleges, encouraging dialogue between the One and the Many could deepen institutional identity while simultaneously establishing permeability in the One, fostering the identities of the Many, and allowing for a deeper relationship with the One. By inviting the secular campus to dialogue about its One, chaplains might draw others into a confirming experience of individual identities while promoting a new rapport together. At the heart of these recommendations is the belief that engagement with the other through meaningful dialogue confirms one's identity even as it grounds it.

I hope that this set of reflections will prompt discussion, critique, and adaptation among my colleagues. *Ad Majorem Dei Gloria.*

"WHAT HAS ATHENS TO DO WITH JERUSALEM?"
The Professor Chaplain

Rev. Dr. J. Diane Mowrey
Queens University of Charlotte, Charlotte, North Carolina

> "Only connect."
>
> E. M. Forester, *Howards End*

The chapel at Queens University sits on one corner of the campus. It is a classical building with Doric columns in front and floor-to-ceiling side windows made of individual handblown panes of glass that diffuse the sunlight and create a warm, inviting interior space. Until this year, the chapel was the first building one saw when driving to campus from Charlotte's city center. Now, a new "green" science and health building rises in front of the chapel, in formerly open space once occupied by trees, grass, and azaleas. If we were given to symbolism (and alas, I am one of those people), we might interpret the prominence of the new science and health building as

---

Rev. Dr. J. Diane Mowrey serves as chaplain and is the Mrs. John R. Irwin Professor of Bible at Queens University of Charlotte in Charlotte, North Carolina. She is a past president of the Presbyterian College Chaplains Association, former associate pastor of Church of the Pilgrims in Washington, D.C., and former assistant professor of English at Hamilton College. She loves to travel, especially with students and colleagues on mission or peace and reconciliation trips, and enjoys spending time with friends or family over coffee or at the beach.

a metaphor for the many ways science and scientific thought have taken over the intellectual and cultural landscape since the Enlightenment. Even in our "postmodern" era, we still give lip service, if not a wholehearted embrace, to a scientific worldview with its reliance on empirical data, and we dismiss, either explicitly or implicitly, and marginalize a religious or spiritual worldview. And so we might lament the passing of an era when chapels, chaplains, and religious commitments were front and center on many campuses, at Queens and in other universities.

Another interpretation of this new arrangement, though, might be to see the chapel, representative of things spiritual, as being embedded more deeply, if less obviously, into our campus culture. Such an image would the reflect findings of a recent UCLA study on spirituality. Surveying over 14,500 college students at 136 colleges from their freshman to junior years, UCLA researchers found the following:

> Today's entering college students report high levels of spiritual interest and involvement. Four in five indicate "having an interest in spirituality" and "believing in the sacredness of life," and nearly two-thirds say that "my spirituality is a source of joy." Many are also actively engaged in a spiritual quest, with nearly half reporting that they consider it "essential" or "very important" to seek opportunities to help them grow spiritually. Moreover, three-fourths of the students say that they are "searching for meaning/purpose in life.[1]

So while the shifting geography of our campuses symbolizes a change in our cultural approach to religion and spirituality, researchers like those with the UCLA study—and university chaplains—recognize that questions of faith remain alive although they may be buried or hidden behind other concerns. This shifting landscape obviously has implications for me and for other chaplains.

As I ponder the chapel's "new location" on campus—is it still the cornerstone of the university? something overshadowed by "science" and dismissed? or important but in less obvious ways?—our new campus geography raises questions that have echoed through the ages, and that form a framework for my chaplaincy. In the third century CE, Tertullian, one of the early Christian church fathers, raised questions about the relationship between reason and faith. He wrote:

> What indeed has Athens to do with Jerusalem? What concord is there between the Academy and the Church? What between heretics and Christians? Our instruction comes from "the porch of Solomon," who had himself taught that "the Lord should be sought in simplicity of heart."[2]

Tertullian was concerned with truth and knowledge, and he was worried about pagans and heretics leading Christians astray. He was also concerned about the priority of a Christian's commitments. In a hierarchy of faith and reason, for Tertullian, faith should come first and would guide and direct the explorations of reason in the academy and in life. Tertullian was among the first to voice a concern about the relationship between faith and reason.

Centuries later, in the opening line of his *Institutes of Christian Faith*, John Calvin would articulate this relationship differently:

> Nearly all the wisdom we possess, that is to say, true and sound wisdom, consists of two parts: the knowledge of God and of ourselves. But, while joined by many bonds, which one precedes and brings forth the other is not easy to discern. In the first place, no one can look upon himself without immediately turning his thoughts to the contemplation of God, in whom he "lives and moves" [Acts 17:28]. For, quite clearly, the mighty gifts with which we are endowed are hardly from ourselves; indeed, our very being is nothing but subsistence in the one God.[3]

Calvin understood the complexity of the bonds between knowledge of self and knowledge of God, which although not coterminous with

Athens and Jerusalem, reflect some of the same tensions and questions. For Calvin, though, everything is of God. As noted by some Calvin scholars, "because all reality and life is God's ... there are no sacred places, if this implies that other places are profane. All the world is sacred."[4] The modern, Western tendency to see the world in a series of dualities—sacred and profane, reason and religion, Athens and Jerusalem—would for Calvin have been a curious perspective. Like Tertullian, Calvin would give first priority to Jerusalem, knowledge of God; but unlike Tertullian, Calvin sees not a hierarchy but a complex relationship where the sacred forms the context for all exploration.

Similar questions about faith and knowledge lie behind both Tertullian and Calvin's thinking: Are these two central arenas of human life in conflict with each other? Does one have priority or dominance over the other? Are they separate realms that should not mix and mingle? Or is there perhaps yet another, third way, a paradoxical relationship not yet seen? Tertullian concluded that one (faith) should have priority over the other; Calvin's vision here is of the interrelationship of faith and reason. Over the years, many other voices have joined into this debate, and it is one that chaplains in particular confront in various ways.

What indeed does Athens have to do with Jerusalem? As a chaplain whose call includes a faculty appointment where I teach two courses a semester, this question is of more than historical (or now geographical) interest to me. During my interview for the position of chaplain, the college president, Dr. Billy O. Wireman, said to me, "We want a chaplain with academic credentials. We want someone who can hold her own with the faculty, especially as we develop our core curriculum." He continued, "One of your challenges will be to make sure that Queens's historical commitment to religious and ethical values is an integral part of that program. That means you'll have to find ways to work with the faculty." My PhD in English (with a minor in religion) is the "entry card," as it were, into the faculty guild, and it puts me on equal footing with my faculty colleagues.

To further Dr. Wireman's vision of a chaplain as one whose role includes teaching, I not only preached a sermon in a local church as part of the call process required by my Presbyterian denomination, but I also taught a class to a group of American literature students and faculty. Teaching a class is required for all applicants for tenure-track faculty positions, and Dr. Wireman knew that any chaplain with faculty status would have to pass the "teaching test." Dr. Wireman envisioned a large part of my chaplaincy to be involved in the academic side of Queens in exploring and developing the connection between Jerusalem and Athens in the curriculum and beyond.

ATHENS AND JERUSALEM: CURRICULUM CONCERNS

The question "What has Athens to do with Jerusalem?" was answered early in my time at Queens when I encountered some faculty colleagues whose actions suggested that their answer to this question is "Nothing!" I had proposed a new course titled "Christian Pacifism." How exciting it would be, I thought, to offer students an opportunity to explore the ideas and lives of people like Dorothy Day, Dietrich Bonhoeffer, Martin Luther King Jr., John Howard Yoder, and Bishop Desmond Tutu. I was surprised, then, when several faculty members raised informal objections to this proposal on the grounds that I would be "teaching a point of view." "Hmmm," I thought, "and when my colleagues teach a course called 'Peace and War' or 'Market Capitalism,' they're not teaching a point of view?" I remember being surprised and upset by the assumptions and conclusions some of my colleagues voiced about my course proposal.

My colleagues' real fear, I suspect, was that I would be using the topic and classroom to influence people's beliefs (which I wouldn't do in the sense they feared) and that I would expect students to be "converted" (although no one used this language) to being Christian and pacifists. (Some probably wouldn't have minded if I were to convert students to pacifism, but most would have had serious concerns about any hint of faith conversion.) In addition, they may also have thought that an apparent faith topic like Christian pacifism could hardly be the stuff of serious academic endeavor. I didn't pursue the idea of teaching the course.

But as it turned out, several years later, after I had been at Queens for a while, I submitted a similar course proposal that was approved without a murmur; more recently, my department and others developed a minor in "Peace Studies and Conflict Resolution." A benefit of years of working together meant either that my colleagues had changed their opinions on the place of faith topics in a classroom (hardly likely in some cases) or that they had begun to see some possible connections between Athens and Jerusalem that did not portend the end of the academic world as they knew it. The debate and tension about the connections between Athens and Jerusalem continued to arise, however, at other points in those early years, so my faculty colleagues and I had had ample opportunities to explore each other's views.

Similar tensions arose as I attempted to fulfill the charge President Wireman gave me upon arrival: to integrate religion into the Queens core program. These discussions and debates often revealed not only the tensions in the academy between Athens and Jerusalem but also the rift in individuals' lives between their own faith and spirituality and how that connects—or not—to their lives as professors. In these discussions sometimes, as Freud noted, "a cigar is just a cigar," but other times it represents something deeper.

When a colleague, in my first few years at Queens, opened a teaching-team meeting with the seemingly innocent comment that "we need to cut some of the units here," I sensed something more than a concern for the number of pages we were assigning the freshmen. So I asked, "Are you referring to all the units or specifically to the Bible unit?" That unit was relatively new at the time, and this professor had expressed doubts about including it at all. "Well, the Bible unit, yes," my colleague responded. "It's too long. We need to shorten it." Objectively that wasn't true; we were assigning most of the *Iliad,* most of Dante's *Inferno,* and four short selections from the Bible. Some other concern lay behind my colleague's objection.

I wish I could say that at the time I recognized the complex, multilayered nature of this resistance to teaching the Bible. Our core program, like most interdisciplinary programs, is built on having faculty teach outside their field of expertise. What we were teaching by example was an attitude of mind, a spirit of inquiry as much as any specific content, but faculty are often nervous about teaching texts in a discipline remote from their own. And as chaplain and religion team member, I had (I thought) addressed my colleagues' fears about teaching the Bible by providing a weeklong seminar on "How to Teach the Bible in Core Programs," bringing in expert teachers and scholars like Dr. James Tabor from the University of North Carolina–Charlotte and faculty from Duke and Colgate and other similar schools.

The concern about teaching the Bible in our core program opened the door to larger issues, both personal and pedagogical. Like my proposal to teach a course on Christian pacifism, the idea of teaching the Bible—especially in a Bible Belt state—raised the ongoing pedagogical question of objectivity in the classroom. On another level, it also touched a nerve for some of my colleagues and raised questions about their own faith journeys. To be sure, as a religion professor wisely said once, teaching the Bible is—and is not—like teaching the *Iliad* or the *Inferno*. The Bible is one of the single most important literary sources for reading and understanding centuries of English literature and Western culture, and so it has a rightful place in any academic curriculum. On the other hand, no one is likely to see the *Iliad* as a living scripture and use the detailed descriptions of ritual sacrifices to Apollo or Aphrodite as instructions on how one should conduct one's own life. Like a charged electron of an atom, so the Bible enters a classroom, creating indeed a different, even exciting, but also difficult classroom situation. And teaching the Bible in a university like Queens, which at the time drew the majority of its students from the South, meant the Bible was an even more charged topic than it might have been in a different context.

The resistance was, I gradually realized, not only intellectual but also emotional and personal. This connection became clearer on the day when another religion colleague and I had the team faculty do an exercise we planned on using with our students. We asked everyone to describe an early memory or experience with the Bible or religion. No censoring, just free-write, we instructed. From that exercise we heard stories of a colleague's great-grandfather who had been a Methodist preacher and circuit rider who had traveled throughout the mountains of North Carolina. Another talked about the home altar and icons her Italian grandmother set up in her bedroom, where she burned votive candles and incense. Others talked about fire-and-brimstone preachers recollected from childhood. At the time (it would no doubt be different now with a younger generation of faculty), everyone had a vivid story, some disturbing, some pleasant. But many of these stories, it seemed, had been packed away in a box and stored deep in their memory. Teaching the Bible—as a literary and cultural text—opened the door to those memories and left my colleagues uncertain what to do with their dusty but vivid recollections. The exercise had raised a practical question in their own lives of how to connect Athens and Jerusalem.

Dr. Wireman as college president liked to remind the faculty that the Chinese character for "crisis" also meant "opportunity." When questions like that about the Bible unit were raised, it felt at times—at least to me, at least at first—like a crisis. From my perspective, finding ways to connect Athens and Jerusalem seemed to offer a richness and depth for our students' academic experience, but obviously some of my colleagues saw things differently, or at the very least were suspicious of faith entering a classroom. These early discussions about curriculum concerns challenged me to find a way to stay true to the charge that Dr. Wireman had articulated when I first arrived as chaplain, but also to respond with pastoral sensitivity and academic integrity to my colleagues' concerns. With time and ongoing discussions, I came eventually to see these challenges as opportunities.

ATHENS AND JERUSALEM: OUTSIDE THE CURRICULUM

Even as I was trying to navigate the waters between Athens and Jerusalem in curricular matters, other avenues for exploring this link presented themselves. At the opening faculty meeting of every academic semester, I introduce myself by using the old line that a chaplain's role is to "comfort the afflicted and afflict the comfortable." At times when a student or another community member dies, my pastoral role to comfort the afflicted is obvious. But sometimes an "affliction" may be as simple as a yearning for a deeper sense of God's presence, a yearning to connect the various parts of one's life.

Because of my accessibility as chaplain to everyone in the community, it seemed natural that during my first few years at Queens a lot of faculty and staff kept stopping me to ask what I thought of the then-popular book *Care of the Soul* by Thomas Moore. To be honest, I had started reading Moore's book and was not impressed. But I could tell by my colleagues' questions that they weren't really looking for me to say, "Well, I think it's a bit thin," or "I really couldn't get into it," or "Maybe we should read the other Thomas More?" While I didn't join with my colleagues' enthusiastic accolades, I also didn't try to squelch their obvious excitement. Finally, someone suggested I gather a group together to discuss Moore's book.

This suggestion formed an ironic counterpoint to the discussions about the Bible curriculum that I had been having at around the same time, especially since some of the same people were involved in both discussions. As a way to stop the seemingly endless barrage of queries and comments about Moore's book, which I knew by that point I'd never read on my own, I agreed. So a group was born—long before book clubs were the thing to do. The idea was simple: everyone who was interested would bring a lunch to a separate dining room, and for six weeks we would talk about the book. And we did. I suggested some basic ground rules: no attention would be paid to titles or campus hierarchies, anything discussed was confidential, and we would meet for only six weeks. While divisions between faculty and staff are not very pronounced at Queens, it was still unusual to have the academic vice president sitting next to a data-entry person and across from the president. Other staff and faculty members were regular attendees, including a chemistry professor who regularly took on the academic vice president in faculty meetings—but for these discussions, everyone left campus politics at the door.

After the first year, some folks said, "Let's do that again, let's have another 'Care of the Soul' group," as they called it. They claimed the title from Moore's book, and it seemed to capture what everyone wanted but didn't really know how to articulate: a different way for our community to gather and "care for our souls," a way to move beyond the defined disciplines and roles we each filled and see ourselves whole. The second year we asked interested faculty and staff to come up with ideas (thankfully no one wanted to reread *Care of the Soul*), and that year we read Wayne Muller's *Sabbath*. At different times the group included a Sufi practitioner, conservative and liberal Christians, seekers, and agnostics, who all came to talk—not about Queens's problems and challenges but about their reactions to Muller or to Henri Nouwen's *Beloved* or about holiday practices and rituals different from their own religious traditions. Folks came because they recognized at some level that we are not only rational academics but also people with a spiritual core.

As week followed week, I had to admit to myself that it ultimately didn't matter that I wouldn't have chosen *Care of the Soul* as our companion for that first journey. What mattered was what emerged as we began those first tentative steps in learning how to care for others' as well as our own souls. What mattered was that we discovered together how God moves in and among us in unexpected ways and that together we could discern the traces of the Spirit's movement in our midst. What mattered was that each of us heard an invitation to move deeper into the mystery of God's presence and that each of us found our own life story expanded and enhanced. What mattered was that together we discovered the wonder and mystery of our lives and the world. The group had found its own way toward a different answer of the relationship between Athens and Jerusalem. The apparent dichotomy, even hostility, between Athens and Jerusalem that would arise in curriculum discussions became less pronounced as colleagues explored this question from a personal perspective. Everyone felt free to define how they experienced the Spirit, the transcendent, the ineffable, and how they connected those experiences with their intellectual lives.

In many ways, "caring for the soul" involves caring not only for the people at the university but also for the university itself, and this responsibility defines in many ways who I am as chaplain. As I occasionally say to our current president, Dr. Pamela Davies, she and I are the only two people who have as our job descriptions to care and focus on the *whole* university. That care can take different shapes at different times, but it always means looking for ways to encourage and support connections that move us out of our narrow compartments toward a wholeness that will integrate head and heart, mind and soul, the tangible and intangible (or any of the other false dualism that can define our lives). Athens and Jerusalem need each other, just as each of us needs to find ways to nurture our own spirits and strengthen our souls, especially in this era that privileges the quantifiable and that threatens to domesticate the Mystery that lies deep at the heart of creation.

Caring for the "soul of the university" suggests a more grandiose image of my role as chaplain than exists in reality. When pastoral concerns arise—an accident, death of a student, cancer—most everyone welcomes the chaplain and looks to me to take the lead. Caring for the soul, and linking Athens and Jerusalem, can also mean raising questions about the moral center of our corporate lives. Fortunately or unfortunately, depending on your point of view, I feel more kinship with Prufrock, who would say, "I am no prophet,"[5] than with a William Sloan Coffin. I'm not sure how I would have fared as a chaplain in the 1960s when chaplains like Coffin were the prophetic voices challenging universities to demonstrate their values through their actions in the board rooms and in the streets. Instead I find myself (along with others at Queens) raising questions, often behind the scenes, about what is right: Are we paying our service employees a living wage? Are we (the university) making decisions that flow from and reflect our core values? Is the financial bottom line, though important to be sure, always the final trump card in crafting university policy? Being seen as a spokesperson for

Jerusalem means raising these and other questions as I attempt to care for the soul of the university. It means seeking ways to make sure that we will not lose our way—or our soul—amidst the pressures of a market-driven world.

Caring for the soul means challenging everyone—the university, faculty and staff colleagues, and students—to find ways to connect parts of their lives that we may have compartmentalized but that are meant to be together. Our educational system encourages that compartmentalization to a large degree in spite of university mission statements that talk about "educating the whole person." Having a "Care of the Soul" lunch discussion group created an opportunity outside the normal academic curriculum where folks could explore the connections between Athens and Jerusalem informally. The challenge always lies in making those connections within the classroom.

ATHENS AND JERUSALEM:
THE CLASSROOM AND BEYOND

The tensions between Athens and Jerusalem heighten, as I was well aware during my early years at Queens, when we try to introduce this exploration into the classroom and curriculum. Historically, faculty and students have learned, appropriately perhaps, to be engaged and even passionate about learning, but to keep our personal lives separate from the classroom. When everyone agrees to focus on the subject matter at hand and to leave anything too personal or spiritual for some other venue, classrooms "work." Is it really relevant to a classroom discussion of the ethics of steroid use, for example, to have a student share about his or her recovery from a different drug addiction? Isn't that "too much information," as many faculty members would lament? In this Facebook era, we are experiencing a shifting of these public/private boundaries. If Calvin was right that wisdom consists in "knowledge of God and knowledge of ourselves,"[6] should that search for wisdom and connections between what might appear to be a purely academic subject and students' own lives and souls be confined solely to chapels, fellowship groups, or therapists' offices?

Classrooms are not, nor should be, group therapy sessions (most faculty would shudder at the thought). On the other hand, students do desire to find connections between their academic lives and their inner lives, as documented by the UCLA spirituality study, among others. Students' sometimes inappropriate comments indicate both the depth of their yearning to be whole and, at times, the pain they live with in our divided and compartmentalized world. Students, like some faculty, seek a middle territory—a third way—between a purely "knowledge for knowledge's sake" approach and a "confessional, group therapy" classroom where anything goes. (Both extremes send chills down my spine.)

Barbara Walvoord identified this gap, what she calls "the great divide," when she researched the teaching of religion in 533 introductory religion courses across numerous universities. She defines the "great divide" as the gap between the goals that faculty regard as primary and those that students prioritize. Faculty generally listed their primary goal for their classes as developing "critical thinking," while students most frequently aspire "to learn factual information, understand other religions and/or their own, and develop their own spiritual and religious lives."[7] Walvoord continues in this groundbreaking study to further observe, "What happens when students who want to work on their own spiritual and religious development meet faculty members' demands for critical thinking? The broadest answer is that colliding worlds create energy."[8] Are Athens and Jerusalem "colliding worlds"? And if so, is the creation of energy from that collision worth the initial disruptions?

Certainly, my educational philosophy, created in the cauldron of the late 1960s' upheavals on college campuses was shaped by reading thinkers like Ivan Ilich and Paulo Freire and by seminary professors like Katie Cannon, Nancy Jay, and Harvey Cox, who taught and lived their theology and welcomed me to explore and experiment with worlds or arenas that potentially might collide. During my undergraduate years, some of my professors took our "readings" to the streets, as they invited their students to protest against the Vietnam War. Consequently, I saw what could happen when universities or professors looked beyond their traditional ivory towers. In these settings, classroom readings and academic assignments can begin to connect to something deep within one's soul and to the world around us.

My undergraduate days laid the groundwork for the later questions that I would find myself pondering: In what ways can the resources encountered in the classroom begin to enrich, expand, and shape our students' lives and stories in meaningful ways? The best professors, of course, are always concerned about challenging their students to integrate academic knowledge into their lives. In recent years the rise of experiential learning seems like one answer to how professors can encourage that integration. A unique feature of the Athens/Jerusalem dichotomy arises because of the focus on the spiritual or faith dimension. In an academic setting, we rarely reflect on how our students can unite these disparate parts of their lives. In my own movement toward some insight into these potentially colliding worlds, I began to explore ways to connect Athens and Jerusalem that would honor the integrity of both realms.

ATHENS AND JERUSALEM ABROAD

One of my ongoing challenges as chaplain is to provide the context in which students, faculty, or staff are encouraged to explore these connections and look for ways to move toward wholeness. In the early discussions about course offerings and the Bible unit in our core curriculum, we as a faculty moved toward one answer: approach "Jerusalem" academically and let students discover for themselves any connections to their inner, spiritual lives. The "Care of the Soul" group offered a different answer for faculty and staff, providing an opportunity for folks to do that exploration on their own terms. Over time, I saw another way to explore these connections—by mixing the academic and the spiritual in overseas trips. Queens has a commitment to offering our traditional undergraduates a three-week overseas trip with faculty members as a way to broaden their horizons and encourage them to become truly global citizens. As chaplain, I built on that international commitment and began offering trips designed to include a spiritual component: a "Peace and Reconciliation" trip to Northern Ireland, and a spring-break trip to Guatemala. Currently we are exploring another connection, with Cameroon.

Combining an academic focus with a spiritual framework for overseas trips creates a space for connections that do not happen regularly in a typical classroom setting. During a trip with students and staff to Northern Ireland to learn about how that country has developed and sustained its peace and reconciliation process, one team member found that questions of reconciliation were not always about political matters. In our evening Bible study reflection one night in the middle of our trip, one participant paused, obviously overcome by an unexpected realization: "As we have been learning about the political and religious reconciliation processes going on here, it occurred to me that I may need to look at my own life. My biological father left when I was a toddler, and I've never wanted to know him. Now I can see that I have some reconciliation work of my own to do." This colleague had taken one step closer to breaking down the barriers he had unconsciously constructed in his own life. He had taken a step toward connecting the external processes of peace and reconciliation we were learning about and the divisions in his own life and soul. Trips like the Northern Ireland "Peace and Reconciliation" trip offer all of us an opportunity for such movement.

No single endeavor in my chaplaincy, however, embodies this opportunity more than our chapel mission trips to Guatemala. Like the Northern Ireland trip or the "Care of the Soul" group, the Guatemala experience offers students and faculty an opportunity to discover how their faith and spirituality connect with their academic lives as well as how our lives in the United States relate to the lives of indigenous communities in developing countries. Queens began its connection with Guatemala in 1993, but because of Guatemala's civil war, we suspended our trips until 2000. At that point, I began offering an annual chapel mission trip to Guatemala during spring break. The trip is part of a three-credit-hour class on Guatemala that is required of all students going on the trip, and the semester's readings and activities (from academic readings to intensive team building to spiritual disciplines) challenge students to connect the dots in their lives, to let themselves be transformed by living in the tensions between Athens and Jerusalem. With the academic course and the trip, students and faculty are challenged to see their lives in different ways.

Over the course of fifteen trips to Guatemala (plus the one to Northern Ireland and another to the Dominican Republic), students have entered into the experience as a way to find answers to life's larger questions—about the purpose for their lives, or how they can participate in easing the world's suffering, or where God is found amidst struggles for peace and justice. By "moving outside their comfort zone," as the students say, students, faculty, and staff who participate in these trips can find their assumptions and worldviews unsettled. Some participants have momentary insights on these trips, but upon return, "normal" life envelops them, and the changes they experienced can become buried. For others the shock waves of their experiences overseas create more permanent and obvious changes. I saw this happen one year on our return from a trip to Guatemala.

The van had just turned into the main street leading to the university. Queens is located in the Myers Park area of Charlotte, an area known for its tree-lined boulevards and gracious, stately homes. It's the area where "old money" lives. No neighborhood could be intentionally designed to contrast more vividly with the dirt-floor, bamboo-walled two-room homes that we had stayed in while in Guatemala. Everyone in the van that night was tired and sad after leaving our new friends in Guatemala. The well of emotions had made us silent for most of the trip back from the airport. Then, as we turned the corner into the Myers Park area, one student half stood, looked out the windows at the signs of wealth and luxury, and shouted, "I can't take it, it's too much! Why do we have so much and others so little?" Then she started crying. Later in her dorm room, she tore down all her posters reflecting our entertainment- and consumer-oriented culture, and she sorted through her closet to find clothes to give away, crying the whole time, and muttering about the disparities she had recently experienced. This experience, plus others, led her to spend two years in the Peace Corps in Africa and then to become a midwife so that she could help provide health care to those in the United States who can't afford it.

The contrast between the relative luxury of our lives in the United States and the poverty of many in Guatemala challenged this student in her core. For her, life could no longer be compartmentalized, and spiritual questions about the meaning and purpose of one's life were no longer abstract questions about career choices. The depth of faith that we encountered in the people of Guatemala, even as they faced poverty and political oppression, opened this student's eyes to a way of being that connected all aspects of one's life.

A similar experience happened to a faculty colleague who was an adviser on one of our Guatemala trips. As a child, my colleague knew the "Power of Being Quiet," as she entitled a talk she gave in chapel for our "This I Believe" series. This childhood attitude was reinforced in later years by her Quaker experiences. But one event during the Guatemala trip cast these earlier experiences of quiet in a different light. She describes the experience as follows:

> The wonder, the curiosity, the instinct to see and to listen—those more secular consequences of being quiet have never disappeared, never left me. But, after Iximiché [a Mayan ruins] they no longer function in my life as narrowly as they did before. Though they continue to guide my intellectual life, my secular life, they also enrich my spiritual life. Indeed, the power of being quiet has led me to realize that these "lives" are not separate, but instead are integrated and interdependent.[9]

For these travelers, the spiritual was no longer consigned to a Sunday experience; instead they, along with many more like them, returned to the United States and to the classroom with their eyes open to new ways of being.

WHY ATHENS AND JERUSALEM? MY STORY

My colleagues' reflections prompted me, too, to wonder why the Athens/Jerusalem tug-of-war spoke so deeply to me. Why over the years have I persisted in raising these questions—for myself, for my colleagues, and for my students? My undergraduate experiences obviously offered me a window into a way of moving beyond this apparent dichotomy, and my seminary education was equally as important. I went to seminary as a "second-career" student, leaving a career in academia as a professor of English. In seminary, questions about what shape my life's story would take as a result of this change were foremost in my mind. Many of those questions, I now see, were ones about how the various parts of my life connected.

During my first year in seminary, I was an intern at the Women's Lunch Place, a program that offered daily lunches to Boston's homeless women. During my year there, I came to know Alice, a woman in her seventies, who had grown up just outside of Boston. She was a college graduate who'd taught music in high school for years. As with many of the women at the Lunch Place, a series of losses meant she found herself on the street for a time. When I knew her, she actually had a small studio apartment, but her financial situation was precarious enough that she couldn't both pay her rent and buy food. The economic realities of her life presented her with difficult choices, but even without these realities, she probably would have come to the Lunch Place in any case. She wanted and needed the companionship of the regular guests, volunteers, and staff at the Lunch Place. Mostly she wanted someone to listen to her, to pay attention, and to walk with her—to listen to her story and to accompany her on this part of her journey.

Her requests were rarely grand: "I'm having trouble cutting my meat today, Diane. Can't you sit down and help me just for a minute?" That request was usually an easy one. On most days, I welcomed Alice's company and pleas for help. It meant I could sit down for a few minutes and have a conversation with her and the other guests. At other times, like when a volunteer group scheduled to help didn't show up at the last second, the few staff people and interns would be left trying to create menus, cook, and serve a hot lunch to over one hundred women. On those days, even Alice's simple requests seemed too much.

And there were other requests. Alice would often be "slow" about gathering her things at the end of the lunch hour, so she'd be one of the last guests to leave. Then, she would grab my arm gently and in her patrician Boston accent say, "Diane, can't you help me carry my bags to my apartment?" Her apartment was about a fifteen-minute walk from the Lunch Place (although Alice could make it into a thirty- or forty-minute endeavor), and her bags certainly weren't heavy. They were plastic grocery bags filled with leftovers she'd gathered for later meals. Her request was hardly unreasonable, but at the end of my eight-hour shift, I felt exhausted. I wanted nothing more than to get on the "T" and be whisked back to my clean apartment, my well-stocked refrigerator, and my Cambridge seminary world.

Now, reflecting back on those experiences and thinking about Athens and Jerusalem, I realize that seminary had become in some ways my "Athens." Ironically, even though we were spending all our waking hours (or so it seemed!) reading, writing, and discussing sacred texts, world religions, and new theologies, we were absorbed by ideas, by the life of the mind. We met amazing people who were doing amazing things, both literally through various speaker series and metaphorically through our studies, but somehow all that I was learning had not yet made the movement from my head to my heart. The "messy" stuff of life (Jerusalem), in an odd way, had ironically been scrubbed and domesticated when it entered our seminary's hallowed halls.

At the Women's Lunch Place, Alice's requests challenged me to see how I, too, had compartmentalized my worlds. I had my seminary world, where we engaged with exciting and challenging ideas, faculty, speakers, and other students. And I had my "service" world, where several times a week I would leave my academic cocoon and go to the Women's Lunch Place. The trip on the "T" nicely kept those two worlds neatly separate, and I had unconsciously made certain that I was in charge of that movement.

Alice's tug on my arm and her requests to walk her to her apartment tugged on the unseen walls I had built between my two worlds. "But as much as ye have done it unto one of the least of these ..." (Matthew 25:40). Jesus's words and the Gospel stories, which had become my story, too, over the years, echoed in my ears. For others the tug might be in the language of a different religious tradition, or it might be in the unformed yearning for "something more." When Alice would ask me to walk her to her apartment, which I sometimes did and sometimes didn't do, I had to answer in practical ways. There were other questions, too, that arose during those seminar years.

No one captured those questions better than Gordon Cosby of the Church of the Savior in Washington, D.C. During my early years at Queens I took students to D.C. on a trip called "Searching for Prophets." During that trip Gordon posed a question to my students that captured vividly what my seminary experiences had encapsulated: "Am I going to be a participant to help God pull off this creation of his reign of peace and justice now, or am I going to watch from the sidelines?" In other words, am I going to keep Athens and Jerusalem separate, or am I going to find ways to connect these two parts of my— our—world and my life? The Gospel stories and Jesus's examples can lie lifeless on the page unless we embody them, and that means letting ourselves walk with people like Alice or with the homeless people my students encountered in D.C. It means letting go of my (our) need to compartmentalize and control all parts of our lives.

But maybe seeking connections between Athens and Jerusalem isn't quite the right way to conceive of this issue. Parker Palmer, a Quaker writer and theologian, explores the contradictions of our lives in his book *The Promise of Paradox.* Early in the book, Palmer suggests a way out of the contradictions that trap us. He writes:

> But there is a third way to respond. A way beyond choosing either this pole or that. Let's call it "living the contradictions." Here we refuse to flee from tension but allow that tension to occupy the center of our lives. And why would anyone walk this difficult path? Because by doing so we may receive one of the great gifts of the

spiritual life—*the transformation of contradiction into paradox*. The poles of either/or, the choices we thought we had to make, may become signs of a larger truth than we had even dreamed. And in that truth, our lives may become larger than we had ever imagined.[10]

Not Athens or Jerusalem, but both, connected or at times in tension, but the tension is ideally one that can indeed lead us into a deeper truth where "our lives may become larger."

The integration of our spiritual and our secular lives continues to be a challenge that we postmoderns face. Like the new science building standing so boldly in front of the chapel at Queens, these two solid structures challenge me to discover a deeper reality than any apparent contradiction between the two. Athens and Jerusalem at times may appear as totally separate and in conflict with each other, or at other times as connected in myriad ways, or even as a paradox to be lived at a deeper level. As Palmer says, by living the contradictions we may discover that "our lives may become larger than we ever imagined." And isn't that what universities are for? And even more: isn't that an ideal role for a chaplain?

CHAPLAINS BREAKING THE SILENCE OF FAITH IN THE ACADEMY
The Charge

Rev. Dr. Lucy A. Forster-Smith
Macalester College, Saint Paul, Minnesota

"The Silence of Faith in the Academy." The posters were hung for an event that featured four remarkable faculty members at Macalester College. The topic, proposed by students from the Council for Religious Understanding, a student group I advised whose purpose was to promote interfaith dialogue and understanding on campus, was intended to help students consider how and why religion and religious faith often felt excluded from public conversation at the college. One outspoken sophomore—who had admitted with a wink and a flip of her pigtails that she loved "raising hell" on campus—relished the irony of discussing and thus giving voice to the silence of people of faith that permeated Macalester College. Though it was only my second year as chaplain, I had quickly discovered that, despite its continued affiliation with the Presbyterian Church (U.S.A.), the college is proudly secular.

Rev. Dr. Lucy A. Forster-Smith serves as chaplain/associate dean for religious and spiritual life at Macalester College in Saint Paul, Minnesota. She is president of the Association of College and University Religious Affairs and past president of the Presbyterian College Chaplains Association. She is an avid walker, smitten with college students, and loves long conversations with her spouse and amazing children.

Four faculty members agreed to speak about their interpretations of the sometimes-strained relationship between religion and a secular campus, to explain the tension that resulted in this "silence" on the part of faith. That evening, the four professors entered a stark classroom with a table carelessly pulled in front of four floor-to-ceiling windows. The neon light hummed overhead. Desks still in disarray from the class that had vacated them an hour earlier waited for an audience. One of the desks by the door held a bag of popcorn, a package of chocolate chip cookies, two jugs of juice, cups, and napkins set out by the pigtailed sophomore and three others from the Council.

I was to moderate the panel. I had offered to be one of the panelists, but Jon, the student who invited me, said that everyone on the Council figured they knew what I'd say so they would rather have me moderate. "Besides," said Jon, "you know how to deal with conflict, so if the faculty begin to get testy, you are our safety."

"Wow," I thought. "I guess that's what they think my role is. Peacekeeper."

Two students came through the door followed by three or four more. The professors, who were used to the formality of the classroom, with clearly defined roles, ready lecture notes, and order in this setting, sat woodenly perched on the edge of their chairs. The student planners chatted nervously with each other, laughing uncontrollably at points. Then one of them, a Christian evangelical from Nigeria, turned away from the others and walked to the classroom door. He looked down the hall and announced in a shockingly resonant voice, "No additional participants are arriving. Let us begin!"

Silence filled the room. The faculty members leaned back in their seats, and a couple of them glanced at the notes they'd brought. Professor Ellen Carson, a brilliant anthropologist, pulled out a manila file folder with her notes. I had run into her the week before and she had joked with me about what she was going to say: "It is easier to come out of the closet as a lesbian than as a Christian at this college." In 1996, few Macalester faculty members were out as either—she was out as both. From the biology department,

Professor Christopher Brown appeared to be reviewing his presentation in his head, staring up at a moth that was circling the light overhead. Before arriving on our campus, he had taught a course on science and religion at another institution, but I had not seen this class in the biology course lists at Macalester. The third panelist, the historian David Cohen, was writing on a yellow legal pad. I wondered if he was jotting notes for his presentation. Likely overwhelmed with commitments, this popular professor was constantly giving his famous lectures on the impact of the Holocaust on contemporary life in America.

The religion department faculty member, the only one in a coat and tie, sat waiting at the end of the table. An enormously popular faculty member, Jack Hanson was known for his brilliant lectures. Accomplished, published, inspiring—tonight, Jack would not disappoint.

The student organizers had done an excellent job of finding a diverse group of thinkers to address the evening's questions: When and how had faith become silent in the academy? Do people of faith have a greater challenge being heard in a secular college or university than they might in a more overtly religious one? Where does religion even fit into a secular institution?

Seated off to the side, I considered my own questions. I had been invited to facilitate this panel, but as the college's chaplain, how was I to think about the larger issues in front of us tonight? Where do chaplains fit into the institutions we serve? Do those of us in secular institutions face distinct challenges in working with administrations that are not always comfortable with us or clear about our role? And I couldn't help but wonder if anyone besides me had noticed the paradox on display that night: that the most unambiguously religious voice on campus, that of the chaplain, was herself "silenced"— present, but not invited to participate in this discussion. With these questions forming in my mind, I stepped into my role as moderator.

THE MESSINESS OF PERSONAL CONVICTION

The first person to speak was Professor Hanson of the religious studies department. "We have to be very careful about allowing belief or conviction into the academic discussion of religion," he began. He told us that religious conviction has no place in the classroom and reminded the audience that the methodology used to study religion is no different than that of studying anthropology, sociology, or any other academic discipline. Advocating for a clear separation between one's religious *life* and one's academic religious *studies*, he argued for absolute quietude from faculty about their own religious or spiritual commitments. Though he did not say it, he implied that the most effective religious studies professor would be the agnostic or atheist, who can stand outside of the discipline and bring a clear-eyed view of the work without complicating the subject with personal conviction, belief, or faith. Professor Hanson held himself to his own standard—he held a seminary degree and was ordained, but he never mentioned this in the context of the classroom. For him, the "silence of faith in the academy" was essential to a secular education.

As I listened to Professor Hanson, I heard an articulation of a tension that often underlies the role of chaplain on campuses like ours: when and where is it appropriate for expressions of faith to appear in a secular context? If Professor Hanson's wariness about allowing personal faith to extend into educational contexts is widely agreed upon, the chaplain in a secular institution will not occupy a public role. In order for the academy to keep its objectivity, its capacity to think critically must be unencumbered by the messiness of personal conviction, whether religious or tied to cultural, gender, or political expression. In this argument, religion on campus needs to remain in the private sphere without influence on institutional mission or academic life.

As I listened to Professor Hanson and thought about my work at Macalester, I grew increasingly uncomfortable. I even wondered if he was implying that my work didn't have a place at a secular institution. I remembered my interview at Macalester: a member of the chaplain search committee had told me outright that I shouldn't get my hopes up about my ministry there, because no one on campus was interested in religion. He meant to be helpful, but it still made for a deeply mixed message. It dawned on me that perhaps part of the reason I wasn't invited to participate on the panel stemmed from an underlying assumption that my practitioner's perspective would somehow complicate the "academic" nature of the discussion. I wondered if Professor Hanson's perspective was the prevailing one at the college.

Despite these thoughts, I knew that my work in the academy was not actually silent. Though the college had some ambivalence about my work, I was hired by the institution to be called on as pastor to the entire campus; to deliver public prayers; to wed and to bury; to awaken dormant dreams and pose big questions about life's meaning and purpose. These roles have been tasked to the chaplaincy throughout the entire history of that position at Macalester.

But, as the search committee member tried to warn me, something important *had* changed between the chaplain and the institution over the years as the college made a clearer divide between religious practice and the academic study of religion. In past decades, chaplains may have taught in the religion department, but not anymore. Though the college hired me for what was at least in name a public role, most of my work, even in my early days at the college, flew entirely under the radar. Students came to my office almost invisibly, without the notice of the campus. Even events such as this one were sparsely attended, by the dozen or so students who dared to show interest in religion or faith, at a place that prided itself on being secular, progressive, liberal, and oriented toward objective truths. And it wasn't just my imagination: in a Princeton Review survey of college campuses where "students ignore God on a regular basis," Macalester once ranked number one.

And yet, I was there at the table that evening, doing my work in public, the important work of holding and hosting a conversation that was not only breaking silence but giving voice to abundant insight. I found myself quite moved by this.

THE INFLUENCE OF HISTORICAL IDENTITY

There was loud applause as Professor Hanson ended his presentation. I realized that I was lost in thought and had abandoned my moderatorial role. The clapping brought me back, and I jumped into action, asking the next panelist to respond to the prompt: "How is faith silent at Macalester and why?"

Professor Cohen, an admired historian of World War II and a Holocaust scholar, began his remarks with a disclaimer: "Faith is not an operative term for me as a Jew. I don't know what that means, so the silence of 'faith,'" he said, his fingers marking air quotes, "isn't quite what I am going to address." What he said next turned out to be almost a direct rebuttal to the previous speaker's call to keep personal religious affiliations out of the classroom. Professor Cohen told us that he always begins his classes on the Holocaust by letting his students know that he is a Jew. He believes it is absolutely essential to be clear with students about the way he reads the historical events surrounding that atrocity.

"It would be ridiculous to try to hide my Jewishness. As a matter of fact, the material I teach has at its core the reality that many of us were forced into hiding, and the hiding was not only physical—our identity as Jews was a source of shame, silence, and threatened by extinction. To hide would be such an abysmal mistake." The audience was riveted by his comments. The other panelists except the religious studies professor were nodding.

As he spoke, Professor Cohen flipped the topic under discussion on its head, challenging the idea of silence in any form in the academy as an affront to academic freedom. He agreed with his religious studies colleague that even when one discloses a perspective, in his case his Jewish identity, care must be taken to provide critical perspective through choice in readings, films, and classroom discussion. "I want students to challenge me. I want a robust discussion. But withholding my Jewishness is not something I choose to do," he said.

The notable contrast between the religious studies faculty member, advocating absolute separation between personal religious identity and academic engagement with his subject, and the history professor, whose disclosure of religious and cultural identity was almost mandated by his subject, was fascinating. I wondered if the contrast between the two voices was puzzling to the students. Both were tenured faculty members, both enormously popular, both brought brilliant insight and depth to their work. But on this particular issue—whether to disclose their religious identity in the classroom—there couldn't have been a sharper contrast.

Dr. Cohen's assumption that in the context of his teaching he needed to disclose his Jewish identity was a powerful reminder to me that chaplains have a clear role as people of faith in the academy. By our title and job description, we are the publicly religious people in the institution. Unlike almost anyone else on campus, it would literally be impossible for a chaplain to keep her identity as a religious person out of view, even if she wanted to.

Yet, Dr. Cohen's presentation reminded me again about my silent role on this panel. Being the unambiguously religious person on a secular campus did carry clear responsibilities—some spoken, some tacit. While I was often invited to participate in the public life of the campus—praying at campus convocations and all-campus dinners, planning and preaching at the annual baccalaureate service—these moments were often seen as institutional "traditions," embellishments to the "real" work of the school. And even then, my efforts were well received as long as my contributions had the distinctly religious language purged—no God language; "holy" didn't communicate; I never, ever mentioned Jesus. I found myself often working to inspire by inference—themes of gratitude, grace, hope, dreams, life, joy, and an awaiting world abounded. My work as the religious figure in a secular context was not entirely private, but it wasn't fully, freely public either.

Dr. Cohen's unhesitating disclosure of his Jewishness, ironically, challenged ways I have silenced the Christian tradition in which I am ordained and out of which the college was founded. On a less personal level, his presentation challenged me to remind the institution of the history that has shaped it, the values that anchor it, and the trust placed in it by church and society to educate the global citizen leaders for the future. There has been a chaplain at Macalester College since the late 1940s. Even before that, there were professors in the religion department and college presidents who were ordained, led religious services and the required chapel program, officiated at weddings and funerals, and offered public prayer.

In my role as chaplain, I often share the college's history that to this day is infused in the institution's values and practices. At all-campus gatherings, I am the one who reminds the participants of the importance of tradition and the fact that colleges like this one were founded by Presbyterians who believed that the life of the mind was a gift of God and must be sharpened and engaged as one is called out to serve the world. When I open the academic year with a prayer, I take a moment before starting to explain why we pray at the convocation. It is a reminder of those who sacrificed, prayed, and were generous with their gifts so that students today could benefit from what people in the past provided. Prayer also allows for moments of public gratitude for the very gift of life. This historical influence is highlighted further every five years or so when the college, through a covenant, officially renews its continuing connection with the Presbyterian Church. We acknowledge the influence of our history on our life today. One of those marks of history is the continued presence of a chaplain.

I also thought, when Cohen spoke, about times when the institution itself exhibits discomfort or embarrassment about its religious history. Often that discomfort arises from a sense that the religious history carries the freight of anti-intellectualism or challenges to academic freedom. It is often the chaplain who encourages the institution to rehearse the narrative of the college or university, not as a means of imposing faith but as a way of respecting what influences the particular identity of the place. Dr. Cohen's reminder that silencing his Jewishness in teaching about the Holocaust is completely counter to the goals of the course itself helped me see that silencing the Presbyterian history of Macalester College erodes the vibrancy of the college's life and in some ways compromises its hospitality to the range of religious and spiritual traditions dwelling on campus. Suppressing the historical identity, even when the institution has severed its ties with the founding body, doesn't fully eliminate its influence; when that secret history inevitably reveals itself through unspoken practices or assumptions, it compromises the carefully cultivated trust among all groups in the campus community.

I remember walking from my office in the chapel to the college's campus center one spring morning. Three students were sitting in the sun, having cigarettes and coffee. One of the students called out to me, "Chaplain, we have a question for you." I stepped into the smoke and morning light. I'd never spoken with these students before. One bearded young man who looked like his shirt had been wadded up in a corner for months said, "We are debating whether this college has a church connection. Sam here says it does, but I said, 'No way.'" He looked at me expectantly. I admit to being as thrown by the questioner as by the question. Students sit out on the campus green in the sunshine and discuss this kind of thing? I explained a bit of the history and affirmed the continuing connection. I then inquired about how the subject came up in their conversation. "Oh, it just seems like this place is different from the University of Minnesota and really different from [Roman Catholic] St. Thomas, where my brother goes," he said. "Some vibe or something."

Call it "vibe" or "campus climate," but clearly students pick up on and are influenced by the presence of religious traditions in the daily life of their school. Students often come to me questioning what faculty will think if they speak about their religious experience or practice. In some classrooms, like Professor Hanson's, personal faith will remain suspect and silent. But there may be times, I heard Professor Cohen suggest, that it is as important to welcome diverse religious perspectives as it is to understand the influence of race or gender or other identities in the classroom. How does a religious perspective influence public health decisions or the ethics of death and dying, for example? Are these perspectives welcomed in the context of higher education?

After a faculty meeting once, I recall talking with a Jewish faculty member who expressed her frustration at the way the meeting was run by what she called "the rigid *Robert's Rules of Order*." She noted that using this process "inhibited rather than opening discussion. I felt like I was in a straightjacket."

I just laughed as she said it. "Yes, it sure is interesting how Presbyterian this place is, even in its secularity," I said. "The motto associated with Presbyterianism is: *We do it decently and in order.* I wonder if 'Robert' was Presbyterian?"

"Oh, of course! Now I get it," she said smiling. The chaplain familiar with the religious tradition that has birthed an institution may be one of the only people on campus able to interpret that tradition's influences on its daily institutional practices and translate them for a diverse community.

WALKING THE TIGHTROPE BETWEEN WORLDS

By the time I raised the night's questions to Professor Brown, the biology faculty member, the students had pulled out their notebooks and were frantically taking notes. He chose to answer by addressing the historical tensions between faith and science. "Far from silent, the debate about their relationship has persisted for centuries," Professor Brown said. "Science and religion, which is sometimes taken up as 'faith and reason,' insist that we engage them." He noted that he had taught a course on science and religion at another college but had not done so at Macalester. He made the point that one usually enters the conversation—yes, the debate—about science and religion from one among several views: assuming the two have nothing in common; assuming one is in service to another; or assuming that God is incalculable and therefore the tools of science are useless when considering religion.

He then spoke about Macalester College's history. The conviction that Macalester would be Christian in purpose, with all knowledge tied to wisdom from Christ, would have been assumed at its founding in the late nineteenth century. "Those early faculty members would not have had any idea what a panel like this one was about," Professor Brown noted. He went on to speak of the easy compatibility between science and religion evident in the college's seal. He held up a photocopied page with the seal on it. We saw two women in flowing gowns, one holding a telescope with a compass at her feet and the other holding a Bible. In the nineteenth century, when the college was founded, these two could sit chatting with little conflict. The motto circling the seal—"Nature and Revelation, the Heavenly Twins," in Latin—presents them as two fully compatible dimensions of human investigation.

Professor Brown recognized that at the core of the science-religion relationship was not only theory, but also how the scientist, him- or herself, brought awe and wonder to what they encountered in labs, observatories, the classroom, the field site. "It is often what we can't know, don't know, long to know, that drives us to religion or spirituality," he stated. "And this is why I am a person of faith. It was biology that led me to a deeper faith."

As he spoke, I thought of a student who had come to me a few months before. She told me about an experience of going to the observatory on campus for her astronomy lab. She shared that she had grown up in a large city in the United States and that because of the intensity of reflected light, she had never had the chance to see stars through a telescope. She described stepping up on the observatory's platform and placing her eye on the lens. The telescope was focused on the rings of Saturn. There they were, those rings that she had seen in photographs. She told me she suddenly felt as if she would weep, not sure if it was for joy or fear or both. And then she remembered that a few weeks earlier the priest at Mass had used an image drawn from the work of another poet-priest—she couldn't remember the exact words, but something like, "The world is filled with God's grandeur, shining like foil."[1] "That was it," she told me. When she saw those rings of Saturn, "it was like God was right there, showing me shining beauty."

While listening to Professor Brown, I realized that tears were welling in my eyes. I knew so clearly that no matter how silent faith sometimes felt in the academy, behind it there were moments when even the most unsuspecting members of our community discovered indescribable wonder and grace. Whether everyone accepts these moments as such or allows him- or herself to consider them in these terms, the Divine is everywhere, surrounding us, if only we have the eyes to see, ears to hear, hearts to trust.

As Brown described the engagement that led him across the precarious tightrope between the two seemingly distinct worlds of science and faith, I thought of how the chaplain walks a similar line—finding the universal in the particular, mystery in the mundane. I thought about how chaplains reside in the secular institution and preside in the realm of faith. We are intimately involved in both worlds—are we also challenged to find integration between them?

Our work as chaplains often takes place in the liminal spaces of the academy. On our campuses, we stand in the spaces that lie between knowing and not knowing, between truth and wonder, between what has come before us and what is yet emerging. I reconsidered my moments of public participation in this light: at commencement, for example, my role is to offer a prayer, but also to look into the faces of those young people who will carry us into the future, our students, and simply say, "Thank you." Clearly, in moments like these, the institution has trusted me with some deeper charge.

Listening to Professor Brown helped me understand that a part of my role in the academy is to be something of a mystic, that is, to be present at moments—both expected and unexpected—when the boundaries between the human and Divine vanish. The mystic chaplain acknowledges what others may sense, may discover, may stumble upon. She reminds others that God is accessible if we can only put ourselves in a position to receive this presence. The chaplain's role is to note these moments as they happen, to receive them when they come, to confirm and affirm them.

My experience is that faith is unbounded, often showing up in the expected places, awakening insight and perspective. But the chaplain's role is also to simply show up in places where others don't. We deal with things that reside in the territory of what is not seen, not certain: death, fear, hopelessness, new life, radical hope, joy. There are times when my work is more about intensifying the questions, probing into the mystery of the student's truth, asking questions that jar them out of the expected. For example, when dealing with students who are in a dilemma—about the work they want to do, the relationship that has them confused, the decision of whether to go to the Mexico/U.S. border to work with immigration rights or to the West Side of Saint Paul, Minnesota, to teach English to immigrants, or any number of other situations—I may challenge them to consider where they will be challenged or uncomfortable, as often as what will help them be at ease. Moving into the complexity of issues often allows the student to realize they hold resources and treasures buried deep underneath the confusion. On the edge or "on edge" is where I understand the Spirit to reside. The Holy Spirit arrives in fire and wind in the Christian Scriptures. Setting the spirit on fire by conviction and compassion is so needed in this world. By trusting that the Spirit of God and the holding power of the universe reside beneath, around, over, and through everything, the chaplain offers reminders of unexpected wonder to others in her community.

Certainly, institutions acknowledge that mystery exists, that knowledge is limited, that humans are finite. But it is rare that they name these truths. The times when institutions come to their knees—when facing tragedy, uncertainty, loss, or grief—are times when they rely on chaplains to provide an unflinching fearlessness. What we offer in those moments is our willingness to look into the face of brokenness and name the longing for wholeness. It is the chaplain who waits, detects, notes, and listens to the power of the deep. She knows how to wait. She also knows how to look into the faces of the community, into the pressing issues that worry the college president or the food server or the secretary, the homesickness, the indiscretion, the fear of being found out. And always, she knows how privileged she is to be invited into these vulnerable moments and into the deeply joyful ones as well.

My tears embarrassed me. We needed to move on to the last panelist.

THE PARTICIPANT OBSERVER

Anthropology professor Carson spoke last. She began her comments with what she termed "a personal confession." She reminded the group that there are many vestiges of a Christian founding at colleges like Macalester. One of note is the term "professor." The word's root meaning does not refer to someone with a PhD who teaches a subject in a particular discipline, she told us. "No," she said. "The original meaning of the word is 'one who professes faith.'"

I noticed a faint tremor make its way down the panel of professors.

Referring to the first speaker, Professor Hanson, she said, "I respect my colleague who spoke earlier and completely support the care he takes to uphold a scholarly and academically rigorous course of study without convictional or confessional assertions in the class-room. But in my field of anthropology, one of our key assumptions is that our scholarly work is inhabited by a *participant observer*, that is, someone who is aware of the impact of her presence."

She told the group that she finds it very important at points along the way to tell her classes that she is a Christian who is also a lesbian. "It shocks them, because they assume that all Christians are anti-gay, that in every Christian context, being gay is a sin. I am both a lesbian and a Christian. This creates cognitive dissonance at a level that other things don't. And then we talk about it. We challenge assumptions, both in the culture and in ourselves."

For her, the presence of her religious faith in the classroom was not merely impossible for her to ignore or avoid, it was essential to her educational philosophy. Not only did she have to acknowledge and interrogate her own perspective and bias as an anthropologist, but she could use the assumed contradictions of her own identity to challenge the perspective and bias of the class. Leaving faith silent, for her, would be to fail in her job as an educator. As she wrapped up her comments she paused and smiled, "I guess this is what we mean by professing."

Dr. Carson's reminder that she inhabits identities that might be understood by some as contradictory made me think too of how chaplains work in contested spaces where our role is to put contra-dictions—like being a lesbian and being a Christian, identities that for some may be assumed to be mutually exclusive—in the same room, hold the tension, and let them instruct.

By locating ourselves squarely in a tradition and inhabiting it fully, chaplains discover that this leads others to trust us. When we are totally transparent about who we are, others not only relax but also are encouraged to explore their own deepest commitments and values, including religious ones. Instead of being silenced by uneasiness with religion, being transparent can open the way for truth telling about this dimension of human life. We can acknowledge our own biases and blind spots and still stand with one another in gracious hospitality. Standing outside of the religious discourse is impossible for a chaplain. It is present wherever we are. For chaplains, the most productive and respectful way to deal with the religious presence we inhabit is to admit it, let it enter the space, interrogate it, and be open to its instruction—participant observers, indeed.

Dr. Carson's words helped me recognize that the chaplain, by her presence, inhabits not only what may seem to be contradictory identities but also contradictory roles. At one moment the chaplain is an insider, an administrator, a staff person, working from a position of leadership and authority; the next moment she is the religious person, the ordained pastor, imam, rabbi, the one whose authority arises from hands of ordination, from a call of God, from the voice of a community or tradition. She not only holds the presence of religion before the institution, but also traffics in unexpected places with unexpected people, carrying on conversations that few others have the courage to engage. When was the last time the academy had an open forum on love? Or failure? Or loss? These essential, troubling questions are the chaplain's domain.

Her liminal status also means the chaplain is well equipped to work in times and places of great uncertainty. In the institution, her authority partly arises from her charge to notice what others overlook or dare not enter. When tragedy strikes, like the day the planes went through the towers in New York, her attention was likely drawn immediately to the student staring at his food in the cafeteria, tears streaming down his face. When others don't notice or are too shy or shaken to respond, the chaplain's job is to stop, to gently inquire if the student would like to talk or to be alone.

There are chaplains in settings where their presence is best expressed through social justice, through challenging institutional practices, standing at the portico of the hurting and hopeless. Their passion is for the dispossessed in society or practices of service and sustainability. Whether they sit late into the night advising students who are planning a campus-wide rally against the investment practices of the institution or accompanying students to the School for the Americas protests, the chaplain works at the radical intersection of imagination and justice. The imagination arises from her theological mind, cultivating the unseen in the seen, the lively hope arising out of the dust underfoot. This work often awakens promise in young adults.

This work calls for abiding joy and also, at times, trembling hearts at its demands. It is not always smooth and easy. It does, I daresay, ask chaplains to stand ready to be asked to do things we never dreamed we'd do. But at its heart, the calling works at the intersection of the chaplain's vocation and those we serve. This work renews the mind, stirs the heart and holds the most pressing issues that arise in our institutions, for the sake of the world. It is a privilege. It is holy.

That night, the four professors who sat in a row considering the silence of faith in the academy addressed key questions about where religion fits in a secular institution. But as I sat there listening and thinking that night—and over the course of many years since—I have come to see that their perspectives also illuminate how chaplains, as publicly religious professionals, find our place on the secular campus today. The panelists spoke from their perspective as faculty, doing what faculty should do: bringing their critical thinking on this subject to the table. The chaplain, too, had ideas about the "silence of faith in the academy"—maybe ideas that were predictable by the student organizers, as they had explained, or maybe not.

But it was certainly clear that I had another role that night. By asking me to perform as moderator, the students had asked me to help, to work, to serve. For the chaplain, the role of faith in the academy is not only an intellectual proposition, but also the foundation of her work, her vocation. Faculty may consider the important issues underlying the silence of faith in the secular academy. But the chaplain doesn't think about whether faith is speaking or silent at 3 a.m. when her sleepy night is rattled awake by a student in crisis. My role was indicated by my very presence, the questions I asked, the confidence the students placed in my work, the regard for the faculty's perspectives—all of these are part of the work of being a chaplain.

The irony that arose from this panel on the silence of faith in the academy was that it gave voice to a conversation I'd been having with myself for some time. I realized quite jarringly that there was another silence I felt the need to break—the long silence of chaplains' lives in the academy, our work and the deep purpose that lands us in expected and unexpected places, the high moments of giving our best and the spent moments when we have come to the end of our rope. Frederick Buechner, theologian, harbinger of light, comes closest to describing the vocation I've found as chaplain when he reflects on a question someone asked of him:

> "I hear you are entering the ministry," the woman said down the long table, meaning no real harm. "Was it your own idea or were you poorly advised?" And the answer that she could not have heard even if I had given it was that it was not an idea at all, neither my own nor anyone else's. It was a lump in the throat. It was an itching in the feet. It was a stirring in the blood at the sound of rain. It was a sickening of the heart at the sight of misery."[1]

Chaplains' work engages the very soul of our universities. We have been working for decades with generations of young adults, nontraditional students, in public universities and private colleges. Our mentoring has guided, challenged, expanded, and grounded untold numbers of global citizen leaders across this planet. We have presided at memorial services for dignitaries and for quiet citizens. We have invoked the Holy at university opening convocations and building dedications. We've reminded our faculty colleagues, when needed, that our students are more than empty vessels to be filled with knowledge. Some of us pray with our trustees, holding the college's fiscal well-being in the arms of a ready spirit of stewardship. We've spent sleepless nights wondering if a student will make it to morning as depression claws at her brilliant mind. We've laughed, cried, bled, died, been born anew in our work—work almost no one, even within our own institutions, fully understands.

Most of the institutions that employ chaplains have long ago left any semblance of sectarianism. The chaplain is no longer the conscience of the campus, no longer a chief advisor to the university president, rarely even solely representing the historical denominational affiliations of these institutions. But if a college or university chaplain is engaged with what composes, reaches for, shuns, or runs from faith, she is also engaging with the question of whether chaplains' work has a place on campus today.

In Saint Paul's letter to the Romans, he talks about creation waiting "with eager longing for the revealing of the children of God." In this, I hear echoes of chaplains. The world is waiting, longing, leaning forward on tiptoe for the gifts of these young people to arise. Our work as chaplains is to help them break their own silences, whatever they may be. Whether it is the silence that results from privileging the past at the expense of expanding the future; the silence that results from hurrying young people into the adult world without attending to their personal, spiritual, and emotional development; the imposed silence of the subjective, artistic, emotional, and heartfelt and in an academy that privileges objective fact and tamed methodology; or any other silence that diminishes human contribution, part of chaplains' calling is to listen, ask questions, invite others to speak, and to speak our own truth freely.

By telling the stories of our vocation, chaplains can invite others to better understand how we work to end silence of all kinds. We invite others to recognize themselves in the struggles we disclose. We challenge seminaries, rabbinical schools, divinity schools to develop courses that recognize the distinct challenges of working on college and university campuses as religious professionals. We trust that our work will capture the imagination of a new generation of practitioners for this field. We dare to share with our readers the world chaplains inhabit, what motivates us to do this work, what jars our faith, what strengthens our conviction. We challenge all to listen attentively to the global moment we are living in, and we extend an invitation to be heard to a world that so longs for a word of hope, possibility, dreams, and peace.

NOTES

FOREWORD

1. See W. H. Auden, "For the Time Being: A Christmas Oratorio" (1941–42).
2. See Langston Hughes, "I Dream a World" (1926).

INTRODUCTION

1. Sharon Daloz Parks, *Big Questions, Worthy Dreams: Mentoring Young Adults in Their Search for Meaning, Purpose and Faith* (San Francisco: Jossey-Bass Publishers, 2000), 146.
2. Kenneth Underwood, *The Church, the University, and Social Policy: The Danforth Study of Campus Ministries* (Middletown, CT: Wesleyan University Press, 1969).
3. Ernest Gordon, *Meet Me at the Door: The Dean of the Princeton Chapel Encounters the New World of College Students* (New York: Harper & Row, 1969).

ROOM TO BREATHE: NURTURING COMMUNITY BY CREATING SPACE, BY REV. DR. SUSAN HENRY-CROWE

1. This description of a typical weekend in Canon Chapel was previously published in Susan Henry-Crowe's article "Emory University's Cannon Chapel as Multireligious Space," *Liturgy* 26, no. 3 (2011): 42–45.

IN COFFIN'S PULPIT: RE-ENVISIONING PROTESTANT RELIGIOUS CULTURE, BY REV. IAN B. OLIVER

1. Gibson Winter, *The Suburban Captivity of the Churches* (New York: Macmillan, 1962).
2. James Carroll, foreword to *Credo*, by William Sloane Coffin (Louisville, KY: Westminster John Knox Press, 2004), xii.
3. Amelia Sargent, cartoon in *The Yale Daily News*, December 8, 2009.

"¡SI, SE PUEDE!": STUDENT MINISTRY IN A MULTICULTURAL SETTING, BY FR. DANIEL REIM, SJ

1. Elizabeth Dias, "Evangelicos," *Time*, April 15, 2013, 24.

2. *Strangers No Longer: Together on the Journey of Hope; A Pastoral Letter Concerning Migration from the Catholic Bishops of Mexico and the United States* (USCCB, January 22, 2003), 3.

3. National Conference of Catholic Bishops, *Communities of Salt and Light: Reflections on the Social Mission of the Parish* (November 1993).

"GOD IS IN THIS PLACE": MENTORING, MINISTERING, AND MAKING MEANING AT STANFORD UNIVERSITY, BY RABBI PATRICIA KARLIN-NEUMANN

1. Frederick Buechner, *Wishful Thinking: A Theological ABC* (New York: Harper & Row, 1973), 95.

2. Jane Lathrop Stanford, address to the Leland Stanford Junior University Board of Trustees, San Francisco, October 3, 1902.

3. David E. Balk, "Grieving: 22 to 30 Percent of All College Students," *New Directions for Student Services* 121 (Spring 2008): 5–14.

4. www.stanford.edu/dept/govcr/documents/founding-grant.pdf, accessed August 26, 2013.

5. Barbara Myerhoff, "Sanctifying Women's Lives through Ritual" (talk delivered at "Illuminating the Unwritten Scroll: Women's Spirituality and Jewish Tradition" Conference, Los Angeles, CA, November 1984).

MY DREAMSICLE JOB: GOOD HUMOR AND BECOMING A CHAPLAIN, BY SHARON M. K. KUGLER

1. Joan Chittister, *Aspects of the Heart: The Many Paths to a Good Life* (New London, CT: Twenty-Third Publications, 2012), 46.

PASSPORTS: THE CHAPLAIN MOVING ACROSS BOUNDARIES, BY REV. DR. RICHARD E. SPALDING

1. Quoted in Parker J. Palmer, "The Grace of Great Things: Reclaiming the Sacred in Knowing, Teaching and Learning," in *The Heart of Learning*, ed. Steven Glazer (New York: Tarcher, 1999), 18.

RELIGIOUS HYBRIDS: A NEW INTERPRETATION, BY REV. K. P. HONG

1. Adapted from the Mumonkan, Case 35. See Zenkai Shibayama, *The Gateless Barrier: Zen Comments on the Mumonkan* (Boston: Shambhala Publications, 1974), 245–248.

2. Joseph Prabhu, "Adieu Raimon, A Dieu," *Journal of Hindu-Christian Studies* 23 (2010): Article 12. Available at: http://dx.doi.org/10.7825/2164-6279.1464.

3. Raimon Panikkar, *The Intra-Religious Dialogue,* 1st ed. (New York: Paulist Press, 1978), 30.

4. Paul Knitter, *Without Buddha I Could Not Be a Christian* (Oxford: Oneworld Publications, 2009), 213.

5. Ibid., 215 (emphasis his).

6. Dany-Robert Dufour, *The Art of Shrinking Heads: On the New Servitude of the Liberated in the Age of Total Capitalism* (Cambridge: Polity Press, 2008), 16.

7. Knitter, *Without Buddha,* 215.

8. Paul Ricoeur, *The Symbolism of Evil* (Boston: Beacon Press, 1967), 349.

9. David Krieger, "Conversion: On the Possibility of Global Thinking in an Age of Particularism," *Journal of the American Academy of Religion* 58 (1990): 227.

10. 1 Corinthians 13:12.

11. Jay Griffiths, "A Tender Wildness," talk delivered at the Annual Biodiversity Forum of Norfolk Biodiversity Partnership, October 2009: http://www.norfolkbiodiversity.org/about/annual_biodiversity_forum.aspx.

12. Emmanuel Levinas, "Ethics as First Philosophy," trans. Sean Hand and Michael Temple, in *The Levinas Reader* (Oxford: Blackwell Publishers, 1989), 76.

STEWARDS OF THE NEW SECULAR, BY REV. DR. SAMUEL H. SPEERS

1. *"Secularity and the Liberal Arts" White Paper* (p. 8), from "Secularity and the Liberal Arts," a Teagle Foundation Working Group from Bucknell University, Macalester College, Vassar College, and Williams College (September 2008), projects.vassar.edu/secularity/whitepaper.

2. The term "stewards of the new secular" borrows from the insightful framings of colleagues in the Teagle Foundation's "Secularity and the Liberal Arts" project. The term "stewards of the secular" is from Richard Spalding; the term "new secular" is from Jonathon Kahn, "'Whose Little Boy Are You?': *The Fire Next Time* as a Black Theology of Belonging," Religion and Race Workshop, "Race and Secularism in America," Syracuse University, October 2012.

3. Charles Taylor, *Varieties of Religion Today: William James Revisited* (Cambridge, MA: Harvard University Press, 2002).

4. David Hollinger, "After Cloven Tongues of Fire: Ecumenical Protestantism and the Modern American Encounter with Diversity," *Journal of American History* 98, no. 1 (2011). I am grateful to Ian Oliver for the reference to this article.

5. Steinman's framing is included in the Teagle *"Secularity and the Liberal Arts" Working Group Papers* (described below). I include the full quotation here because it so lucidly distills the cultural shifts this paper explores: "In the last mid-century, the question of religious diversity at liberal arts colleges, whether explicitly elite Protestant or culturally so, might have been framed as: *How open are these religiously grounded institutions to religious difference and indifference in their students?* Now as our colleges have evolved into institutions of what might be called the consensus of elite secularity, rooted in liberal Protestantism, the questions of religious diversity might be more accurately framed as: *How open are these secular institutions to religious expression and experience in the classroom that falls outside the consensus? Should we teach in ways that break with that consensus? What if any religious expression should be encouraged or discouraged?"* See projects.vassar.edu/secularity/ whitepaper, p. 2.

6. Charles Taylor, *A Secular Age* (Cambridge, MA: Belknap Press, 2007), 12.

7. Ibid., 13.

8. Ibid., 3.

9. My chaplain colleagues in the Teagle project include the editor of this book, Lucy Forster-Smith, as well as Rena Blumenthal, Ian Oliver, and Richard Spalding, who are each contributors.

10. See Jonathon Kahn's excellent essay "Reconceiving the Secular and the Practice of the Liberal Arts" (November 24, 2010), Social Science Research Council's blog *The Immanent Frame*, http://blogs.ssrc.org/tif/2010/11/24/ reconceiving-the-secular-and-the-practice-of-the-liberal-arts. See also the project website with my White Paper and all the working group papers at http://projects.vassar.edu/secularity.

11. See Pierre Bourdieu and Loïc J. D. Wacquant, *An Invitation to Reflexive Sociology* (Chicago: University of Chicago, 1992), 73.

12. "Secular, Not Secularist" was the title of Jeffrey Stout's keynote address at the "Varieties of Secular Experience Conference" at Vassar College, November 13, 2008.

13. Jeffrey Stout, "2007 Presidential Address: The Folly of Secularism," *Journal of the American Academy of Religion* 76, no. 3 (2008): 533.

14. Ibid., 534.

15. Jeffrey Stout, *Democracy and Tradition* (Princeton, NJ: Princeton University Press, 2004), 97. This passage from *Democracy and Tradition* helps clarify the "secular, not secularist" distinction he makes in his article "The Folly of Secularism" (542). Although he uses the term "secularize" in one and

"secular" in the other, both carry the same generous ethic he distinguishes from "secularist."

16. See Kahn, "Reconceiving the Secular." As noted in Kahn's article, the notion that vital dialogue requires participants to acknowledge the contestable quality of what matters most to them comes from William Connolly. See Connolly, *Why I Am Not a Secularist* (Minneapolis: University of Minnesota Press, 1999), 7, 39.

17. I am drawing here on David Bebbington's work on the defining traits of evangelicals, as cited by leading religious historian and evangelical scholar Mark Noll. See Bebbington, *Evangelicalism in Modern Britain: A History from the 1730s to the 1980s* (London: Unwin Hyman, 1989), 2–19, cited in Mark A. Noll, *The Scandal of the Evangelical Mind* (Grand Rapids: William B. Eerdmans, 1994), 8. Noll is citing a study of evangelism in Britain but thinks Bebbington's analysis applies in the U.S. context as well.

18. B. A. Gerrish, *A Prince of the Church: Schleiermacher and the Beginnings of Modern Theology* (Philadelphia: Fortress Press, 1984), 43.

19. B. A. Gerrish, *Tradition and the Modern World: Reformed Theology in the 19th Century* (Chicago and London: University of Chicago Press, 1978), 7.

20. See Bruce Lincoln, *Holy Terrors: Thinking about Religion after September 11* (Chicago: University of Chicago Press, 2003), 1. As Lincoln notes, Judaism, Islam, and Roman Catholicism, for example, all suggest other ways of understanding religion—in terms of material and communal practices and disciplines.

21. Janet R. Jakobsen, "Ethics after Pluralism," in *After Pluralism: Reimagining Religious Engagement*, eds. Courtney Bender and Pamela E. Klassen (New York: Columbia University Press, 2010), 48.

22. See Nicholas Wolterstorff, "Epilogue," in *Religion, Scholarship, and Higher Education: Perspectives, Models, and Future Prospects; Essays from the Lilly Seminar on Religion and Higher Education*, ed. Andrea Sterk (Notre Dame, IN: University of Notre Dame, 2002), 248. Wolterstorff attributes the phrase "educational Christendom" to an unnamed seminar participant.

23. Though he resists claiming any ownership of the phrase "stewards of the secular," Richard Spalding offered this as one way to describe the task of our faculty-chaplain working group.

24. On some campuses we have visited with the secularity workshop, it turns out that the presumption for students is that they are religious rather than nonreligious, while for faculty the presumption is toward nonreligious. Yet for the majority of campuses involved in the project, Tiffany's secular—or hidden Protestant—default seems to be the norm.

25. When I spoke to Blumenthal about my interest in "faded Protestantism" for this essay, she quipped back that "faded Protestants" are the missing third term to current cultural acceptance of "secular Jews" and "lapsed Catholics" as a category of identification. It may not make sense yet to add "lapsed Catholics" and "faded Protestants" to our religious preference card, but the day may come. The question of the religious life of the increasing number of young adults who do not identify any religious affiliations, the so-called nones, is a critical emerging issue for campus chaplaincy.

THE ONE AND THE MANY: OLD LANGUAGE, NEW ENGAGEMENT, BY FR. ROC O'CONNOR, SJ

1. Jeanne Halgren Kilde, *Nature and Revelation: A History of Macalester College* (Minneapolis: University of Minnesota Press, 2010), 54.

2. Minutes of the Board of Trustees of Macalester College, January 2, 1958, as quoted in ibid., 202.

3. Ibid., 217.

4. Ibid., 218.

5. Kilde, *Nature and Revelation*, 308. She summarizes a talk by Yahya Armajani, "What It Takes to Be a Christian College," September 19, 1967, as found in David Hopper Papers, Committee on Church Relatedness Folder, Macalester College Archives.

6. "Polarity, n. *Oxford English Dictionary Online*, Oxford University Press.

"WHAT HAS ATHENS TO DO WITH JERUSALEM?": THE PROFESSOR CHAPLAIN, BY REV. DR. J. DIANE MOWREY

1. *The Spiritual Life of College Students: A National Study of College Students' Search for Meaning and Purpose* (Spirituality in Higher Education, Higher Education Research Institute, UCLA), 4.

2. Tertullian, Prescription Against Heretics, chapter 7, http://www.newadvent.org/fathers/0311.htm (retrieved August 6, 2013).

3. John Calvin, *Institutes of the Christian Religion*, ed. John T. McNeill (Philadelphia: Westminster Press, 1960), vol. I, i., p. 35.

4. Margaret P. Cowan, Roger P. Ebertz, and Mary E. Shields, "The Vocation of Teaching: Themes and Models from the Presbyterian Tradition," *Teaching Theology and Religion* 5, no. 3 (2002): 150.

5. See "The Love-Song of J. Alfred Prufrock" (1915) by T.S. Eliot.

6. John Calvin, Institutes, vol. I, i., p. 35.

7. Barbara E. Walvoord, *Teaching and Learning in College Introductory Religion Courses* (Malden, MA: Blackwell Publishing, 2008), 6.

8. Ibid., 7.

9. Dr. Suzanne Cooper-Guasco, "The Power of Being Quiet" (unpublished essay).

10. Parker J. Palmer, *The Promise of Paradox: A Celebration of Contradictions in the Christian Life* (Notre Dame, IN: Ave Maria Press, 1980), 19.

CHAPLAINS BREAKING THE SILENCE OF FAITH IN THE ACADEMY: THE CHARGE, BY REV. DR. LUCY A. FORSTER-SMITH

1. See "God's Grandeur" (1877) by Gerard Manly Hopkins.

2. Frederick Buechner, *The Alphabet of Grace* (San Francisco: Harper, 1970), 109–110.

Inspiration

Perennial Wisdom for the Spiritually Independent: Sacred Teachings—Annotated & Explained

Annotation by Rami Shapiro; Foreword by Richard Rohr

Weaves sacred texts and teachings from the world's major religions into a coherent exploration of the five core questions at the heart of every religion's search.

5½ x 8½, 336 pp, Quality PB Original, 978-1-59473-515-8 **$16.99**

Finding God Beyond Religion: A Guide for Skeptics, Agnostics & Unorthodox Believers Inside & Outside the Church

By Tom Stella; Foreword by The Rev. Canon Marianne Wells Borg

Reinterprets traditional religious teachings central to the Christian faith for people who have outgrown the beliefs and devotional practices that once made sense to them.

6 x 9, 160 pp, Quality PB, 978-1-59473-485-4 $16.99

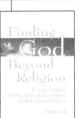

How Did I Get to Be 70 When I'm 35 Inside?: Spiritual Surprises of Later Life *By Linda Douty*

Encourages you to focus on the inner changes of aging to help you greet your later years as the grand adventure they can be. 6 x 9, 208 pp, Quality PB, 978-1-59473-297-3 **$16.99**

Fully Awake and Truly Alive: Spiritual Practices to Nurture Your Soul

By Rev. Jane E. Vennard; Foreword by Rami Shapiro

Illustrates the joys and frustrations of spiritual practice, offers insights from various religious traditions and provides exercises and meditations to help us become more fully alive.

6 x 9, 208 pp, Quality PB, 978-1-59473-473-1 **$16.99**

Saving Civility: 52 Ways to Tame Rude, Crude & Attitude for a Polite Planet

By Sara Hacala

Provides fifty-two practical ways you can reverse the course of incivility and make the world a more enriching, pleasant place to live.

6 x 9, 240 pp, Quality PB 978-1-59473-314-7 **$16.99**

Spiritually Healthy Divorce: Navigating Disruption with Insight & Hope

By Carolyne Call

A spiritual map to help you move through the twists and turns of divorce.

6 x 9, 224 pp, Quality PB, 978-1-59473-288-1 **$16.99**

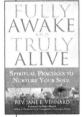

Who Is My God? 2nd Edition

An Innovative Guide to Finding Your Spiritual Identity

By the Editors at SkyLight Paths

Provides the Spiritual Identity Self-Test™ to uncover the components of your unique spirituality. 6 x 9, 160 pp, Quality PB, 978-1-59473-014-6 **$15.99**

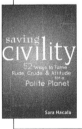

Journeys of Simplicity: Traveling Light with Thomas Merton, Bashō, Edward Abbey, Annie Dillard & Others *By Philip Harnden*

Invites you to consider a more graceful way of traveling through life. PB includes journal pages to help you get started on your own spiritual journey.

5 x 7¼, 144 pp, Quality PB, 978-1-59473-181-5 **$12.99**

5 x 7¼, 128 pp, HC, 978-1-893361-76-8 **$16.95**

Or phone, fax, mail or e-mail to: SKY LIGHT PATHS Publishing

An imprint of Turner Publishing Company

4507 Charlotte Avenue • Suite 100 • Nashville, Tennessee 37209

Tel: (615) 255-2665 • www.skylightpaths.com

Prices subject to change.

Spirituality of the Seasons

Autumn: A Spiritual Biography of the Season
Edited by Gary Schmidt and Susan M. Felch; Illus. by Mary Azarian
Rejoice in autumn as a time of preparation and reflection. Includes Wendell Berry, David James Duncan, Robert Frost, A. Bartlett Giamatti, E. B. White, P. D. James, Julian of Norwich, Garret Keizer, Tracy Kidder, Anne Lamott, May Sarton.
6 x 9, 320 pp, b/w illus., Quality PB, 978-1-59473-118-1 **$18.99**

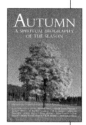

Spring: A Spiritual Biography of the Season
Edited by Gary Schmidt and Susan M. Felch; Illus. by Mary Azarian
Explore the gentle unfurling of spring and reflect on how nature celebrates rebirth and renewal. Includes Jane Kenyon, Lucy Larcom, Harry Thurston, Nathaniel Hawthorne, Noel Perrin, Annie Dillard, Martha Ballard, Barbara Kingsolver, Dorothy Wordsworth, Donald Hall, David Brill, Lionel Basney, Isak Dinesen, Paul Laurence Dunbar. 6 x 9, 352 pp, b/w illus., Quality PB, 978-1-59473-246-1 **$18.99**

Summer: A Spiritual Biography of the Season
Edited by Gary Schmidt and Susan M. Felch; Illus. by Barry Moser
"A sumptuous banquet.... These selections lift up an exquisite wholeness found within an everyday sophistication." — ★ *Publishers Weekly* starred review
Includes Anne Lamott, Luci Shaw, Ray Bradbury, Richard Selzer, Thomas Lynch, Walt Whitman, Carl Sandburg, Sherman Alexie, Madeleine L'Engle, Jamaica Kincaid.
6 x 9, 304 pp, b/w illus., Quality PB, 978-1-59473-183-9 **$18.99**

Winter: A Spiritual Biography of the Season
Edited by Gary Schmidt and Susan M. Felch; Illus. by Barry Moser
"This outstanding anthology features top-flight nature and spirituality writers on the fierce, inexorable season of winter.... Remarkably lively and warm, despite the icy subject." — ★ *Publishers Weekly* starred review
Includes Will Campbell, Rachel Carson, Annie Dillard, Donald Hall, Ron Hansen, Jane Kenyon, Jamaica Kincaid, Barry Lopez, Kathleen Norris, John Updike, E. B. White.
6 x 9, 288 pp, b/w illus., Deluxe PB w/ flaps, 978-1-893361-92-8 **$18.95**

Spirituality / Animal Companions

Blessing the Animals: Prayers and Ceremonies to Celebrate God's Creatures, Wild and Tame *Edited and with Introductions by Lynn L. Caruso*
5¼ x 7¼, 256 pp, Quality PB, 978-1-59473-253-9 **$15.99**; HC, 978-1-59473-145-7 **$19.99**

Remembering My Pet: A Kid's Own Spiritual Workbook for When a Pet Dies
By Nechama Liss-Levinson, PhD, and Rev. Molly Phinney Baskette, MDiv; Foreword by Lynn L. Caruso
8 x 10, 48 pp, 2-color text, HC, 978-1-59473-221-8 **$16.99**

What Animals Can Teach Us about Spirituality: Inspiring Lessons from Wild and Tame Creatures *By Diana L. Guerrero* 6 x 9, 176 pp, Quality PB, 978-1-893361-84-3 **$16.95**

Spirituality—A Week Inside

Making a Heart for God: A Week Inside a Catholic Monastery
By Dianne Aprile; Foreword by Brother Patrick Hart, OCSO
6 x 9, 224 pp, b/w photos, Quality PB, 978-1-893361-49-2 **$16.95**

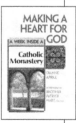

Waking Up: A Week Inside a Zen Monastery
By Jack Maguire; Foreword by John Daido Loori, Roshi
6 x 9, 224 pp, b/w photos, Quality PB, 978-1-893361-55-3 **$16.95**

Spiritual Poetry—The Mystic Poets

Experience these mystic poets as you never have before. Each beautiful, compact book includes a brief introduction to the poet's time and place, a summary of the major themes of the poet's mysticism and religious tradition, essential selections from the poet's most important works, and an appreciative preface by a contemporary spiritual writer.

Hafiz
The Mystic Poets
Translated and with Notes by Gertrude Bell
Preface by Ibrahim Gamard
Hafiz is known throughout the world as Persia's greatest poet, with sales of his poems in Iran today only surpassed by those of the Qur'an itself. His probing and joyful verse speaks to people from all backgrounds who long to taste and feel divine love and experience harmony with all living things.
5 x 7¼, 144 pp, HC, 978-1-59473-009-2 **$16.99**

Hopkins
The Mystic Poets
Preface by Rev. Thomas Ryan, CSP
Gerard Manley Hopkins, Christian mystical poet, is beloved for his use of fresh language and startling metaphors to describe the world around him. Although his verse is lovely, beneath the surface lies a searching soul, wrestling with and yearning for God.
5 x 7¼, 112 pp, HC, 978-1-59473-010-8 **$16.99**

Tagore
The Mystic Poets
Preface by Swami Adiswarananda
Rabindranath Tagore is often considered the Shakespeare of modern India. A great mystic, Tagore was the teacher of W. B. Yeats and Robert Frost, the close friend of Albert Einstein and Mahatma Gandhi, and the winner of the Nobel Prize for Literature. This beautiful sampling of Tagore's two most important works, *The Gardener* and *Gitanjali,* offers a glimpse into his spiritual vision that has inspired people around the world.
5 x 7¼, 144 pp, HC, 978-1-59473-008-5 **$16.99**

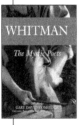

Whitman
The Mystic Poets
Preface by Gary David Comstock
Walt Whitman was the most innovative and influential poet of the nineteenth century. This beautiful sampling of Whitman's most important poetry from *Leaves of Grass,* and selections from his prose writings, offers a glimpse into the spiritual side of his most radical themes—love for country, love for others and love of self
5 x 7¼, 192 pp, HC, 978-1-59473-041-2 **$16.99**

Prayer / Meditation

Men Pray: Voices of Strength, Faith, Healing, Hope and Courage
Created by the Editors at SkyLight Paths
Celebrates the rich variety of ways men around the world have called out to the Divine—with words of joy, praise, gratitude, wonder, petition and even anger—from the ancient world up to our own day.
5 x 7¼, 192 pp, HC, 978-1-59473-395-6 **$16.99**

Honest to God Prayer: Spirituality as Awareness, Empowerment, Relinquishment and Paradox
By Kent Ira Groff
For those turned off by shopworn religious language, offers innovative ways to pray based on both Native American traditions and Ignatian spirituality.
6 x 9, 192 pp, Quality PB, 978-1-59473-433-5 **$16.99**

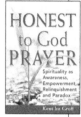

Sacred Attention: A Spiritual Practice for Finding God in the Moment
By Margaret D. McGee
Framed on the Christian liturgical year, this inspiring guide explores ways to develop a practice of attention as a means of talking—and listening—to God.
6 x 9, 144 pp, Quality PB, 978-1-59473-291-1 **$16.99**

Women of Color Pray: Voices of Strength, Faith, Healing, Hope and Courage
Edited and with Introductions by Christal M. Jackson
Through these prayers, poetry, lyrics, meditations and affirmations, you will share in the strong and undeniable connection women of color share with God.
5 x 7¼, 208 pp, Quality PB, 978-1-59473-077-1 **$15.99**

Living into Hope: A Call to Spiritual Action for Such a Time as This
By Rev. Dr. Joan Brown Campbell; Foreword by Karen Armstrong
6 x 9, 208 pp, HC, 978-1-59473-283-6 **$21.99**

Praying with Our Hands: 21 Practices of Embodied Prayer from the World's Spiritual Traditions *By Jon M. Sweeney; Photos by Jennifer J. Wilson; Foreword by Mother Tessa Bielecki; Afterword by Taitetsu Unno, PhD*
8 x 8, 96 pp, 22 duotone photos, Quality PB, 978-1-893361-16-4 **$16.95**

Secrets of Prayer: A Multifaith Guide to Creating Personal Prayer in Your Life
By Nancy Corcoran, CSJ
6 x 9, 160 pp, Quality PB, 978-1-59473-215-7 **$16.99**

Three Gates to Meditation Practice: A Personal Journey into Sufism, Buddhism, and Judaism *By David A. Cooper* 5½ x 8½, 240 pp, Quality PB, 978-1-893361-22-5 **$16.95**

Prayer / M. Basil Pennington, OCSO

Finding Grace at the Center, 3rd Edition: The Beginning of Centering Prayer *With Thomas Keating, OCSO, and Thomas E. Clarke, SJ; Foreword by Rev. Cynthia Bourgeault, PhD* A practical guide to a simple and beautiful form of meditative prayer. 5 x 7¼,128 pp, Quality PB, 978-1-59473-182-2 **$12.99**

The Monks of Mount Athos: A Western Monk's Extraordinary Spiritual Journey on Eastern Holy Ground *Foreword by Archimandrite Dionysios*
Explores the landscape, monastic communities and food of Athos.
6 x 9, 352 pp, Quality PB, 978-1-893361-78-2 **$18.95**

Psalms: A Spiritual Commentary *Illus. by Phillip Ratner*
Reflections on some of the most beloved passages from the Bible's most widely read book. 6 x 9, 176 pp, 24 full-page b/w illus., Quality PB, 978-1-59473-234-8 **$16.99**

The Song of Songs: A Spiritual Commentary *Illus. by Phillip Ratner*
Explore the Bible's most challenging mystical text.
6 x 9, 160 pp, 14 full-page b/w illus., Quality PB, 978-1-59473-235-5 **$16.99**
HC, 978-1-59473-004-7 **$19.99**

Women's Interest

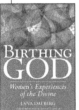

Birthing God: Women's Experiences of the Divine
By Lana Dalberg; Foreword by Kathe Schaaf
Powerful narratives of suffering, love and hope that inspire both personal and collective transformation. 6 x 9, 304 pp, Quality PB, 978-1-59473-480-9 **$18.99**

On the Chocolate Trail: A Delicious Adventure Connecting Jews, Religions, History, Travel, Rituals and Recipes to the Magic of Cacao
By Rabbi Deborah R. Prinz
Take a delectable journey through the religious history of chocolate—a real treat! 6 x 9, 272 pp, 20+ b/w photographs, Quality PB, 978-1-58023-487-0 **$18.99***

Women, Spirituality and Transformative Leadership
Where Grace Meets Power
Edited by Kathe Schaaf, Kay Lindahl, Kathleen S. Hurty, PhD, and Reverend Guo Cheen
A dynamic conversation on the power of women's spiritual leadership and its emerging patterns of transformation. 6 x 9, 288 pp, HC, 978-1-59473-313-0 **$24.99**

Spiritually Healthy Divorce: Navigating Disruption with Insight & Hope
By Carolyne Call A spiritual map to help you move through the twists and turns of divorce. 6 x 9, 224 pp, Quality PB, 978-1-59473-288-1 **$16.99**

New Feminist Christianity: Many Voices, Many Views
Edited by Mary E. Hunt and Diann L. Neu
Insights from ministers and theologians, activists and leaders, artists and liturgists who are shaping the future. Taken together, their voices offer a starting point for building new models of religious life and worship.
6 x 9, 384 pp, Quality PB, 978-1-59473-435-9 **$19.99**; HC, 978-1-59473-285-0 **$24.99**

Bread, Body, Spirit: Finding the Sacred in Food
Edited and with Introductions by Alice Peck 6 x 9, 224 pp, Quality PB, 978-1-59473-242-3 **$19.99**

Dance—The Sacred Art: The Joy of Movement as a Spiritual Practice
By Cynthia Winton-Henry 5½ x 8½, 224 pp, Quality PB, 978-1-59473-268-3 **$16.99**

Daughters of the Desert: Stories of Remarkable Women from Christian, Jewish and Muslim Traditions
By Claire Rudolf Murphy, Meghan Nuttall Sayres, Mary Cronk Farrell, Sarah Conover and Betsy Wharton
5½ x 8½, 192 pp, Illus., Quality PB, 978-1-59473-106-8 **$14.99** Inc. reader's discussion guide

The Divine Feminine in Biblical Wisdom Literature
Selections Annotated & Explained
Translation & Annotation by Rabbi Rami Shapiro; Foreword by Rev. Cynthia Bourgeault, PhD
5½ x 8½, 240 pp, Quality PB, 978-1-59473-109-9 **$16.99**

Divining the Body: Reclaim the Holiness of Your Physical Self
By Jan Phillips 8 x 8, 256 pp, Quality PB, 978-1-59473-080-1 **$18.99**

Honoring Motherhood: Prayers, Ceremonies & Blessings
Edited and with Introductions by Lynn L. Caruso
5 x 7¼, 272 pp, Quality PB, 978-1-58473-384-0 **$9.99**; HC, 978-1-59473-239-3 **$19.99**

Next to Godliness: Finding the Sacred in Housekeeping
Edited by Alice Peck 6 x 9, 224 pp, Quality PB, 978-1-59473-214-0 **$19.99**

ReVisions: Seeing Torah through a Feminist Lens
By Rabbi Elyse Goldstein 5½ x 8½, 224 pp, Quality PB, 978-1-58023-117-6 **$16.95***

The Triumph of Eve & Other Subversive Bible Tales
By Matt Biers-Ariel 5½ x 8½, 192 pp, Quality PB, 978-1-59473-176-1 **$14.99**

White Fire: A Portrait of Women Spiritual Leaders in America
By Malka Drucker; Photos by Gay Block 7 x 10, 320 pp, b/w photos, HC, 978-1-893361-64-5 **$24.95**

Woman Spirit Awakening in Nature: Growing Into the Fullness of Who You Are
By Nancy Barrett Chickerneo, PhD; Foreword by Eileen Fisher
8 x 8, 224 pp, b/w illus., Quality PB, 978-1-59473-250-8 **$16.99**

Women of Color Pray: Voices of Strength, Faith, Healing, Hope and Courage
Edited and with Introductions by Christal M. Jackson
5 x 7¼, 208 pp, Quality PB, 978-1-59473-077-1 **$15.99**

* A book from Jewish Lights, SkyLight Paths' sister imprint

Bible Stories / Folktales

Abraham's Bind & Other Bible Tales of Trickery, Folly, Mercy and Love *By Michael J. Caduto*
New retellings of episodes in the lives of familiar biblical characters explore relevant life lessons. 6 x 9, 224 pp, HC, 978-1-59473-186-0 **$19.99**

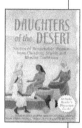

Daughters of the Desert: Stories of Remarkable Women from Christian, Jewish and Muslim Traditions *By Claire Rudolf Murphy, Meghan Nuttall Sayres, Mary Cronk Farrell, Sarah Conover and Betsy Wharton*
Breathes new life into the old tales of our female ancestors in faith. Uses traditional scriptural passages as starting points, then with vivid detail fills in historical context and place. Chapters reveal the voices of Sarah, Hagar, Huldah, Esther, Salome, Mary Magdalene, Lydia, Khadija, Fatima and many more. Historical fiction ideal for readers of all ages.
5½ x 8½, 192 pp, Quality PB, 978-1-59473-106-8 **$14.99** Inc. reader's discussion guide

The Triumph of Eve & Other Subversive Bible Tales
By Matt Biers-Ariel
These engaging retellings of familiar Bible stories are witty, often hilarious and always profound. They invite you to grapple with questions and issues that are often hidden in the original texts.
5½ x 8½, 192 pp, Quality PB, 978-1-59473-176-1 **$14.99**
Also available: **The Triumph of Eve Teacher's Guide**
8½ x 11, 44 pp, PB, 978-1-59473-152-5 **$8.99**

Wisdom in the Telling
Finding Inspiration and Grace in Traditional Folktales and Myths Retold
By Lorraine Hartin-Gelardi
6 x 9, 192 pp, HC, 978-1-59473-185-3 **$19.99**

Religious Etiquette / Reference

How to Be a Perfect Stranger, 5th Edition: The Essential Religious Etiquette Handbook *Edited by Stuart M. Matlins and Arthur J. Magida*
The indispensable guidebook to help the well-meaning guest when visiting other people's religious ceremonies. A straightforward guide to the rituals and celebrations of the major religions and denominations in the United States and Canada from the perspective of an interested guest of any other faith, based on information obtained from authorities of each religion. Belongs in every living room, library and office. Covers:

African American Methodist Churches • Assemblies of God • Bahá'í Faith • Baptist • Buddhist • Christian Church (Disciples of Christ) • Christian Science (Church of Christ, Scientist) • Churches of Christ • Episcopalian and Anglican • Hindu • Islam • Jehovah's Witnesses • Jewish • Lutheran • Mennonite/Amish • Methodist • Mormon (Church of Jesus Christ of Latter-day Saints) • Native American/First Nations • Orthodox Churches • Pentecostal Church of God • Presbyterian • Quaker (Religious Society of Friends) • Reformed Church in America/Canada • Roman Catholic • Seventh-day Adventist • Sikh • Unitarian Universalist • United Church of Canada • United Church of Christ

"The things Miss Manners forgot to tell us about religion."
—*Los Angeles Times*

"Finally, for those inclined to undertake their own spiritual journeys ... tells visitors what to expect." —*New York Times*

6 x 9, 432 pp, Quality PB, 978-1-59473-294-2 **$19.99**

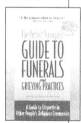

The Perfect Stranger's Guide to Funerals and Grieving Practices: A Guide to Etiquette in Other People's Religious Ceremonies *Edited by Stuart M. Matlins*
6 x 9, 240 pp, Quality PB, 978-1-893361-20-1 **$16.95**

The Perfect Stranger's Guide to Wedding Ceremonies: A Guide to Etiquette in Other People's Religious Ceremonies *Edited by Stuart M. Matlins*
6 x 9, 208 pp, Quality PB, 978-1-893361-19-5 **$16.95**

Judaism / Christianity / Islam / Interfaith

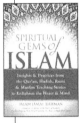

Spiritual Gems of Islam: Insights & Practices from the Qur'an, Hadith, Rumi & Muslim Teaching Stories to Enlighten the Heart & Mind
By Imam Jamal Rahman
Invites you—no matter what your practice may be—to access the treasure chest of Islamic spirituality and use its wealth in your own journey.
6 x 9, 256 pp, Quality PB, 978-1-59473-430-4 **$16.99**

All Politics Is Religious: Speaking Faith to the Media, Policy Makers and Community *By Rabbi Dennis S. Ross; Foreword by Rev. Barry W. Lynn*
Provides ideas and strategies for expressing a clear, forceful and progressive religious point of view that is all too often overlooked and under-represented in public discourse. 6 x 9, 192 pp, Quality PB, 978-1-59473-374-1 **$18.99**

Religion Gone Astray: What We Found at the Heart of Interfaith
By Pastor Don Mackenzie, Rabbi Ted Falcon and Imam Jamal Rahman
Welcome to the deeper dimensions of interfaith dialogue—exploring that which divides us personally, spiritually and institutionally.
6 x 9, 192 pp, Quality PB, 978-1-59473-317-8 **$16.99**

Getting to the Heart of Interfaith: The Eye-Opening, Hope-Filled Friendship of a Pastor, a Rabbi & an Imam *By Pastor Don Mackenzie, Rabbi Ted Falcon and Imam Jamal Rahman*
6 x 9, 192 pp, Quality PB, 978-1-59473-263-8 **$16.99**

Hearing the Call across Traditions: Readings on Faith and Service
Edited by Adam Davis; Foreword by Eboo Patel
6 x 9, 352 pp, Quality PB, 978-1-59473-303-1 **$18.99**

How to Do Good & Avoid Evil: A Global Ethic from the Sources of Judaism
By Hans Küng and Rabbi Walter Homolka; Translated by Rev. Dr. John Bowden
6 x 9, 224 pp, HC, 978-1-59473-255-3 **$19.99**

Blessed Relief: What Christians Can Learn from Buddhists about Suffering
By Gordon Peerman 6 x 9, 208 pp, Quality PB, 978-1-59473-252-2 **$16.99**

Christians & Jews—Faith to Faith: Tragic History, Promising Present, Fragile Future *By Rabbi James Rudin*
6 x 9, 288 pp, HC, 978-1-58023-432-0 **$24.99***   Quality PB, 978-1-58023-717-8 **$18.99***

Christians & Jews in Dialogue: Learning in the Presence of the Other *By Mary C. Boys and Sara S. Lee; Foreword by Dorothy C. Bass* 6 x 9, 240 pp, Quality PB, 978-1-59473-254-6 **$18.99**

InterActive Faith: The Essential Interreligious Community-Building Handbook
Edited by Rev. Bud Heckman with Rori Picker Neiss; Foreword by Rev. Dirk Ficca
6 x 9, 304 pp, Quality PB, 978-1-59473-273-7 **$16.99**; HC, 978-1-59473-237-9 **$29.99**

The Jewish Approach to God: A Brief Introduction for Christians
By Rabbi Neil Gillman, PhD 5½ x 8½, 192 pp, Quality PB, 978-1-58023-190-9 **$16.95***

The Jewish Approach to Repairing the World (Tikkun Olam): A Brief Introduction for Christians *By Rabbi Elliot N. Dorff, PhD, with Rev. Cory Willson*
5½ x 8½, 256 pp, Quality PB, 978-1-58023-349-1 **$16.99***

The Jewish Connection to Israel, the Promised Land: A Brief Introduction for Christians *By Rabbi Eugene Korn, PhD* 5½ x 8½, 192 pp, Quality PB, 978-1-58023-318-7 **$14.99***

Jewish Holidays: A Brief Introduction for Christians *By Rabbi Kerry M. Olitzky and Rabbi Daniel Judson* 5½ x 8½, 176 pp, Quality PB, 978-1-58023-302-6 **$16.99***

Jewish Ritual: A Brief Introduction for Christians
By Rabbi Kerry M. Olitzky and Rabbi Daniel Judson 5½ x 8½, 144 pp, Quality PB, 978-1-58023-210-4 **$14.99***

Jewish Spirituality: A Brief Introduction for Christians *By Rabbi Lawrence Kushner*
5½ x 8½, 112 pp, Quality PB, 978-1-58023-150-3 **$12.95***

* A book from Jewish Lights, SkyLight Paths' sister imprint

Spirituality

The Passionate Jesus: What We Can Learn from Jesus about Love, Fear, Grief, Joy and Living Authentically
by The Rev. Peter Wallace
Reveals Jesus as a passionate figure who was involved, present, connected, honest and direct with others and encourages you to build personal authenticity in every area of your own life.
6 x 9, 208 pp, Quality PB, 978-1-59473-393-2 **$18.99**

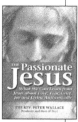

Gathering at God's Table: The Meaning of Mission in the Feast of Faith
by Katharine Jefferts Schori
A profound reminder of our role in the larger frame of God's dream for a restored and reconciled world. 6 x 9, 256 pp, HC, 978-1-59473-316-1 **$21.99**

The Heartbeat of God: Finding the Sacred in the Middle of Everything
by Katharine Jefferts Schori; Foreword by Joan Chittister, OSB
Explores our connections to other people, to other nations and with the environment through the lens of faith. 6 x 9, 240 pp, HC, 978-1-59473-292-8 **$21.99**

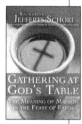

A Dangerous Dozen: Twelve Christians Who Threatened the Status Quo but Taught Us to Live Like Jesus
by the Rev. Canon C. K. Robertson, PhD; Foreword by Archbishop Desmond Tutu
Profiles twelve visionary men and women who challenged society and showed the world a different way of living. 6 x 9, 208 pp, Quality PB, 978-1-59473-298-0 **$16.99**

Decision Making & Spiritual Discernment: The Sacred Art of Finding Your Way *By Nancy L. Bieber*
Presents three essential aspects of Spirit-led decision making: willingness, attentiveness and responsiveness. 5½ x 8½, 208 pp, Quality PB, 978-1-59473-289-8 **$16.99**

Laugh Your Way to Grace: Reclaiming the Spiritual Power of Humor
by Rev. Susan Sparks A powerful, humorous case for laughter as a spiritual, healing path. 6 x 9, 176 pp, Quality PB, 978-1-59473-280-5 **$16.99**

Bread, Body, Spirit: Finding the Sacred in Food
Edited and with Introductions by Alice Peck 6 x 9, 224 pp, Quality PB, 978-1-59473-242-3 **$19.99**

Claiming Earth as Common Ground: The Ecological Crisis through the Lens of Faith
By Andrea Cohen-Kiener; Foreword by Rev. Sally Bingham
6 x 9, 192 pp, Quality PB, 978-1-59473-261-4 **$16.99**

Creating a Spiritual Retirement: A Guide to the Unseen Possibilities in Our Lives
By Molly Srode 6 x 9, 208 pp, b/w photos, Quality PB, 978-1-59473-050-4 **$14.99**

Creative Aging: Rethinking Retirement and Non-Retirement in a Changing World
By Marjory Zoet Bankson 6 x 9, 160 pp, Quality PB, 978-1-59473-281-2 **$16.99**

Keeping Spiritual Balance as We Grow Older: More than 65 Creative Ways to Use Purpose, Prayer, and the Power of Spirit to Build a Meaningful Retirement
By Molly and Bernie Srode 8 x 8, 224 pp, Quality PB, 978-1-59473-042-9 **$16.99**

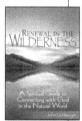

Hearing the Call across Traditions: Readings on Faith and Service
Edited by Adam Davis; Foreword by Eboo Patel 6 x 9, 352 pp, Quality PB, 978-1-59473-303-1 **$18.99**

Honoring Motherhood: Prayers, Ceremonies & Blessings
Edited and with Introductions by Lynn L. Caruso
5 x 7¼, 272 pp, Quality PB, 978-1-58473-384-0 **$9.99**; HC, 978-1-59473-239-3 **$19.99**

The Losses of Our Lives: The Sacred Gifts of Renewal in Everyday Loss
By Dr. Nancy Copeland-Payton 6 x 9, 192 pp, HC, 978-1-59473-271-3 **$19.99**

Renewal in the Wilderness: A Spiritual Guide to Connecting with God in the Natural World *By John Lionberger* 6 x 9, 176 pp, b/w photos, Quality PB, 978-1-59473-219-5 **$16.99**

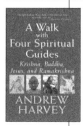

Soul Fire: Accessing Your Creativity
By Thomas Ryan, CSP 6 x 9, 160 pp, Quality PB, 978-1-59473-243-0 **$16.99**

A Spirituality for Brokenness: Discovering Your Deepest Self in Difficult Times
By Terry Taylor 6 x 9, 176 pp, Quality PB, 978-1-59473-229-4 **$16.99**

A Walk with Four Spiritual Guides: Krishna, Buddha, Jesus, and Ramakrishna
By Andrew Harvey 5½ x 8½, 192 pp, b/w photos & illus., Quality PB, 978-1-59473-138-9 **$15.99**

Spiritual Practice

Fly-Fishing—The Sacred Art: Casting a Fly as a Spiritual Practice
By Rabbi Eric Eisenkramer and Rev. Michael Attas, MD; Foreword by Chris Wood, CEO, Trout Unlimited; Preface by Lori Simon, executive director, Casting for Recovery
Shares what fly-fishing can teach you about reflection, awe and wonder; the benefits of solitude; the blessing of community and the search for the Divine.
5½ x 8½, 160 pp, Quality PB, 978-1-59473-299-7 **$16.99**

Lectio Divina—The Sacred Art: Transforming Words & Images into Heart-Centered Prayer *By Christine Valters Paintner, PhD*
Expands the practice of sacred reading beyond scriptural texts and makes it accessible in contemporary life. 5½ x 8½, 240 pp, Quality PB, 978-1-59473-300-0 **$16.99**

Writing—The Sacred Art: Beyond the Page to Spiritual Practice
By Rami Shapiro and Aaron Shapiro
Push your writing through the trite and the boring to something fresh, something transformative. Includes over fifty unique, practical exercises.
5½ x 8½, 192 pp, Quality PB, 978-1-59473-372-7 **$16.99**

Conversation—The Sacred Art: Practicing Presence in an Age of Distraction
By Diane M. Millis, PhD; Foreword by Rev. Tilden Edwards, PhD
Cultivate the potential for deeper connection in every conversation.
5½ x 8½, 192 pp, Quality PB, 978-1-59473-474-8 **$16.99**

Pilgrimage—The Sacred Art: Journey to the Center of the Heart
By Dr. Sheryl A. Kujawa-Holbrook
Explore the many dimensions of the experience of pilgrimage—the yearning heart, the painful setbacks, the encounter with the Divine and, ultimately, the changed orientation to the world. 5½ x 8½, 240 pp, Quality PB, 978-1-59473-472-4 **$16.99**

Dance—The Sacred Art: The Joy of Movement as a Spiritual Practice
By Cynthia Winton-Henry 5½ x 8½, 224 pp, Quality PB, 978-1-59473-268-3 **$16.99**

Giving—The Sacred Art: Creating a Lifestyle of Generosity
By Lauren Tyler Wright 5½ x 8½, 208 pp, Quality PB, 978-1-59473-224-9 **$16.99**

Haiku—The Sacred Art: A Spiritual Practice in Three Lines
By Margaret D. McGee 5½ x 8½, 192 pp, Quality PB, 978-1-59473-269-0 **$16.99**

Hospitality—The Sacred Art: Discovering the Hidden Spiritual Power of Invitation and Welcome *By Rev. Nanette Sawyer; Foreword by Rev. Dirk Ficca*
5½ x 8½, 208 pp, Quality PB, 978-1-59473-228-7 **$16.99**

Labyrinths from the Outside In, 2nd Edition: Walking to Spiritual Insight—A Beginner's Guide *By Rev. Dr. Donna Schaper and Rev. Dr. Carole Ann Camp*
6 x 9, 208 pp, b/w illus. and photos, Quality PB, 978-1-59473-486-1 **$16.99**

Practicing the Sacred Art of Listening: A Guide to Enrich Your Relationships and Kindle Your Spiritual Life *By Kay Lindahl* 8 x 8, 176 pp, Quality PB, 978-1-893361-85-0 **$16.95**

Recovery—The Sacred Art: The Twelve Steps as Spiritual Practice *by Rami Shapiro, Foreword by Joan Borysenko, PhD* 5½ x 8½, 240 pp, Quality PB, 978-1-59473-259-1 **$16.99**

Running—The Sacred Art: Preparing to Practice *By Dr. Warren A. Kay; Foreword by Kristin Armstrong* 5½ x 8½, 160 pp, Quality PB, 978-1-59473-227-0 **$16.99**

The Sacred Art of Chant: Preparing to Practice
By Ana Hernández 5½ x 8½, 192 pp, Quality PB, 978-1-59473-036-8 **$16.99**

The Sacred Art of Fasting: Preparing to Practice
By Thomas Ryan, CSP 5½ x 8½, 192 pp, Quality PB, 978-1-59473-078-8 **$15.99**

The Sacred Art of Forgiveness: Forgiving Ourselves and Others through God's Grace
By Marcia Ford 8 x 8, 176 pp, Quality PB, 978-1-59473-175-4 **$18.99**

The Sacred Art of Listening: Forty Reflections for Cultivating a Spiritual Practice
By Kay Lindahl; Illus. by Amy Schnapper 8 x 8, 160 pp, b/w illus., Quality PB, 978-1-893361-44-7 **$16.99**

The Sacred Art of Lovingkindness: Preparing to Practice
By Rabbi Rami Shapiro; Foreword by Marcia Ford 5½ x 8½, 176 pp, Quality PB, 978-1-59473-151-8 **$16.99**

Thanking & Blessing—The Sacred Art: Spiritual Vitality through Gratefulness
By Jay Marshall, PhD; Foreword by Philip Gulley 5½ x 8½, 176 pp, Quality PB, 978-1-59473-231-7 **$16.99**

Professional Spiritual & Pastoral Care Resources

College & University Chaplaincy in the 21st Century
A Multifaith Look at the Practice of Ministry on Campuses across America
Edited by The Rev. Dr. Lucy Forster-Smith

Examines experiences and perspectives that arise at the intersection of religious practice, distinct campus culture, student counseling, and the challenges of the secular context of today's college or university campus.

6 x 9, 368pp, HC, 978-1-59473-516-5 **$40.00**

Professional Spiritual & Pastoral Care
A Practical Clergy and Chaplain's Handbook
Edited by Rabbi Stephen B. Roberts, MBA, MHL, BCJC

An essential resource integrating the classic foundations of pastoral care with the latest approaches to spiritual care, specifically intended for professionals who work or spend time with congregants in acute care hospitals, behavioral health facilities, rehabilitation centers and long-term care facilities.

6 x 9, 480 pp, HC, 978-1-59473-312-3 **$50.00**

Disaster Spiritual Care
Practical Clergy Responses to Community, Regional and National Tragedy
Edited by Rabbi Stephen B. Roberts, BCJC, and Rev. Willard W.C. Ashley, Sr., DMin, DH

The definitive guidebook for counseling not only the victims of disaster but also the clergy and caregivers who are called to service in the wake of crisis.

6 x 9, 384 pp, HC, 978-1-59473-240-9 **$50.00**

Learning to Lead: Lessons in Leadership for People of Faith
Edited by Rev. Williard W.C. Ashley Sr., MDiv, DMin, DH

In this multifaith, cross-cultural and comprehensive resource for both clergy and lay persons, contributors who are experts in the field explore how to engage spiritual leaders and teach them how to bring healing, faith, justice and support to communities and congregations.

6 x 9, 384 pp, HC, 978-1-59473-432-8 **$40.00**

How to Be a Perfect Stranger, 5th Edition
The Essential Religious Etiquette Handbook
Edited by Stuart M. Matlins and Arthur J. Magida

The indispensable guidebook to help the well-meaning guest when visiting other people's religious ceremonies. Covers: **African American Methodist Churches • Assemblies of God • Bahá'í Faith • Baptist • Buddhist • Christian Church (Disciples of Christ) • Christian Science (Church of Christ, Scientist) • Churches of Christ • Episcopalian and Anglican Hindu • Islam • Jehovah's Witnesses • Jewish • Lutheran • Mennonite/Amish • Methodist Mormon (Church of Jesus Christ of Latter-day Saints) • Native American/First Nations • Orthodox Churches • Pentecostal Church of God • Presbyterian • Quaker (Religious Society of Friends) • Reformed Church in America/Canada • Roman Catholic • Seventh-day Adventist • Sikh • Unitarian Universalist • United Church of Canada • United Church of Christ**

6 x 9, 432 pp, Quality PB, 978-1-59473-294-2 **$19.99**

"The things Miss Manners forgot to tell us about religion."
—*Los Angeles Times*

The Perfect Stranger's Guide to Funerals and Grieving Practices
A Guide to Etiquette in Other People's Religious Ceremonies
Edited by Stuart M. Matlins 6 x 9, 240 pp, Quality PB, 978-1-893361-20-1 **$16.95**

Jewish Pastoral Care, 2nd Edition: A Practical Handbook from Traditional & Contemporary Sources *Edited by Rabbi Dayle A. Friedman, MSW, MAJCS, BCC*
6 x 9, 528 pp, Quality PB, 978-1-58023-427-6 **$30.00**
(A book from Jewish Lights, SkyLight Paths' sister imprint)

Caresharing: A Reciprocal Approach to Caregiving and Care Receiving in the Complexities of Aging, Illness or Disability *By Marty Richards*
6 x 9, 256 pp, Quality PB, 978-1-59473-286-7 **$16.99**; HC, 978-1-59473-247-8 **$24.99**

InterActive Faith: The Essential Interreligious Community-Building Handbook
Edited by Rev. Bud Heckman with Rori Picker Neiss
6 x 9, 304 pp, Quality PB, 978-1-59473-273-7 **$16.99**; HC, 978-1-59473-237-9 **$29.99**

About SKYLIGHT PATHS Publishing

SkyLight Paths Publishing is creating a place where people of different spiritual traditions come together for challenge and inspiration, a place where we can help each other understand the mystery that lies at the heart of our existence.

Through spirituality, our religious beliefs are increasingly becoming a part of our lives—rather than *apart* from our lives. While many of us may be more interested than ever in spiritual growth, we may be less firmly planted in traditional religion. Yet, we do want to deepen our relationship to the sacred, to learn from our own as well as from other faith traditions, and to practice in new ways.

SkyLight Paths sees both believers and seekers as a community that increasingly transcends traditional boundaries of religion and denomination—people wanting to learn from each other, *walking together, finding the way.*

For your information and convenience, at the back of this book we have provided a list of other SkyLight Paths books you might find interesting and useful. They cover the following subjects:

Buddhism / Zen	Global Spiritual	Monasticism
Catholicism	Perspectives	Mysticism
Children's Books	Gnosticism	Poetry
Christianity	Hinduism /	Prayer
Comparative	Vedanta	Religious Etiquette
Religion	Inspiration	Retirement
Current Events	Islam / Sufism	Spiritual Biography
Earth-Based	Judaism	Spiritual Direction
Spirituality	Kabbalah	Spirituality
Enneagram	Meditation	Women's Interest
	Midrash Fiction	Worship

Or phone, fax, mail or e-mail to: SKYLIGHT PATHS Publishing
An imprint of Turner Publishing Company
4507 Charlotte Avenue • Suite 100 • Nashville, Tennessee 37209
Tel: (615) 255-2665 • www.skylightpaths.com
Prices subject to change.

**For more information about each book,
visit our website at www.skylightpaths.com**

Printed in the USA
CPSIA information can be obtained
at www.ICGtesting.com
JSHW022205140824
68134JS00018B/880